KV-576-409

Contents

Chapter 1

Visual Selective Attention

P. M. A. RABBITT

It would be artificial and unhelpful to consider only the papers published on visual selective attention during the last year. The context of some twenty years work is necessary in order to understand why some questions have arisen, others have changed, and some have been entirely neglected.

It is revealing that theories of visual and of auditory selective attention should have so little in common. For a surprisingly long time, theories of auditory selective attention have been constructed to describe performance only in a single, rather limited, range of experimental tasks in which subjects shadow or monitor continuous speech, or lists of words, presented to them dichotically or binaurally, (e.g. Broadbent 1958, 1972; Deutsch and Deutsch 1963; Treisman 1969; Kahneman 1973). Pioneering work on the psychophysics of auditory selective attention by Moray (Moray 1970, Moray et al. 1976) has only recently allowed the effects of joint and independent variations in signal information load, of temporal pacing of signals, of signal duration and of signal intensity to be studied under conditions in which the precise degree of synchrony of events in separate channels can be guaranteed. This is an illustration that human experimental psychology has been very much a 'paradigm driven' enquiry, in which theories have grown up to explain data from particular tasks rather than to describe the interactions of factors common to many experimental situations and all sensory modalities.

Precise control over signal parameters, especially of rate and duration of display presentation, has always been much easier in visual than in auditory experiments. Work on visual selective attention has perhaps suffered from the fact that too many rather than too few paradigms have been investigated. Careful quantitative studies are the rule. The problem is to find a way of talking about disparate sets of very precise data in terms of a common theory. Since the range of *paradigms* used is very confusing, the reader may find it helpful to review the literature in terms of the various different usages which the word 'attention' has acquired, and hence to review the various different kinds of question which have arisen. Posner and Boies (1971) provide such an introduction. We may here consider three of the usages they distinguish. The first is 'attention' meaning the maintenance of vigilance in order to detect the occurrence of some sensory events rather than others over long periods of time. We shall not review any of this vast literature, but the reader is urged to consider the logical continuities between models for selective attention discussed below, and by Treisman (1969) and Moray (1970) with the models used to account for vigilance effects in reviews by Broadbent (1958, 1972) Kahneman (1973) and Poulton (1970).

A second usage of 'attention' is to describe the gradual development of perceptual skills specific to particular tasks, such as detection of birds among foliage, of town names on time-tables or of compositors' errors on galley proofs. People learn to select from complex displays characteristics which are critical for particular decisions, while minimizing distraction from other characteristics momentarily irrelevant to them. A final usage is in the description of sudden, and short-lasting, changes in perceptual sensitivity for some sensory events and not for others. It is with these last two usages that this review is concerned.

DEVELOPED SKILLS OF PERCEPTUAL SELECTION

The Unit of Analysis in Visual Perception Processing

All theoretical descriptions of selective attention face the problem that the units in which evidence from the external world is processed by the CNS must be specified. Neisser (1963, 1967) discussed his classic work on visual search in terms of Selfridge's (1959) 'Pandemonium' model for computer recognition of symbols. The essential premise is that it is theoretically possible to specify, for the human perceptual system, a list of all possible discriminable stimulus 'features'. Each of these features is independently discriminable because a particular 'analyzer' in the perceptual system responds when it is present and not when it is absent. A representation of input as a sub-set of detached features among the total set of all possible features, is therefore theoretically possible. The simultaneous activation of particular subsets of feature analyzers activates other, higher order analyzers known as 'demons'. This 'coding down' continues through an indeterminate hierarchy of levels until a distinction relevant to a required decision may be made (Selfridge 1959; Selfridge and Neisser 1960).

The basic unit of processing is therefore a 'feature', and the structure of these models allows description in terms of an information transmission matrix in which each cell corresponds to a particular analyzer and may be in an 'on' or 'off' condition. An excellent review of pattern perception, considered in these terms, is provided by Garner (1962). An empirical point demonstrated by Fitts, Weinstein, Rappaport, Anderson and Leonard (1956) and by Anderson and Leonard (1958) is that not all possible differences between the 'feature lists' activated by two distinct displays are necessary, or are in fact used, to discriminate between them. Some of these features may be redundant and others critical to such discriminations. Garner (1962, ch. 6) gives an excellent theoretical review of the role of redundancy in discriminations between complex displays. Neisser (1963) and Rabbitt (1967) have both showed that visual search is easier when all targets share a single critical feature (e.g. a curved line) not possessed by any of the background items on a display. Rabbitt (1967) further showed that even when no *single* critical feature could be specified, subjects improved with practice by discovering and using the minimum number of features necessary to distinguish target from background symbols.

Some important assumptions left open by most discussions of feature analyzer models are brought out in Keeley and Doherty's (1968) discussion of an empirical comparison of the effects of two kinds of redundancy on tachistoscopic discrimination threshold for displays of symbols. They presented the same symbol four times, or simultaneously presented four versions of the same symbol. One set of symbols were Landholdt Cs with their gaps orientated in one of four directions. Subjects had to specify gap direction. Repeated presentation of symbols increased probability of gap detection but simultaneous multiple presentation did not. When different symbols to be discriminated from each other, differing in terms of more than one feature (e.g. the letters A and U), both simultaneous and successive multiple presentation increased discrimination probability.

There are obvious methodological problems with interpretation of this result, but Keeley and Doherty (1968) make the interesting suggestion that if only one feature analyzer can be deployed to recognise a gap in a Landholt C, an increase in the number of gaps simultaneously presented would not improve performance. In the case of letters A and U any one of a number of feature analyzers may be simultaneously deployed to recognize the many possible critical features. The value of this suggestion is not so much that it may be correct, as that it shows that when 'feature analyzer' models specify a list of all possible discriminable stimulus 'features', and when a particular structure designated as a 'feature' occurs in many locations of the same display, we cannot assume that there are necessarily several precisely corresponding 'analyzers' on to which these replicated features map in a one-to-one fashion. That is to say, models of this kind must not only specify a listing of all the different kinds of analyzers which are available, but must further specify which of these analyzers can be activated independently and which cannot.

At any one time there is always a reciprocity between abstract models for perceptual processes and the metrics which researchers find useful to analyse their empirical data. The influence of information theory has been apparent in the formulation of binary, 'on/off' coding structures such as the analyzer 'demons' in Selfridge's (1959, 1966) Pandemonium model, in the binary 'processing nodes' in Feigenbaum's (1963) EPAM recognition model, and the 'operators' in Uhr and Vossler's (1963) and Uhr's (1966) models. A more recent, and extremely useful model put forward by Rumelhart (1970) still uses the concept of 'operators' which can, to some extent, be regarded in the same way as 'analyzers'. However, Rumelhart's (1970) multi-component model begins to take into consideration cases in which detection of any individual 'component' is a probabilistic, rather than an 'all or none' process.

Perceptual 'Features' and Perceptual 'Dimensions'

When discussing differences between two dimensional monochrome symbols of constant size we may define discriminative 'features' as particular components (straight lines, curves, angles, gaps, etc.) which are either present or absent in particular cases. A quite different problem arises when stimuli may be ranked along *continuous dimensions* such as colour brightness or size. How are such variations to be 'digitalized' as features? More to the point, are variations along one continuum, such as size, to be equated with variations along another, such as colour? It must be borne in mind when discussing such dimensions of difference between stimuli that, while some of them may correspond to continua of operation of sense organs (e.g. brightness or wavelength of light), not all of them do so. Symbol shape is a 'continuum' of difference only in an arbitrary sense. We must distinguish continua determined by the physics or physiology of sense organs from those determined by arbitrary linguistic conventions adopted by experimenters to communicate with their subjects and each other.

Therefore two kinds of questions tend to be confounded. First there is the problem as to how far the neurophysiological apparatus encoding one dimension, such as colour, is distinct from that encoding another, such as brightness. Second there is the separate, functional question as to whether the subject can process more information in unit time if stimuli differ in terms of two or more of these continua than if they differ in terms of one continuum alone. A different form of this second question has been raised by experiments which have asked whether people can check for variations on several display dimensions simultaneously ('in parallel') or whether they can only check for variations along one dimension at a time ('in series'). (See Egeth 1966; Hawkins 1969; Barber 1969; Beller 1970; Saraga and Shallice 1973. See also a theoretical discussion by Townsend 1971 b.).

In visual search tasks it is clear that subjects *can* make judgements serially, and test first for differences along one sensory dimension in order to reduce the number of judgements which they may have to make upon another. Green and Anderson (1956) showed that when symbols on a display differed both in colour and shape, if the colour of a particular target symbol was specified in advance, the time taken to find it varied with the total number of other symbols *of that colour* rather than with the total number of all symbols of all colours on the display. It thus seemed that subjects were tested first for symbol colour and only then, conditionally, for symbol shape. Green and Anderson (1955) reported similar findings when size and shape were independently varied. Very recent work has shown that when text is printed in lines of alternate colours people can very efficiently read material printed in one colour without any interference from material printed in the other (Neisser 1969; Willows and McKinnon 1973). The selective capabilities of subjects are quite remarkable, and it seems possible for them to follow one of two simultaneously superimposed episodes presented overlapping each other on a TV screen, with little distraction from the other (Neisser 1976; Neisser and Becklen 1975).

A number of experiments have tested how far subjects can improve their search among symbols if they are pre-cued to scan only those which have a specified value on one or another dimension of difference. Advance cues, whether for spatial location (Sperling 1960), for colour (Brown 1960; von Wright 1968, 1970, 1975, 1977) or for brightness (von Wright 1968) all improve search performance. This again suggests that subjects can efficiently reduce the number of symbols which they inspect for differences in terms of one dimension (i.e. shape) by making this analysis conditional upon the outcome of others.

In very lucid and complete reviews of multidimensional perceptual processing Garner (1974a, b) introduces the idea that in cases like those discussed above, judgements of spatial location, colour or brightness may under some circumstances be *separable* from each other, and from judgements of shape. However Garner also presents evidence that certain other pairs of dimensions such as colour and brightness may sometimes have to be processed *integrally* rather than separately. Evidence from this comes from Garner (1970), Garner and Felfoldy (1970) and Felfoldy and Garner (1971) who describe many tasks in which decisions based on joint variations in two different stimulus dimensions (e.g. colour and brightness) are made faster than decisions based on either dimension alone, indicating that both dimensions must be processed simultaneously, and integrally, rather than successively and separately.

A new set of problems has been raised by Treisman *et al.* (1977) who presents experiments showing that when multidimensional stimuli are identified in terms of conjunctions of attributes, a complex model is necessary to account for the ways in which separate dimensions are extracted and then subsequently mutually related.

How Many Tests can be Made Simultaneously?

Obviously the amount of evidence which a man can process from a display at any one moment is limited, if for no other reason than because he cannot focus the whole display at once. A further question is whether the number of units of perceptual analysis which can be processed at a single fixation may not also be limited. It is not easy to clearly specify what such units of analysis may be. The conventional empirical solution has therefore been to use familiar symbols, such as letters or digits, and to test how variations in information load achieved by variations in the vocabulary of such symbols used in search tasks affects the time taken to scan displays.

Neisser (1963) and Neisser, Novik and Lazar (1963) found that highly practised subjects could scan displays as rapidly to find any of ten specified targets as to find one. Kaplan and Carvellas (1965), Kaplan, Carvellas and Metlay (1966) and Shurtleff and Marsetta (1968) found that less practised subjects showed an increase in scanning time with the number of targets specified for search (N_T). Rabbitt (1964) found effects of N_T on search time even for practised subjects.

A visual search task is a special case of a signal categorization task in which people recognize symbols as being members of two classes (i.e. 'target' or 'background'). Another example of such a task is Sternberg's (1966) well known memory search paradigm. The question arises why even highly practised subjects continue to show a systematic increase of RT with NT (size of the positive 'memory set') in Sternberg's tasks (Sternberg 1975) but not with N_T (size of the remembered positive target set) in Neisser's (1963, 1967) reported studies.

This question has been formally tested by combining both tasks so that subjects search displays of varying size for varying numbers of specified target items. RT as a function of display size (scanning rate) and RT as a function of target set (memory set) size can then be calculated separately (Sternberg and Scarborough 1969; Nickerson 1966). Even with considerable practice some variation in search time with memory set size is usually observed, although the data are fitted by the assumption that subjects make an exhaustive scan through the memory set for each display item in turn, terminating their scan of a display when a target is located. Slopes of both functions (relating RT to display size and to memory set size) reduce with practice but the memory set size slope has not yet been observed to reach zero (Burrows and Murdock 1969). Some logical and methodological differences between various visual search experiments on one side and memory search experiments on the other which may account for this are reviewed by Rabbitt (1978).

The amount of practice which subjects are given turns out to be especially critical. Rabbitt, Cumming and Vyas (1978) confirmed Neisser's (1963) results in a different task in which the effects of high error rates (Wattenbarger 1969) and low target frequency (Rabbitt 1966) were controlled. After twenty to thirty days' practice scanning time did not vary with target set size between two and eight items. But at this level of practice, both in visual search tasks (Rabbitt, Cumming and Vyas 1978) and in memory search tasks (Kristoffersen 1977) no change in performance was observed when subjects were transferred from a familiar to a novel background or negative set of items. It seems that extended practice does not simply allow people to perform the same functional operations faster and more accurately, but actually allows them to develop new ways of discriminating between stimuli on a display.

May More than One Categorization of Stimuli be Made at Once?

Selective attention always implies a categorization of stimuli into two arbitrary sets, i.e. 'target' and 'background' items. A given set of symbols on a display may be separated into the classes 'rounded' and 'angular', 'those with names beginning with T and others' or 'letters and digits'. In any given search task only one of these categorizations will be required. The question is whether other categorizations may not also simultaneously be made, and whether the outcomes of these categorizations may help or hinder performance on a particular set task.

Obviously some symbols are visually more similar than others and discriminations among these will be relatively slow, as Neisser (1963); Rabbitt (1967); Clement and Carpenter (1970); Townsend (1971a); Vingilis, Blake and Theodor (1977) and Krumhansl and Thomas (1977) have shown. A very complete review of such effects of discrimination difficulty is given by Krueger (1975). Letters of the alphabet may be distinguished from each other by particular component graphemic units such as lines, curves and angles and by the relationships between them (Naus and Schillman 1976). A recent very interesting suggestion is that such graphemic units (letter fragments) can be identified at shorter tachistoscopic exposure durations if they are presented in the context of their component letters than if they are presented in isolation (Schendel and Shaw 1976).

Since letters of the alphabet can be distinguished from each other purely in terms of graphemic cues it is not logically necessary for people to name any of the letters they encounter while searching a display. However they sometimes appear to do this, since Kruger (1970) reports that visual search is slower when target and background letters have acoustically similar names (e.g. V and T) than when their names are distinct (e.g. V and S). Thus if all names are accessed, and if subjects distinguish between letters in terms of their phonological representations as well as their shapes, in this task, as in binary classification experiments, it may take longer to recognize acoustically similar letters as being different (Posner 1970).

The argument becomes more complicated when subjects search for individual letters in lists of words. Krueger and Weiss (1976) found that specified target letters were located faster in lists of words than in random letter strings. Reicher (1969) and Wheeler (1970) report a similar 'Word Context Effect' (WCE) for detection of component letters in tachistoscopically presented single words. However Björk and Estes (1973), Massaro (1973) and Thompson and Massaro (1973) find that no WCE is obtained in a task in which all forced choice target alternatives are specified to subjects before rather than after presentation of the display.

Contextual effects are of course not confined to artificial stimuli such as letters and words, but are also demonstrable when the efficiency with which people scan and recall objects in their environment is investigated. Biederman (1972), Biederman, Glass and Stacey (1973) and Biederman, Rabinowitz, Glass and Stacey (1974) have tested subjects' efficiency at scanning structured, real-life scenes as compared with pictures in which the elements of these scenes are randomly transposed. Both initial identification and subsequent recall is better for the structured scenes.

On balance it still seems possible that both Letter Context Effects (LCEs) and WCEs exist (Schendel and Shaw 1976). If they do, we may choose between two kinds of explanation, which are not mutually exclusive. First *graphemic* context provided by familiar words e.g. shapes of spaces between letters, shapes and lengths of words, etc.) may improve recognition of particular unit letters within words (Krueger 1975). Second it is possible that search for letters embedded in words is faster because entire familiar groups of letters forming words can be simultaneously processed as units. The phonological representations of these words are then extracted and scanned to detect component letters by their *sound*. Demonstrations that word recognition and letter recognition are affected by word *pronounceability* as well as by orthographic legitimacy and familiarity render this plausible (Rubenstein, Richter and Kay 1975, Barron 1975).

Striking demonstrations by Corcoran (1966, 1967) and Corcoran and Weening (1968) show that when subjects search continuous text, target letters are detected better when they are in voiced rather than in unvoiced word positions (e.g. voiced Ps are detected better than silent Ps). These experiments have been replicated and extended by Healy (1976) who shows that a complicating factor is the frequency of occurrence of the word incorporating the target letter. She suggests that the more frequently a word is encountered the more likely it is to be processed as a graphemic unit rather then as a string of individual letters. If processed as a graphemic unit a word is more likely to be converted into its phonological representation and its individual component letters are less likely to be detected if they are not voiced. Recent work by Smith and Jones (1977) supports some of Healy's findings but indicates that the effect is much more complex than she suspected.

Target and background symbols on a display may be drawn from different pre-learnt categories or classes such as letters and digits. This can facilitate visual search. Rabbitt (1962), Ingling (1971) and Brand (1971) found that a subject could find a target letter among background digits as rapidly when he was told to look for 'any letter' as when he was told to look for a particular symbol (e.g. the letter K).

Sperling, Budianski, Spivak and Johnstone (1971) report the same result, estimating a scanning rate for paced visual search of eight msec to thirteen msec per symbol. Egeth, Atkinson, Gilmore and Marcus (1973) also found that search for digits among letters on tachistoscopically presented displays was very efficient indeed.

One possible line of explanation is that all digits have common graphemic features not possessed by any letters, and vice versa (see discussions by Rabbitt (1978) and others). A witty experiment by Jonides and Gleitman (1972) showed that this cannot be the whole story because observers locate the symbol 'O' faster among letters when told to search for 'zero' than when told to search for 'Oh'. Two more recent studies by Jonides and Gleitman (1976) and Gleitman and Jonides (1976) pursue the idea that subjects can sometimes recognise the category to which a symbol belongs before they can identify it as an individual letter or digit, and that this categorization can provide a cue for target localization among symbols from a different category. Note that experiments by Nickerson (1973) which show that subjects take longer to name the categories of symbols (e.g. 'letter' or 'digit') than to name the symbols themselves (e.g. 'One' or 'Ay') are beside this point. Response frequencies probably differ.

Explanations of categorization effects based on the presence or absence of common graphemic features also do not explain results by Karlin and Bower (1976) who found that a target word designated only by its taxonomic noun class can be located faster among background words all drawn from a different, common class than among words from different, heterogenous classes. Replications and extensions of this work by Henderson (1978) and Fletcher and Rabbitt (1978) suggest that these effects are due to relative variations in speed of search among noun classes in long term memory rather than on physical characteristics of displays.

Control Processes in Visual Search and Reading

Many studies have shown that subjects can systematically vary the amount of information which they take in during a single ocular fixation (inter-saccadic interval) as a function of the information load of the material which they are required to read (Morton 1970). Recent, technologically impressive, studies have displayed text on a computer cathode ray tube display and fed input from eye-movement recording apparatus into the computer to arrange that the text is presented legibly at the point of visual fixation but is systematically degraded at various visual angles about the fixation point. As the eyes move so does the 'window' of clear text on the display (Rayner 1975; Rayner and McConkie 1973; McConkie and Rayner 1974). Subjects can thus be shown to use such coarse cues as word length, word shape and initial and terminal letters of words, which they perceive in peripheral vision to modify the amplitude and timing of the eye movements they make while reading. The same points have been indirectly demonstrated by the use of text with gaps between words omitted or infilled with dummy characters, or with random alternations of upper and lower case letters (Smith, Lott and Cromwell 1969; Fisher 1975). Similar points emerge from studies of the relative efficiencies with which people can scan lists of letters printed in reversed orientation (Frith 1974). An excellent recent overall review of research on reading has been produced by Cohen (1978) and see Chapter 12.

In summary, it is now clear that reading does not merely involve the successive fixation and encoding of successive 'quanta' or 'packages' of information from a printed page. It is, rather, an adaptively controlled process in which the size of successive perceptual samples is varied according to difficulty of context, and in which subjects use this context, together with preliminary inspection of critical cues obtained from peripheral vision, to develop and use 'hypotheses' as to what is to come next. These 'hypotheses' govern their ongoing perceptual selectivity. The hypothesis framed at any one moment determines which cues are sought to confirm or disconfirm it. Confirmation of an hypothesis allows a decision to be based on fewer perceptual cues than would otherwise be necessary. In other words this is the way in which subjects take advantage of redundancy in continuous text.

Our understanding of the operation of another kind of control process in visual selective attention has been advanced by experiments using the technique of rapid serial visual presentation of successive displays (RSVP) first reported by Sperling, Budiansky, Spivak and Johnstone (1971) and more extensively used by Lawrence (1971) who displayed successions of single words printed in lower case, and asked his subjects to detect and name any word printed in upper case. Subjects usually made errors by reporting a lower case word which occurred immediately, or shortly *after* the target word. They also reported a convincing subjective impression of 'seeing' this incorrect word in upper case. It seemed that capital letters might trigger a recognition response which encouraged subjects to begin a sample of the display. When displays rapidly changed, the latency of the recognition response caused a later word to be identified by mistake, and upper case letters to be perceptually 'attributed' to it.

Fischler (1975) has shown that the error distribution obtained in such tasks depends on factors such as syllabic length which affect recognition latency of the first of two adjacent target words. Frankish (1977) reports a series of experiments which suggest that the appearance of a cue on a target display may in fact allow the subject to *stop* continuously sampling information from successive displays and to begin processing information available in his short term memory store. These experiments again all suggest that visual search can sometimes be regarded as a 'two stage' process, in which initial decisions made on the basis of some stimulus characteristics conditionally determine how other decisions are later made on the basis of other cues.

A final series of theoretical and empirical studies have examined how subjects may optimize scanning strategies for search of complex displays (Sheridan and Johannsen 1977) or may optimize the way in which they visually fixate and sample information from more than one signal source, when the probability of occurrence of critical information varies systematically from source to source and from time to time (Senders 1973). Recent work has adapted a mathematical theory of search optimization developed by Koopman (1956a, b, 1957) to visual search of displays (Shaw and Shaw 1977). In short, such studies tend to force us to regard a human subject as adaptively using predictions made on the basis of past experience of his environment in order to optimize his decisions as to when, where and how to obtain information which he needs to guide his decisions. They force us to recognize that the stochastic models of his environment which a subject develops and uses to guide his information processing, may be very complex indeed.

FACTORS BRINGING ABOUT MOMENTARY CHANGES IN PERCEPTUAL SELECTIVITY

Experiments in Cueing and Priming

We have seen that subjects use current information to guide their sampling behaviour. They can also more efficiently process complex displays if they are pre-cued to select some parts of them and not others by spatial position (Sperling 1960), colour (Brown 1960; von Wright 1975, 1977) or brightness (von Wright 1970). Such advance information, reducing the amount of analysis which must be conducted on a display, must be distinguished from advance information given in 'priming' experiments in which subjects are alerted to become more receptive to some classes of complex stimuli and less sensitive to others (see Posner and Klein 1973; and Posner and Boies 1971 for a theoretical discussion).

Meyer, Schvaneveldt and Ruddy (1974, 1975) have shown that presentation of a single noun such as DOCTOR will facilitate recognition of a subsequently presented semantically associated noun such as NURSE but not of an unassociated noun such as BUTTER. It seems from recent work that such 'priming' may facilitate encoding of graphemic cues from visually degraded displays as well as probably increasing the availability of some verbal responses more than others (Meyer and Schvaneveldt 1971).

Discussions of such effects are usually carried on in terms of modifications of the 'logogen' theory for word recognition, first developed by Morton (1970). A 'logogen' is envisaged as an internal representation of a linguistic or other concept which may be activated by sensory input, or may be activated by internal associations with other activated logogens, or which may have its threshold for activation altered by either sensory input or internal associations. Activation of any one logogen may therefore affect the probability of subsequent activation of other logogens. This provides a powerful explanatory rubric to interpret shifts in attentional selectivity and response availability. Posner and Snyder (1975) modify a version of the 'logogen' theory already adapted by Keele (1973) to explain their finding that if subjects are pre-cued by presentation of a particular letter of the alphabet they make subsequent binary comparisons faster when these include the cue letter, and slower when they do not. They extend Keele's (1973) model by postulating that analysis of any particular display activates a set of corresponding 'coding pathways' in the information processing system. This activation endures for some time, facilitating subsequent analysis of any stimulus requiring re-use of any or all of the same pathways. Pathways in the coding system are not only activated by external input. They may also be activated by internal representations or logogens. Thus the presentation of one stimulus may result in facilitation of the encoding of another, conceptually related but physically different stimulus (Rabbitt, Jordan and Vyas 1978).

Experiments Showing Sequential Effects in Continuous Tasks

It is well known that when signals and responses are immediately repeated during continuous tasks subjects respond faster (Bertelson 1961, 1963, 1965, Rabbitt 1968; Kornblum 1969). The question has been whether this facilitation is entirely due to facilitation of response programming by repetition (Bertelson 1965; Rabbitt 1965, 1966) or whether repetitions of *stimuli* also facilitate perceptual analysis by modifying attentional selectivity. In Posner and Snyder's (1975) terminology we wish to know whether perceptual analytic pathways activated by presentation of one display may not facilitate *perceptual* analysis of the next.

Bertelson and Tisseyre (1966) found that variations in stimulus probability affected RT more than did variations in response probability, suggesting that at least two separate sources of facilitation were operative. Similar results had already been obtained by La Berge and Tweedy (1964) and were later clarified and extended by La Berge, Tweedy and Ricker (1967); La Berge, Legrand and Hobbie (1969) by Hinrichs and Craft (1971) and Hinrichs and Kraintz (1970). La Berge, Legrand and Hobbie (1969) comment 'The nature of selection in the present task seems to amount to a biassing of the speed of perception of a particular stimulus'. These and subsequent data led to the formulation of a model of priming in visual selective attention put forward by La Berge (1975, 1977). It seems clear that overall *probability* of occurrence of one signal against others can 'attune' perceptual selectivity for it in some way. An ingenious experiment by Ellis and Gotts (1977) showing that repetition of displays facilitate RT even when responses are *not* also repeated, emphasises this point.

In continuous visual search tasks similar effects have been shown for repetitions of target symbols on successively presented displays (Rabbitt, Cumming and Vyas 1977a), especially when their spatial positions are also repeated. Repetitions of background items on successive displays also facilitates displays analysis, especially if they recur in the same spatial positions (Rabbitt, Cumming and Vyas 1978). These effects, with other demonstrations that repetition of both relevant and irrelevant characteristics of successive displays reduces RT (Eichelman 1970; Jordan, Rabbitt, and Vyas 1977; Rabbitt, Jordan and Vyas 1978; Rabbitt and Rodgers 1978), can be very economically explained in terms of the assumptions borrowed from Keele (1973) by Posner and Snyder (1975).

REFERENCES

Anderson, N. S. and Leonard, J. A. 1958. 'The recognition, naming and reconstruction of visual figures as a function of contour redundancy.' *J. exp. Psychol. 56*, 262-70.

Barber, D. 1969. 'Reaction times and error rates for "same" – "different" judgements of multidimensional stimuli.' *Percep. & Psychophys. 6* 169-74.

Barron, J. 1975. 'Successive stages in word recognition.' In S. Dornic and P. M. A. Rabbitt (eds) *Attention and performance V*. New York: Academic Press.

Beller, H. K. 1970. 'Parallel and serial stages in matching.' *J. exp. Psychol. 84*, 213-19.

Bertelson, P. 1961. 'Sequential redundancy and speed in a serial two-choice responding task.' *Quart. J. exp. Psychol. 12,* 90-102.

Bertelson, P. 1963. 'S–R relationships and reaction times for new versus repeated signals in a serial task.' *J. exp. Psychol. 65,* 478-84.

Bertelson, P. 1965. 'Serial choice reaction time as a function of response versus signal-and-response repetition.' *Nature 206* (4980), 217-18.

Bertelson, P. and Tisseyre, F. 1966. 'Choice reaction time as a function of stimulus versus response frequency of occurrence.' *Nature 212* 1069-70.

Biederman, I. 1972. 'Perceiving real world scenes.' *Science 177,* 77-80.

Biederman, I., Glass, A. L. and Stacey, E. W. I. 1973. 'Searching for objects in real world scenes.' *J. exp. Psychol. 97,* 22-7.

Biederman, I., Rabinowitz, J. C., Glass, A. L. and Stacey, E. W. Jr 1974. 'On the information extracted at a glance from a scene.' *J. exp. Psychol. 103,* 597-600.

Björk, E. L. and Estes, W. K. 1973. 'Letter identification in relation to linguistic context and masking conditions.' *Memory and Cognition 1,* 217-23.

Brand, J. 1971. 'Classification without identification in visual search.' *Quart. J. exp. Psychol. 23,* 178-86.

Broadbent, D. E. 1958. *Perception and communication.* London: Pergamon Press.

Broadbent, D. E. 1972. *Decision and stress.* New York and London: Academic Press.

Brown, J. 1960. 'Evidence for a selective process during perception of tachistoscopically presented stimuli.' *J. exp. Psychol. 59,* 176-81.

Burrows, D. and Murdock, B. B. Jr 1969. 'Effects of extended practice on high speed scanning.' *J. exp. Psychol. 82,* 231-7.

Clement, D. E. and Carpenter, J. S. 1970. 'Relative discriminability of visually presented letter pairs using a same-different choice reaction-time task.' *Psychonom. Sci. 20,* 363-5.

Cohen, G. 1978. 'Reading.' Chapter in course book in 'Cognitive Psychology'. Course for the Open University.

Corcoran, D. W. J. 1966. 'An acoustic factor in letter cancellation.' *Nature* 210, 658.

Corcoran, D. W. J. 1967. 'Acoustic factors in proof reading.' *Nature 214,* 851-2.

Corcoran, D. W. J. and Weening, D. L. 1968. 'Acoustic factors in visual search.' *Quart. J. exp. Psychol. 20,* 83-5.

Deutsch, J. A. and Deutsch, D. 1963. 'Attention: some theoretical considerations.' *Psychol. Rev. 70,* 80-90.

Egeth, H. 1966. 'Parallel versus serial processes in multidimensional stimulus discrimination.' *Percep. & Psychophys. 1,* 245-52.

Egeth, H., Atkinson, J., Gilmore, G. and Marcus, N. 1973. 'Factors affecting processing rate in visual search.' *Percep. & Psychophys. 13,* 394-402.

Eichelman, W. H. 1970. 'Stimulus and response repetition effects for naming letters at two response stimulus intervals.' *Percep. & Psychophys. 7,* 94-6.

Ellis, J. G. and Gotts, G. H. 1977, 'Serial reaction times as a function of the nature of repeated events.' *J. exp. Psychol Human Percept. & Perform. 3,* 234-42.

Feigenbaum, E. A. 1963. 'The simulation of verbal learning behaviour.' In E. A. Feigenbaum and J. Feldman (eds) *Computers and thought*. New York: McGraw Hill.

Felfoldy, G. L. and Garner, W. R. 1971. 'The effects on speeded classification of implicit and explicit instructions regarding stimulus dimensions.' *Percep. & Psychophys. 9,* 289-92.

Fischler, I. 1975. 'Detection and identification of words and letters in simulated visual search of word lists.' *Memory and Cognition 3*, 175-82.

Fisher, D. F. 1975. 'Reading and visual search.' *Memory and Cognition 3,* 188-96.

Fitts, P. M., Weinstein, M., Rappaport, M., Anderson, N. S. and Leonard, J. A. 1956. 'Stimulus correlates of visual pattern recognition: a probability approach.' *J. exp. Psychol. 51,* 1-11.

Fletcher, C. B. and Rabbitt, P. M. A. 1978. 'Categorization and visual search.' Talk at Meeting of Experimental Psychology Society, Durham, July 1976.

Frankish, C. 1977. Paper submitted for publication.

Frith, U. 1974. 'A curious effect with reversed letters explained by a theory of schema.' *Percep. & Psychophys. 16*, 113-16.

Garner, W. R. 1962. *Uncertainty and structure as psychological concepts.* New York: Academic Press.

Garner, W. R. 1970. 'The stimulus in information processing.' *Amer. Psychologist 25,* 350-8.

Garner, W. R. 1974a. 'Attention and selection of stimuli and attributes.' In E. C. Carterette and M. P. Friedman (eds) *Handbook of perception vol. 2,* New York: Academic Press.

Garner, W. R. 1974b. *The processing of information and structure*. Potomac, Md: Lawrence Erlbaum Associates. Distributed by John Wiley, N.Y. and London.

Garner, W. R. and Felfoldy, G. L. 1970. 'Integrality of stimulus dimensions in various types of information processing.' *Cogn. Psychol. 1,* 225-41.

Gleitman, H. and Jonides, J. 1976. 'The cost of categorisation in visual search: incomplete processing of targets and field items.' *Percep. & Psychophys. 20,* 281-8.

Green, B. F. and Anderson, L. K. 1955. 'Size coding in a visual search task.' *M.I.T. Research Reports XVI.*

Green, B. F. and Anderson, L. K. 1956. 'Colour coding in a visual search task.' *J. exp. Psychol. 51,* 19-24.

Hawkins, H. L. 1969. 'Parallel processing in complex visual discrimination.' *Percep. & Psychophys. 5,* 56-64.

Healy, A. F. 1976. 'Detection errors on the word *The*: Evidence for reading units larger than letters.' *J. exp. Psychol.: Human Percept. & Perform. 2,* 235-42.

Henderson, L. 1978. 'Semantic effects in visual search through word lists for physically defined targets.' Brit. Psychol. Soc. Ann. Meeting, York 1976.

Hinrichs, J. V. and Craft, J. L. 1971. 'Verbal expectancy and probability in two-choice reaction time.' *J. exp. Psychol. 83,* 367-71.

Hinrichs, J. V. and Kraintz, P. L. 1970. 'Expectancy in choice reaction time: anticipation of stimulus or response?' *J. exp. Psychol. 85,* 330-4.

Ingling, N. W. 1971. 'Categorization: a mechanism for rapid interaction processing.' *J. exp. Psychol. 94*, 239-43.

Jonides, J. and Gleitman, H. 1972. 'A conceptual category effect in visual search: O as letter or as digit.' *Percep. & Psychophys. 1*, 172-4.

Jonides, J. and Glêitman, H. 1976. 'The benefit of categorization in visual search: target location without identification.' *Percep. & Psychophys. 20*, 289-98.

Jordan, T. C. and Rabbitt, P.M.A. 1977. 'Response times to stimuli of increasing complexity as a function of ageing.' *Brit. J. Psychol. 68*, 189-201.

Kahneman, D. 1973. *Attention and effort*. New Jersey, U.S.A.: Prentice Hall, Englewood Cliffs.

Kaplan, I. T. and Carvellas, T. 1965. 'Scanning for multiple targets.' *Percep. & Mot. Skills 21*, 239-43.

Kaplan, I. T., Carvellas, T. and Metlay, W. 1966 'Visual search and immediate memory.' *J. exp. Psychol. 71*, 488-93.

Kaplan, G. A., Yonas, A. and Shurcliff, A. 1966. 'Visual and acoustic confusibility in a visual search task.' *Percep. & Psychophys. 1*, 172-4.

Karlin, M. B. and Bower, G. H. 1976. 'Semantic category effects in visual word search.' *Percep. & Psychophys. 19*, 417-24.

Keele, S. W. 1973. *Attention and human performance*. Pacific Palinades, California: Goodyear.

Keeley, S. M. and Doherty, M. E. 1968. 'Simultaneous and successive presentations of single-featured and multi-featured visual forms: implications for the parallel processing hypothesis.' *Percep. & Psychophys. 4*, 296-8.

Koopman, B. O. 1956a. 'The theory of search. Part 1. Kinematic bases.' *Operations Research 4*, 324-46.

Koopman, B. O. 1956b. 'The theory of search. Part 2. Target detection.' *Operations Research 4*, 503-31.

Koopman, B. O. 1957. 'The theory of search. Part III. The optimum distribution of searching effort.' *Operations Research 5*, 613-26.

Kornblum, S. 1969. 'Segmential determinants of information processing in serial and discrete reaction time.' *Psychol. Rev. 76*, 113-31.

Kristofferson, M. W. 1977. 'The effects of practice with one positive set in a memory scanning task can be completely transferred to a new set.' *Memory and Cognition 5*, 177-86.

Krueger, L. E. 1970. 'The effect of acoustic confusability on visual search.' *Amer. J. Psychol. 83*, 389-400.

Krueger, L. E. 1975. 'Familiarity effects in visual information processing.' *Psychol. Bull. 82*, 949-74.

Krueger, L. E. and Weiss, M. E. 1976. 'Letter search through words and nonwords: the effect of fixed, absent or mutilated targets.' *Memory and Cognition 4*, 200-6.

Krumhansl, C. L. and Thomas, E. A. C. 1977, 'Effect of level of confusability on reporting letters from briefly presented visual displays.' *Percep. & Psychophys. 21*, 269-79.

La Berge, D. 1975, 'Acquisition of automatic processing in perceptual and associate learning.' In P. M. A. Rabbitt and S. Dornic (eds) *Attention and Performance V*. London: Academic Press.

La Berge, D. 1977. Chapter in S. Dornic (ed.) *Attention and performance VI*. Potomac Md.: Lawrence Erlbaum, in press.

La Berge, D. and Tweedy, J. R. 1964. 'Presentation probability and choice time.' *J. exp. Psychol. 68,* 477-81.

La Berge, D., Tweedy, J. R. and Ricker, J. 1967. 'Selective attention: incentive variables and choice time.' *Psychonom. Sci. 8,* 341-2.

La Berge, D., Legrand, R. and Hobbie, R. K. 1969. 'Functional identification of perceptual and response biases in choice reaction time.' *J. exp. Psychol. 79,* 295-9.

Lawrence, D. H. 1971. 'Two studies of visual search for word targets with controlled rates of presentation.' *Percep. & Psychophys. 10,* 85-9.

McConkie, G. W. and Rayner, K. 1974. 'Identifying the span of the effective stimulus in reading.' Final report O.E.G., 2-71-0531, submitted to the Office of Education, July 1974.

Massaro, D. W. 1973. 'Perception of letters, words and non-words.' *J. exp. Psychol. 100,* 349-53.

Meyer, D. E. and Schvaneveldt, R. W. 1971, 'Facilitation in recognizing pairs of words: evidence of a dependance between retrieval operations.' *J. exp. Psychol. 90,* 227-34.

Meyer, D. E., Schvaneveldt, R. W. and Ruddy, M. G. 1974. 'Functions of the graphemic and phonemic codes in visual word recognition.' *Memory and Cognition 2,* 309-23.

Meyer, D. E., Schvaneveldt, R. W. and Ruddy, M. G. 1975. 'Loci of contextual effects on word recognition.' In P. M. A. Rabbitt and S. Dornic (eds) *Attention and Performance V.* London: Academic Press.

Moray, N. 1970. *Attention: selective processes in vision and hearing.* London: Hutchinson.

Moray, N., Fitter, M., Ostry, D., Favreau, D. and Nagy, V. 1976. 'Attention to pure tones.' *Quart. J. exp. Psychol. 28,* 271-83.

Morton, J. 1970. In D. Norman (ed.) *Models of memory.* New York: John Wiley.

Naus, M. J. and Schillman, R. J. 1976. 'Why a Y is not a V; a new look at the distinctive features of letters.' *J. exp. Psychol. Human Percep. and Perform. 2,* 394-400.

Neisser, U. 1963. 'Decision time without reaction time: experiments in visual scanning.' *Amer. J. Psychol. 76,* 376-85.

Neisser, U. 1967. *Cognitive psychology.* New York: Appleton Century Crofts.

Neisser, U. 1969. 'Selective reading: a method for the study of visual attention.' Paper presented to the 19th International Congress of Psychology (Conference abstracts).

Neisser, U. 1976. *Cognition and reality.* San Francisco: W. H. Freeman.

Neisser, U., Novik, R. and Lazar, R. 1963. 'Searching for ten targets simultaneously.' *Percep. & Mot. Skills 17,* 955-61.

Neisser, U. and Becklen, R. 1975. 'Selective looking: attending to visually-specified events.' *Cogn. Psychol. 7,* 480-94.

Nickerson, R. S. 1966. 'Response times with a memory dependent decision task. *J. exp. Psychol. 72,* 761-9.

Nickerson, R. S. 1973. 'Can characters be classified directly as digits versus letters or must they be identified first?' *Memory and Cognition I,* 477-84.

Posner, M. I. 1970. 'On the relationship between letter names and superordinate categories.' *Quart. J. exp. Psychol. 22,* 279-87.

Posner, M. I. and Boies, S. J. 1971. 'Components of attention.' *Psychol. Rev. 78,* 391-408.

Posner, M. I. and Klein, R. M. 1973. 'On the functions of consciousness.' In S. Kornblum (ed.) *Attention and performance IV*. London: Academic Press.

Posner, M. I. and Snyder, C. R. R. 1975. 'Facilitation and inhibition in the processing of signals.' In P. M. A. Rabbitt and S. Dornic (eds) *Attention and performance V*. London: Academic Press.

Poulton, E. C. 1970. *Environment and human efficiency*. Springfield, Ill.: Charles Thomas.

Rabbitt, P. M. A. 1962. 'Perceptual discrimination and the choice of responses.' Unpublished Ph.D. thesis, University of Cambridge.

Rabbitt, P. M. A. 1964. 'Ignoring irrelevant information.' *Brit. J. Psychol. 55*, 403-14.

Rabbitt, P. M. A. 1965. 'Response facilitation on repetition of a limb movement.' *Br. J. Psychol. 56*, 303-4.

Rabbitt, P. M. A. 1966. 'Times for transitions between hand and foot responses in a self-paced task.' *Quart. J. exp. Psychol. 18*, 334-9.

Rabbitt, P. M. A. 1967. 'Ignoring irrelevant information.' *Amer. J. Psychol.* 80, 1-13.

Rabbitt, P. M. A. 1968. 'Repetition effects and signal classification strategies in serial choice-response tasks.' *Quart. J. exp. Psychol. 20*, 232-40.

Rabbitt, P. M. A., Cumming, G. and Vyas, S. M. 1977a 'Sequential factors in visual search.' In S. Dornic (ed.) *Attention and performance VI*. Potomac Md.: Lawrence Erlbaum.

Rabbitt, P. M. A., Cumming, G. and Vyas, S. M. 1978, 'Modulation of selective attention by sequential effects in visual search.' *Quart. J. exp. Psychol.* (in press).

Rabbitt, P. M. A., Jordan, T. C. and Vyas, S. M. 1978. 'Attentional priming in serial, self-paced choice-response tasks.' In press with *J. exp. Psychol: Human Percep. and Perform.*

Rabbitt, P. M. A. 1978. 'Visual selective attention.' In E. Carterette and M. Friedman (eds) *Handbook of perception VI*. New York: Academic Press.

Rabbitt, P. M. A. and Rodgers, B. 1976. Paper in press.

Rayner, K. 1975. 'The perceptual span and peripheral cues in reading.' *Cogn. Psychol. 7*, 65-81.

Rayner, K. and McConkie, G. W. 1973. 'A computer technique for identifying the perceptual span in reading.' Paper presented at the Eastern Psychological Association meeting, Washington D.C. (Text available from authors.)

Reicher, G. M. 1969. 'Perceptual recognition as a function of the meaningfulness of the material.' *J. exp. Psychol. 81*, 275-80.

Rubenstein, H., Richter, M. L. and Kay, E. J. 1975. 'Pronounceability and the visual recognition of nonsense words.' *J. verb. Learn. verb. Behav. 14*, 651-7.

Rumelhart, D. E. 1970. 'A multicomponent theory of the perception of briefly presented visual displays.' *J. Math. Psychol. 7*, 191-218.

Saraga, E. and Shallice, T. 1973, 'Parallel processing of the attributes of single stimuli.' *Percep. & Psychophys. 13*, 261-70.

Schendell, J. D. and Shaw, P. 1976. *Percep. & Psychophys. 19*, 383-93.

Selfridge, O. G. 1959. 'Pandemonium: a paradigm for learning.' In *The mechanisation of thought processes*. London: H.M. Stationery Office.

Selfridge, O. G. 1966. 'Pandemonium: a paradigm for learning.' In L. Uhr (ed.) *Pattern recognition*. New York: Wiley.

Selfridge, O. G. and Neisser, U. 1960. 'Pattern recognition by machine.' *Sci. Am. 203,* 60-8.

Senders, J. W. 1973. *Visual scanning behaviour in visual search.* Washington D.C.: National Academy of Sciences.

Shaw, M. L. and Shaw, P. 1977. 'Optimal allocation of cognitive resources to spatial locations.' *J. exp. Psychol.: Human Percep. & Perform. 3,* 201-11.

Sheridan, T. and Johannsen, G. (eds) 1977. *Monitoring behaviour and supervising control.* N.Y.: Plenum Press.

Shurtleff, D. A. and Marsetta, N.Y. 1968. 'Visual search in a letter cancelling task re-examined.' *J. exp. Psychol. 77,* 19-23.

Smith, F., Lott, D. and Cromwell, B. 1969. 'The effect of type-size and case alternation on word identification.' *Amer. J. Psychol. 82,* 248-53.

Smith, P. T. and Jones, S. 1977.

Sperling, G. 1960. 'The information available in brief visual presentations.' *Psycholog. Monog. 74,* No. 11.

Sperling, G., Budianski, J., Spivak, J. G. and Johnstone, M. L. 1971. 'Extremely rapid visual search: the maximum rate of scanning letters for the presence of a numeral.' *Science 174,* 307-10.

Sternberg, S. 1966. 'High speed scanning in human memory.' *Science 153,* 652-4.

Sternberg, S. 1975. 'Memory scanning. New findings and current controversies.' *Quart. J. exp. Psychol. 27,* 1-32.

Sternberg, S. and Scarborough, D. L. 1969. 'Parallel testing of stimuli in visual search.' Paper presented at the international symposium on visual information processing and control of motor activity. Bulgaria, July 1969.

Thompson, M. and Massaro, D. W. 1973. 'Visual information and redundancy in reading.' *J. exp. Psychol. 98,* 49-54.

Townsend, J. T. 1971a. 'Theoretical analysis of an alphabetic confusion matrix.' *Percep. & Psychophys. 9,* 40-50.

Townsend, J. T. 1971b. 'A note on the identifiability of parallel and serial processes.' *Percep. & Psychophys. 10,* 161-3.

Treisman, A. M. 1969. 'Strategies and models of selective attention.' *Psycholog. Rev. 76,* 282-99.

Treisman, A. M. 1977. 'Focussed attention in the perception and retrieval of multidimensional stimuli.' *Percep. & Psychophys.* In press.

Treisman, A. M., Sykes, M. and Gelade, G. 1977. 'Selective attention and stimulus integration.' In S. Dornic (ed.) *Attention and performance VI.* Potomac Ma.: Lawrence Erlbaum.

Uhr, L. 1966. 'Pattern recognition.' In L. Uhr (ed.) *Pattern recognition.* New York: Wiley.

Uhr, L. and Vossler, C. 1963. 'A pattern recognition program that generates, evaluates and adjusts its own operators.' In E. A. Feigenbaum and J. Feldman (eds) *Computers and thought.* New York: McGraw Hill.

Vingilis, E., Blake, J. and Theodor, L. 1977. 'Recognition versus recall of visually versus acoustically confusable letter matrices.' *Memory and Cognition 5,* 146-50.

von Wright, J. M. 1968. 'Selection in visual immediate memory.' *Quart. J. exp. Psychol. 20,* 62-8.

von Wright, J. M. 1970. 'On selection in visual immediate memory.' *Acta Psychol. 33,* 280-92.

von Wright, J. M. 1975. Chapter in Rabbitt, P. M. A. and S. Dornic (eds) *Attention and performance VI*. London: Academic Press.

von Wright, J. M. 1977, Chapter in S. Dornic, (ed.) *Attention and performance VI*. Potomac Md.: Erlbaum.

Wattenbarger, B. L. (1969). 'Speed and accuracy set in visual search performance. (Ph.D. thesis) University of Michigan.

Wheeler, D. D. 1970. 'Processes in word recognition.' *Cogn. Psychol. 1,* 59-85.

Willows, D. M. and McKinnon, G. E. 1973. 'Selective Reading: Attention to the "unattended" lines.' *Canad. J. Psychol. 27,* 292-304.

Chapter 2

Verbal Remembering

MICHAEL W. EYSENCK

INTRODUCTION

Theoretical approaches to human memory are considerably more complex than even ten years ago. In part, this is attributable to the contemporary view that remembering cannot be sharply divided off from other processes: an information-processing analysis recognizes that attentional, perceptual, and cognitive processes are necessary components of a complete theory of memory. In addition, there is a growing awareness that memory traces are more complicated than was previously thought to be the case. It is now customary to argue that memory traces comprise attributes, features, tags, nodes and associative links, in contrast to the former emphasis on trace strength.

In an excellent analysis of changing theoretical views of the crucial concept of the memory trace, Tulving and Watkins (1975) pointed out that memory traces will appear to be differentiated primarily along the quantitative dimension of trace strength if a single measure of retention is used. If we discover that common words are better recalled than rare words, the interpretation is likely to be that trace strength is positively related to word frequency. Much more complete information about the memory trace can be obtained if there is successive probing of a given trace with two or more different types of retrieval cue. If, for example, subjects told to process phonemically can subsequently recall a word when given a rhyming cue but not a semantic cue, whereas those told to process semantically can recall to the semantic cue only,

*Thanks are due to the Social Science Research Council for financial assistance during the preparation of the manuscript, and to Christine Eysenck for critical comments on an earlier draft of this chapter.

then this indicates that the processing instructions have produced qualitatively different memory traces. Tulving and Watkins (1975) indicated one way in which information from successive probes could be combined to describe the trace in their reduction method.

Remembering of information depends on the structure of memory, the processes involved in the storage of information, and the processes involved in accessing that information subsequently. The following sections consider these various inter-related factors. Work on sentence memory is evaluated by Eysenck (1977a).

STRUCTURAL MODELS

The consensus view of the structure of human memory from the standpoint of the nineteen sixties was provided by Murdock (1967) with his 'modal model'. This model distinguished between sensory store, primary memory and secondary memory. Attention causes information to pass from the modality-specific sensory store to primary memory, and rehearsal allows information to be transferred from primary to secondary memory. Forgetting is due to decay from the sensory store, to displacement from primary memory, and to interference from secondary memory.

Many aspects of this formulation were effectively criticized by Craik and Lockhart (1972), who pointed out that it was too inflexible. It is also true that the role of rehearsal was exaggerated, and it is difficult to see how visually presented information could be rehearsed in primary memory *before* contact has been made with secondary memory.

The simple assumption that primary memory represents the contents of consciousness, or the currently active portion of secondary memory, has merit (for a review, see Watkins 1974a). The most obvious prediction from such a viewpoint is that information can be accessed more rapidly in primary memory than in secondary memory, and this result has been obtained several times (e.g. Mohs and Atkinson 1974).

Current thinking about primary memory or short-term memory owes much to Baddeley and Hitch (1974). They required subjects to perform reasoning, prose comprehension or free recall learning tasks while simultaneously holding sequences of up to six random digits in short-term memory. The results indicated that subjects could hold up to three items with virtually no effect on task performance, but a decrement occurred when more than three items had to be retained. These, and other, findings were interpreted in terms of a working memory system which operates as a central executive, and a supplementary articulatory loop with a capacity of approximately three items. Since use of the articulatory loop is optional, the hypothesis is able potentially to interpret both the numerous phonemic similarity effects in short-term memory, and their occasional absence.

Baddeley, Thomson, and Buchanan (1975) found that there was a systematic relationship between articulation time and the immediate memory span for words, such that memory span was equivalent to the number of words that could be read aloud in approximately two seconds. On the assumption that memory span relies on the articulatory loop, the implication is that the articulatory loop is time-based, and hence has a temporally limited capacity.

It has frequently been assumed that primary memory underlies the recency effect in free recall. Richardson and Baddeley (1975) argued that, if the articulatory-loop component of working memory were involved in producing the recency effect, then articulatory suppression would have its greatest detrimental effect on the last few items in the list. In fact, the adverse effects of suppression were constant across all list positions, indicating that the articulatory loop is not involved in the recency effect.

Hitch and Baddeley (1976) explored the characteristics of the central working-memory executive. In an experiment in which subjects had to repeat six digits out loud a number of times while performing a sentence-verification task, they found that the concurrent digit load interfered more severely with performance for the more grammatically complex sentences. This finding suggested that working memory is an executive system with a limited capacity for information processing.

Since the information in working or primary memory has already contacted long-term memory (if it had not, it would appear novel to the subject), it may be fruitful to think of primary or working memory as a stage of response pre-programming (i.e. as an output buffer). The eye-voice span, in which the words spoken by a reader lag behind the point fixated by him may exemplify the working of this system.

LEVELS OF PROCESSING

An interesting approach to memory was proposed by Craik and Lockhart (1972) and Craik (1973). The essence of their formulation was expressed in the following terms by Craik (1973): 'Trace persistence is a positive function of the depth of analysis. "Depth" is defined in terms of the meaningfulness extracted from the stimulus rather than in terms of the number of analyses performed upon it' (p. 48). The reason that deep levels of processing enhance retention is that deep processing enables the subject to make substantial use of learned rules and past knowledge. Craik and Lockhart (1972) also pointed out that deep levels of processing might or might not facilitate retention, contingent upon the retrieval environment. Finally, they claimed that memory was unaffected by repetition of processing at a constant depth.

Subsequent theoretical extensions of the original formulation have emphasized additional factors that are related to depth of encoding. For example, Craik and Tulving (1975) maintained that the depth of encoding and the spread or elaboration of encoding within the variegated encoding domains are both importantly related to retention. Lockhart, Craik, and Jacoby (1976) emphasized the importance of trace distinctiveness: 'The beneficial effect of depth of encoding is that deeper, richer encodings are also more distinctive and unique' (p. 86).

The levels-of-processing approach has frequently been examined experimentally by utilizing incidental-learning paradigms, since they give the experimenter control over the subject's information-processing activities. For example, Craik (1973) presented a list of words one at a time, and required his subjects to answer questions either involving shallow levels of processing (e.g. 'Is the word in capital letters?') or deep levels (e.g. 'Is the word a member of the following category: ---?'). Deeply encoded words were much better remembered than shallowly encoded words. The common finding that semantic encodings are better remembered than phonemic encodings is consistent with the general approach.

The importance of spread or elaboration of encoding at the semantic level of processing was demonstrated by Klein and Saltz (1976). Their processing tasks required subjects to rate nouns in terms of semantic attribute dimensions. Recall was superior for words rated on two dimensions than for words rated on a single dimension. Of those words rated on two dimensions, recall was higher where the two dimensions were independent (pleasant-unpleasant and big-little) than where the dimensions were related (pleasant-unpleasant and fast-slow).

While the levels approach has the undeniable advantage over other approaches of avoiding paradigm specificity, there are several difficulties with the Craik-Lockhart formulation (cf., Eysenck 1977b):

(1) There is no independent measure of processing depth. It was originally argued that deeper levels of processing take longer than shallow levels, but there are several exceptions (e.g. Craik and Tulving 1975). The problem was expressed in the following terms by

Eysenck (1978): 'In view of the vagueness with which depth is defined, there is the danger of using retention-test performance to provide information about the depth of processing, and then using the putative depth of processing to "explain" the retention-test performance, a self-defeating exercise in circularity'. The concept of spread or elaboration is equally vague.

(2) There has been some theoretical confusion about whether memory traces differ quantitatively or qualitatively, or both. Use of the term 'depth', and the claim that depth of processing can be defined in terms of the amount of meaningfulness extracted from the stimulus suggest that traces differ quantitatively. However, Craik and Lockhart (1972) argued that perceptual processing involves the qualitatively different stages of analysis of physical features, pattern recognition, and the extraction of meaning, and that the memory trace is based upon this perceptual analysis. Qualitative differences were obtained by Davies and Cubbage (1976), who found that more homophone errors were made following rhyme encoding, whereas more synonym errors were made after categorical encoding.

(3) It is hard to distinguish between the effects of depth, elaboration and distinctiveness, since deep encodings are usually more elaborate and distinctive than shallow encodings. The most promising interpretation of the data may be that physical (e.g. phonemic) encodings of a to-be-remembered item are relatively invariant across different situations, making the intra-experimental physical encoding non-distinctive, and thus poorly remembered. A related viewpoint is developed by Moscovitch and Craik (1976).

(4) Nelson (1977) has investigated the hypothesis of Craik and Lockhart (1972) that repetition of processing at a constant depth does not enhance retention. In contradistinction to the hypothesis, Nelson found that repetition of processing at either the phonemic or the semantic level significantly facilitated retention. Moreover, this effect was obtained with tests of uncued recall, cued recall and recognition.

RETRIEVAL

Sternberg Paradigm

In order to investigate any one of the three successive stages of acquisition, storage, and retrieval, it is necessary to take the other two stages into account. Sternberg (1975) attempted to arrange conditions where acquisition and storage were perfect, thus permitting observation of retrieval uncomplicated by failures at the previous stages. He studied the time people take to decide whether a particular test item is or is not among those in a previously memorized set, and found it to be an increasing linear function of the number of items in the set. Since the slope of the function for 'yes' decisions is approximately the same as that for 'no' decisions, Sternberg argued that subjects engaged in serial exhaustive searches, i.e. they searched through all the items in the set. If subjects were to terminate their searches when they found the critical item, the slope for 'yes' decisions would be approximately half that for 'no' decisions.

Corballis (1975) discussed several criticisms of Sternberg's hypothesis. For example, contrary to the exhaustive-scan assumption, several investigators have obtained a recency effect, with faster reaction times being found for more recent items. While Sternberg's hypothesis predicts a linear relationship between set size and reaction time, several researchers have reported functions which are negatively accelerated, and more closely approximated by a logarithmic function than by a linear one. Furthermore, Baddeley and Ecob (1973) found that reaction times were faster for items that were repeated in the memory set, a finding inconsistent with the notion of a serial-exhaustive search.

It is possible that there is no search process through the memorized set, but that the subject's reaction time is based on the strength or familiarity of stored information about the test item. Reaction times might increase as a function of the size of the memory set because increasing the size of the memory set would reduce the average familiarity of the items in it. If the more recent items are stronger or more familiar, decisions concerning them will have short latencies. However, while strength hypotheses account for serial-position effects, they often cannot explain why the relationship between set size and reaction time should be linear.

Atkinson and Juola (1974) have argued for a model incorporating elements from the Sternberg and strength theories. Initially, the subjective familiarity of the test stimulus is evaluated against a double criterion. The subject makes a fast positive response if the test stimulus has very high familiarity, and a fast negative response if the test stimulus has very low familiarity. If the subjective familiarity of the test item is intermediate, a serial search of the memorized set is undertaken. This model is intuitively reasonable and in accord with most of the evidence.

Since the great majority of studies in this area have found that error rates increase as the set size increases, there is the continual problem that reaction times for different set sizes may be differentially affected by speed-accuracy tradeoff. Reed (1976) argued for the value of taking response accuracy as the dependent variable, and manipulating the time available for processing of the test stimulus. In his response-signal method, the experimenter controls the lag between the onset of the probe and a signal instructing the subject to respond. The subject must respond as rapidly as possible after the response signal.

On the simplest assumptions from Sternberg's exhaustive-scan model, no information will be available before the search or scan is completed, and full information thereafter. This would mean that accuracy would increase dramatically around that time lag corresponding to the scan time. There should be comparable speed-accuracy curves for all list lengths, with the large accuracy increases taking place thirty to forty msec later for each additional item, since Sternberg found this to be the search rate per item. In fact, none of these predictions was upheld, and longer lists required longer processing-time intervals for accurate responding than would be predicted by Sternberg. While strength models would predict that maximal accuracy would vary inversely with list length, maximal accuracy was actually affected very little by list length. The obtained data were best explained in terms of a model proposed by Theios, Smith, Haviland, Traupmann and Moy (1973), who claimed that subjects performed a self-terminating scan.

Recall and Recognition

Watkins, Ho and Tulving (1976) have discussed the popular two-stage theory of recall and recognition. This theory assumes that a person's knowledge comprises a network of nodes, many of which correspond to words in the person's vocabulary, together with associative links among the nodes. Memory for specific events is carried in the form of tags attached to the appropriate nodes. Recall requires the two stages of searching through the network for the right node, followed by a decision process based on whether or not the node is appropriately tagged. Recognition provides direct access to the appropriate node, and thus bypasses the search process.

This theory predicts that recognition will be unaffected by changes in context between study and test. In fact, Tulving (1976) has reviewed evidence indicating that recognition performance is typically better when the context at input and test is the same. For example, if the word 'JAM' is presented at input in the phrase 'strawberry JAM', then it is better remembered when tested in that phrase than in the phrase 'traffic JAM'. To handle this, Anderson and Bower (1974) argued that some words (especially homographic words) could be represented in the associative network by more than one node. Recognition can now be affected by context changes if different nodes are accessed at input and at test.

Watkins *et al.* (1976) demonstrated a difficulty with this revised theory. They presented pairs of strange faces to their subjects, followed by a recognition test with each face presented in the context of the same or a different face. They found that performance was better in the same-context condition than the different-context condition. The two-stage theory would presumably argue that each new face presented at input resulted in the creation of a new node in the associative network, complete with the appropriate tag. With such stimuli, context could not bias the selection of nodes, since there is only one relevant node for each stimulus. This prediction of no context effect was disconfirmed by the results.

The effects of context on recognition memory can be accounted for within the framework of Tulving's encoding specificity principle, which was expressed in the following words by Wiseman and Tulving (1976): 'A to-be-remembered (TBR) item is encoded with respect to the context in which it is studied, producing a unique trace which incorporates information from both target and context. For the TBR item to be retrieved, the cue information at the time of retrieval must appropriately match the trace of the item-in-context' (p. 349). One implication of this approach is that much forgetting is cue-dependent (i.e. the retrieval cue does not access the appropriate trace information) rather than trace-dependent (i.e. loss of information from the trace).

The two-stage theory predicts that recognition will always equal or exceed recall, since recall comprises two fallible stages, only the second of which is involved in recognition, whereas the encoding specificity principle allows for the possibility that recall could exceed recognition. This surprising result has been obtained mainly where the context and target words form a cohesive Gestalt, as in a study by Watkins (1974b). Subjects learned paired associates such as 'SPANI-EL' and 'EXPLO-RE', followed by tests of recognition (e.g. 'EL' and 'RE') or cued recall (e.g. 'SPANI-?' and 'EXPLO-?'). Recall was substantially superior to recognition (sixty-seven per cent versus nine per cent), presumably because the Gestalten of 'SPANIEL' and 'EXPLORE' were more readily evoked by the retrieval cue used for recall than that used for recognition. In other words, there was an associative asymmetry between the abilities of the two parts of a unified whole to reinstate that unified whole.

Salzberg (1976) argued that it was the most concrete or salient component of an encoded unit that provided the most reliable access to it. He found that cued recall only exceeded recognition where the retrieval cue on the recall test comprised the more concrete part of the previously learned paired associate (e.g. 'cloud' in the paired associate 'cloud-BLACK').

Tulving (1976) has shown that encoded traces are specific to the environmental context prevailing at the time of input, and that highly specific retrieval cues may be required to gain access to stored information. However, there are doubts as to the empirical testability of the encoding specificity principle. Tulving claims that identical processes are used in recall and recognition, which may be incorrect. Paivio (1976) correlated recognition and recall scores for seventy-two items, and found that the correlations were mostly non-significant. Broadbent and Broadbent (1975) compared recognition for those items that could not be recalled from a list with recognition for all list items. In several experiments they found that the non-recalled items showed no recognition disadvantage.

CONCLUSIONS

An encouraging development in the past few years has been the emergence of general theories that have considerable application outside the limitations of a specific experimental task. All the above theoretical approaches have this characteristic. While such approaches are generally imprecise both with respect to defining major theoretical concepts and the generating of specific predictions, they are to be preferred to precise analyses of the utterly trivial.

There are several useful summaries of memory research which have recently appeared. These include a chapter by Peterson (1977), and books by Crowder (1976), Gregg (1975) and Eysenck (1977a).

REFERENCES

Anderson, J. R. and Bower, G. H. 1974. 'A propositional theory of recognition memory.' *Memory and Cognition 2,* 406-12.

Atkinson, R. C. and Juola, J. F. 1974. 'Search and decision processes in recognition memory.' In D. H. Krantz, R. C. Atkinson and P. Suppes (eds) *Contemporary developments in mathematical psychology.* London: W. H. Freeman.

Baddeley, A. D. and Ecob, J. R. 1973. 'Reaction time and short-term memory: Implications of repetition effects for the high-speed exhaustive scan hypothesis.' *Quart J. exp. Psychol. 25,* 229-40.

Baddeley, A. D. and Hitch, G. 1974. 'Working memory.' In G. H. Bower (ed.) *The psychology of learning and motivation 8*. London: Academic Press.

Baddeley, A. D., Thomson, N. and Buchanan, M. 1975. 'Word length and the structure of short-term memory.' *J. verb. Learn. verb. Behav. 14,* 575-89.

Broadbent, D. E. and Broadbent, M. H. P. 1975. 'The recognition of words which cannot be recalled.' In P. M. A. Rabbitt and S. Dornic (eds) *Attention and performance V,* 575-90.

Corballis, M. C. 1975. 'Access to memory: An analysis of recognition times.' In P. M. A. Rabbitt and S. Dornic (eds) *Attention and performance V,* 591-612.

Craik, F. I. M. 1973. 'A "Levels of Analysis" view of memory.' In P. Pliner, L. Krames and T. M. Alloway (eds) *Communication and affect: language and thought*. London: Academic Press.

Craik, F. I. M. and Lockhart, R. S. 1972. 'Levels of processing: A framework for memory research.' *J. verb. Learn. verb. Behav. 11,* 671-84.

Craik, F. I. M. and Tulving, E. 1975. 'Depth of processing and the retention of words in episodic memory.' *J. exp. Psychol.: Gen. 104,* 268-94.

Crowder, R. G. 1976. *Principles of learning and memory*. London: Wiley.

Davies, G. and Cubbage, A. 1976. 'Attribute coding at different levels of processing'. *Quart. J. exp. Psychol. 28,* 653-60.

Eysenck, M. W. 1977. *Human memory: theory, research, and individual differences*. Oxford: Pergamon.

Eysenck, M. W. 1978. 'Levels of processing: a critique.' *Brit. J. Psychol. 69*.

Gregg, V. H. 1975. *Human memory*. London: Methuen.

Hitch, G. J. and Baddeley, A. D. 1976. 'Verbal reasoning and working memory.' *Quart. J. exp. Psychol. 28,* 603-21.

Klein, K. and Saltz, E. 1976. 'Specifying the mechanisms in a levels-of-processing approach to memory.' *J. exp. Psychol.: Hum. Learn. Mem. 2,* 671-9.

Lockhart, R. S., Craik, F. I. M. and Jacoby, L. 1976. 'Depth of processing recognition, and recall.' in J. Brown (ed.) *Recall and recognition*. London: Wiley.

Mohs, R. C. and Atkinson, R. C. 1974. 'Recognition time for words in short-term, long-term, or both memory stores.' *J. exp. Psychol. 102,* 830-5.

Moscovitch, M. and Craik, F. I. M. 1976. 'Depth of processing, retrieval cues, and uniqueness of encoding as factors in recall.' *J. verb. Learn. verb. Behav.* 15, 447-58.

Murdock, B. B. 1967. 'Recent developments in short-term memory.' *Brit. J. Psychol. 58,* 421-33.

Nelson, T. O. 1977. 'Repetition and depth of processing.' *J. verb. Learn. verb. Behav. 16,* 151-71.

Paivio, A. 1976. 'Imagery in recall and recognition.' In J. Brown (ed.) *Recall and recognition*. London: Wiley.

Peterson, L. R. 1977. 'Verbal learning and memory.' In M. R. Rozenweig and L. W. Porter (eds) *Annual review of psychology 28*. Palo Alto: Annual Reviews Inc.

Reed, A. V. 1976. 'List length and the time course of recognition in immediate memory.' *Memory and Cognition 4,* 16-30.

Richardson, J. T. E. and Baddeley, A. D. 1975. 'The effect of articulatory suppression in free recall.' *J. verb. Learn. verb. Behav. 14,* 623-9.

Salzberg, P. M. 1976. 'On the generality of encoding specificity.' *J. exp. Psychol.: Hum. Learn. Mem. 2,* 586-96.

Sternberg, S. 1975. 'Memory scanning: new findings and current controversies.' *Quart. J. exp. Psychol. 27,* 1-32.

Theios, J., Smith, P. G., Haviland, S. E., Traupmann, J. and Moy, M. C. 1973, 'Memory scanning as a serial self-terminating process.' *J. exp. Psychol. 97,* 323-36.

Tulving, E. 1976. 'Ecphoric processes in recall and recognition.' In J. Brown (ed.) *Recall and recognition.* London: Wiley.

Tulving, E. and Watkins, M. J. 1975. 'Structure of memory traces.' *Psychol. Rev. 80,* 352-73.

Watkins, M. J. 1974a. 'The concept and measurement of primary memory.' *Psychol. Bull. 81,* 695-711.

Watkins, M. J. 1974b. 'When is recall spectacularly higher than recognition?' *J. exp. Psychol. 102,* 161-3.

Watkins, M. J., Ho, E. and Tulving, E. 1976. 'Context effects in recognition memory for faces.' *J. verb. Learn. verb. Behav. 15,* 505-17.

Wiseman, S. and Tulving, E. 1976. 'Encoding specificity: relation between recall superiority and recognition failure.' *J. exp. Psychol.: Hum. Learn. Mem. 2,* 349-61.

Chapter 3

Conditioning

N. J. MACKINTOSH

INTRODUCTION

The study of simple conditioning, it is sometimes difficult to believe, was once regarded as a central topic in psychology, which would advance our understanding of all human behaviour. A more common attitude today is that conditioning is a dull and mechanical form of learning, whose rather trivial laws (such as contiguity and reinforcement) are fully understood and do not merit further study. We should be able to reject the first attitude without accepting the second. The analysis of conditioning will probably never succeed in telling us how young children learn to speak their native language or older children learn the differential calculus. On the other hand, research of the past ten years has shown that our traditional theories are quite inadequate to encompass the central facts of conditioning. We can now see that conditioning is not reducible to the strengthening of stimulus-response associations by the automatic action of a process called reinforcement. It is more profitably viewed as a matter of detecting and learning about relations between events; it is the process whereby organisms typically discover what signals or causes such events of consequence to themselves as food or water, danger or safety (Testa 1974; Rescorla 1975).

The strong hold gained by stimulus-response theory over the minds of a generation of psychologists arose partly from the historical accident that many early experiments, certainly those which found their way into textbooks, were fortuitously restricted to producing data appropriate to the theory. Thorndike placed cats in a puzzle box and observed that they learned an arbitrary response, such as pressing a panel, which gained their release from the box and access to food. Pavlov restrained dogs on a conditioning stand and observed that they learned to salivate at the sound of a bell which regularly preceded the delivery of food. In each case the experimenter recorded an increase in the probability of a particular response in the presence of a particular stimulus situation. What could be more natural than to suppose that conditioning consisted in the strengthening of stimulus-response connections? Natural it may have been, but certainly not necessary. Instead of treating the response of salivating or panel pressing as what is learned, we could regard it simply as a convenient *index* that the subject has detected certain relationships in its environment. Thorndike arranged a particular relationship between his subjects' behaviour and a particular outcome (thus performing the first experiment on instrumental conditioning); and his cats, by changing their behaviour appropriately, showed that they had learned this relationship. Pavlov arranged a particular relationship between an external stimulus and a particular outcome (thus performing the first experiment on classical conditioning); and his dogs, by salivating to that stimulus, showed that they had learned this relationship.

VARIETIES OF CONDITIONING

Most of our traditional conceptions of conditioning have given a totally false impression of the nature of conditioning because they have been based on far too restricted a set of observations. Thus classical conditioning, it is often assumed, applies only to local reflexes such as salivation, leg flexion, or blinking. It is clear, however, that a process of classical conditioning will endow initially neutral stimuli with the properties of goals which will elicit approach or avoidance behaviour depending on their relation to an appetitive reinforcer such as food (Hearst and Franklin 1977). Experiments on conditioned suppression and enhancement (Blackman 1977) may be viewed as studies of emotional or motivational interactions generated by the classical pairing of stimuli and reinforcers. Experiments on taste-aversion conditioning (Revusky and Garcia 1970; Riley and Baril 1976) show that classical conditioning plays an essential role in the regulation of food intake.

We should accept that classical conditioning can produce a wide variety of changes in behaviour. Frequently, moreover, these changes are only with difficulty described as increases in the probability of any readily specifiable response. In conditioned suppression and in taste-aversion conditioning, for example, conditioning is measured as a decline in the frequency of responding or a decline in the consumption of a particular substance. Similarly, although Thorndike's cats, or their modern equivalent, Skinner's rats, will learn to press a panel or lever if rewarded with food for doing so, they will rapidly learn to stop pressing the lever if this response produces an electric shock in addition to the food. How is a theory which regards conditioning as the formation of stimulus-response associations to explain cases of conditioning which result in a decline in responding?

Finally, the textbook examples of conditioning experiments are restricted to the arrangement of only one of several possible relationships between events. In Pavlov's or Thorndike's experiments, the conditioned stimulus (CS) or response is positively correlated with the occurrence of the reinforcer. If we view conditioning as a matter of learning relationships, there is no need to confine our attention to this particular contingency. It is as easy to arrange a negative correlation between a stimulus and a reinforcer as a positive one. Following Pavlov, we can say that the positive correlation, in which the CS signals an increase in the probability of a reinforcer, produces excitatory conditioning, while the negative correlation, in which a CS signals a decrease in the probability of a reinforcer, produces inhibitory conditioning. Although Pavlov himself devoted heroic efforts to the study of inhibitory conditioning, until recently it has received scant attention from western psychologists (Rescorla 1975). In part, this is probably again because stimulus-response theory has been content to ignore, because it could not easily explain, a form of learning which typically produces a decline in the probability of a CR.

DISTINCTION BETWEEN CLASSICAL AND INSTRUMENTAL CONDITIONING

Fifty years ago, Miller and Konorski (1928) drew a sharp distinction between classical or Pavlovian and instrumental or operant conditioning. The reality or importance of this distinction continues to cause dispute (Gray 1975; Hearst 1975). All are agreed on the reality of the operational distinction: in a classical conditioning experiment, the experimenter arranges a relationship between a stimulus (the CS) and a reinforcer regardless of the subject's behaviour; in an instrumental experiment, he arranges a relationship between the subject's behaviour and a reinforcer. It seems obvious that the question whether this operational distinction is of any theoretical importance must reduce to the question whether the subject's behaviour is *in fact* modified by stimulus-reinforcer relations alone in some situations, and by response-reinforcer relations in others. The reason why the question cannot be answered simply by reference to the experimenter's operations, is that those operations may fail to specify the actual controlling relationships. Thus in an operationally defined instrumental experiment, food may be given to a pigeon only when it pecks an illuminated response key, or to a rat only when it runs down an alley into a goal box. But each of these experimental arrangements also contains various implicit stimulus-reinforcer relationships. If the pigeon receives food for pecking the key, then a close view of the illuminated key is reliably associated with the delivery of food; to a rat rewarded in a particular goal box, that goal box is a reliable signal for food. Is it not possible that these stimulus-reinforcer relationships are responsible for the observed change in the pigeon's and rat's behaviour? Conversely, in operationally defined classical experiments, a dog may salivate to a CS signalling food, or flex its leg to a CS signalling shock to the paw. But although the experimenter may deliver food or shock regardless of the subject's behaviour, there are two ways in which a response-reinforcer relationship may operate. First, as soon as a conditioned response (CR) occurs, it will in fact be followed by the reinforcer, and this temporal contiguity may increase the probability of the CR; secondly, and more plausibly, the dog may learn that salivating makes dry food more palatable, or flexing its leg makes a shock to the paw less painful. Is it not possible that these implicit response-reinforcer relationships are responsible for the increase in salivation and leg flexion?

One experimental procedure for answering this question is to add an explicit response-reinforcer contingency to an otherwise classical experiment. If, for example, dogs flex their legs to a CS signalling shock because this reduces the pain of the shock, the implication is that they would learn even more rapidly if this response enabled them to avoid the shock altogether. Wahlsten and Cole (1972) compared the performance of dogs trained on the straightforward classical contingency where the CR had no scheduled consequence and those trained on this avoidance contingency, with results shown in Figure 3.1a. The explicit avoidance schedule produced reliably better learning; the implication is that the flexion response can be modified by its instrumental consequences. Figure 3.1b, however, shows the results of a comparable study of the eyeblink response in rabbits to a CS signalling shock to the cheek (Coleman 1975). In this case, animals that could avoid the shock by blinking actually responded rather less than animals trained on the strict classical contingency. The implication is that *this* response is not modified by its consequences and must therefore have

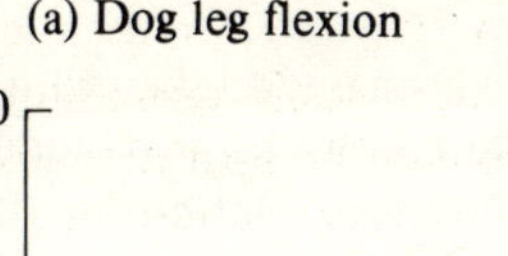

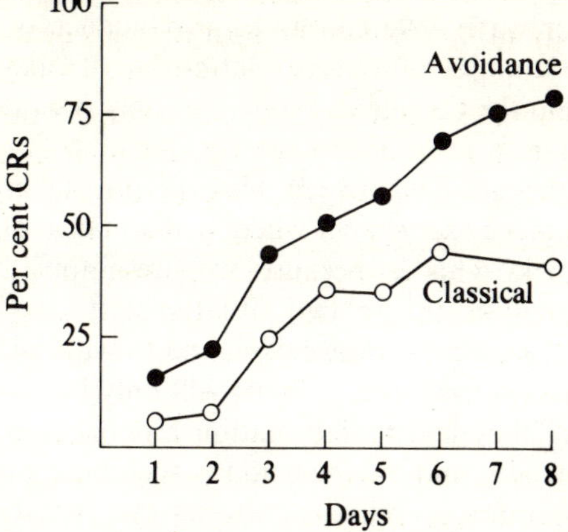

Figure 3.1a

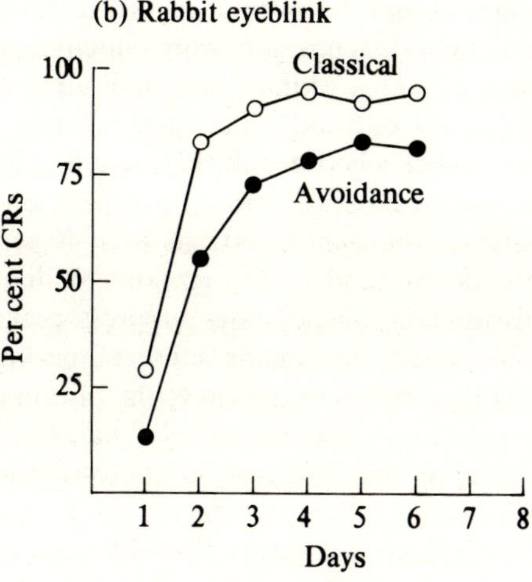

Figure 3.1b

been conditioned by the classical, stimulus-reinforcer relationship alone.

Similar experiments have been undertaken with appetitive reinforcers such as food or water. We can add an avoidance or omission contingency to the stimulus-reinforcer relationship of Pavlov's experiment by arranging that the CS signals food – but only provided that the dog does not salivate in response to the CS. At first glance, it may not be easy to see the parallel between this experimental arrangement and that of an avoidance experiment where performance of the CR avoids an electric shock. This is because we are implicitly applying an instrumental analysis to the two situations: it pays the animal to perform the CR in the avoidance case, and to withhold the CR in the appetitive omission case. But animals will only behave in this instrumental manner if they detect these relationships between their behaviour and its consequences, and can then modify their behaviour accordingly. The stimulus-reinforcer relationships in the two experiments are identical: a CS sometimes signals reinforcement and sometimes not, and this should be sufficient to ensure that the CS will elicit a CR. On a Pavlovian analysis, dogs will learn that the CS signals food and will therefore come to salivate to the bell even though this costs them food.

In fact, although the omission contingency clearly suppresses the tendency to salivate, the remarkable result is that dogs will continue to salivate on a considerable proportion of trials (Herendeen and Shapiro 1975). Even more striking results have been obtained in experiments on 'autoshaping' in pigeons (Hearst and Jenkins 1974). As Brown and Jenkins (1968) discovered, in the absence of any explicit response-reinforcer contingency, a pigeon will come to approach and peck the response-key of a Skinner box if illumination of the key signals the availability of food. Such pecking has been shown to depend on the contingency between the key light and food (Gamzu and Williams 1973), and pigeons will continue to peck on more than fifty per cent of trials for thousands of trials even if pecking invariably causes the omission of food (Schwartz and Williams 1972). Even though the omission contingency does suppress pecking to a certain extent, it is obvious that the major cause of pecking must be the classical stimulus-reinforcer contingency: the pigeon cannot help approaching and contacting a visual stimulus signalling the availability of food even if such approach and contact causes the loss of food (see also Hearst 1977).

Once again, the evidence suggests that different response systems differ in their sensitivity to instrumental contingencies. At one extreme, rabbits show no detectable tendency to suppress jaw movement and swallowing responses to a CS signalling the delivery of water even when such responses cause the omission of water (Gormezano and Hiller 1972). At the other extreme, although rats will come to approach and contact a lever whose appearance signals the delivery of food in the absence of a response contingency, they will rapidly learn not to if such responses cause the omission of food (Locurto, Terrace, and Gibbon 1976).

The distinction between classical and instrumental conditioning, then, is not merely operational. Some responses appear to be readily modifiable by their consequences while others do not; stimulus-reinforcer relationships appear sufficient to generate some changes in behaviour but not others. The distinction is surely not an absolute one: although many responses may be affected more by one process than the other, many are affected by both. Careful analysis has suggested that the precise form of the dog's leg flexion response or the pigeon's key peck, for example, may depend on whether classical or instrumental contingencies are in effective control (Wahlsten and Cole 1972; Schwartz 1977). In the final analysis, indeed, the question at issue is not whether a particular response is only modifiable by one contingency and never by the other: it is whether we can separate the effects of the two types of contingency, and whether animals can learn both kinds of relationship. Thus many historical attempts to find intrinsic characters of classically and instrumentally conditionable responses are largely misconceived and should not detain us long. The most venerable of these attempts, of course, was the suggestion that autonomic responses were classically, and skeletal responses instrumentally, conditioned. Although earlier claims for the modifiability of autonomic responses by instrumental contingencies (Di Cara and Miller 1969) must now be regarded with some scepticism in the light of subsequent failure of replication (Miller and Dworkin 1974), there can hardly be doubt that such skeletal responses as blinking, pecking, or swallowing are subject to classical conditioning. If we are to draw this sort of distinction, it is imperative to stress that it will be one of degree only; at present, the most plausible suggestions seem to be that more reflexive responses are likely to be more subject to classical contingencies, and responses providing substantial intrinsic feedback are likely to be more subject to instrumental contingencies (Mackintosh 1974, 132-8).

SELECTIVE ASSOCIATION IN CONDITIONING

The parallels between classical and instrumental conditioning remain as important as the differences. The differences arise because the former depends on learning a stimulus-reinforcer relationship and the latter a response-reinforcer relationship, and because reinforcers are events with two distinct properties: they elicit or release certain consummatory responses to produce classical conditioning, and they set up goals to produce instrumental conditioning. The parallels arise because the same learning mechanism is used to associate related events regardless of the nature of those events. The phenomena observed in one type of conditioning experiment are, with hardly an exception, also observed in the other. As Kimble (1961) noted, acquisition is affected in similar ways by such variables as contiguity between stimulus or response and reinforcer; extinction and spontaneous recovery, conditioned inhibition, generalization and discrimination, all occur in both types of experiment. Moreover, the one exception which Kimble claimed to find, that partial reinforcement has different effects in classical and instrumental experiments, should be examined with some caution (Mackintosh 1974, 72-5; Leonard 1975).

Perhaps the most important recent development in the study of conditioning, however, has been the discovery that the central proposition of most traditional theories of conditioning is plainly incorrect. The proposition, a legacy of conditioning theory's links with classical associationist theory, is that successful conditioning depends solely on arranging an appropriate temporal relationship between a stimulus or response and an adequate reinforcer. Temporal contiguity between such events is both sufficient and necessary for conditioning to occur.

That temporal contiguity is not necessary for conditioning has been demonstrated most notably by experiments on taste-aversion conditioning. If rats are given a novel substance to eat or drink and are subsequently made sick by such treatments as X-irradiation or injections of lithium chloride or apomorphine, they will show a marked reluctance to eat or drink that substance again, even though the interval between ingestion and sickness (the events to be associated) is counted in minutes or hours rather than seconds (Revusky and Garcia 1970; Riley and Baril 1976).

It is not only the law of temporal contiguity that is violated by these results. The rat is more likely to show an aversion to the flavour or odour of food or drink rather than its visual characteristics or the place in which it was consumed, let alone the numerous other events that must have preceded the onset of sickness (Garcia and Koelling 1966). These peculiarities have led some to suppose that taste-aversion conditioning represents a unique adaptive specialization of learning which may not obey the same laws as other, more arbitrary forms of conditioning (Rozin and Kalat 1971; Seligman 1970), while others have queried the validity of the original experiments (Bitterman 1976; Krane and Wagner 1975). As Revusky (1971) has noted, however, there are numerous parallels between taste-aversion conditioning and other, more conventional paradigms. The two most important are that although conditioning occurs over longer intervals than those usually effective in other paradigms, it still varies inversely with the length of interval separating ingestion and sickness (Revusky 1968; Andrews and Braveman 1975), and an aversion produced by making a rat sick after ingesting one substance does not generalize completely to other flavours (Nowlis 1974; Domjan 1975). These results can only mean that the aversion is a consequence of associating the specific substance ingested with the subsequent sickness.

It is not only in taste-aversion conditioning that strict temporal contiguity is unnecessary for successful conditioning. Lett (1974, 1975) has reported that rats are capable of learning a simple spatial or brightness discrimination in a T-maze with an interval between correct choice and reinforcement as long as an hour. In simple runway experiments, it is well established that rats can use the outcome of one trial as a cue to predict the outcome of the next. Trained on an alternating sequence of reinforced and nonreinforced trials, they rapidly learn that a reward on one trial means no reward on the next (and vice-versa) and run appropriately (Mackintosh 1974, 161-4). Although the majority of earlier studies found no convincing evidence of successful alternation learning at very long intertrial intervals (e.g. Amsel, Hug and Surridge, 1969), it is now clear that learning is possible with a twenty-four hour interval between trials (Jobe, Mellgren, Feinberg, Littlejohn and Rigby 1977).

We must accept, therefore, that the association span of the rat is in principle capable of bridging very long intervals. Why then does it not always do so? Why do delays of reinforcement of only a few seconds sometimes completely prevent conditioning? Conversely, why do not animals associate any and every event of the preceding hour with the eventual occurrence of a particular reinforcer? The answer is to be found in another set of experiments which have established that contiguity between stimulus or response and reinforcement is not sufficient to ensure conditioning. Perhaps the best known example is Kamin's blocking experiment (Kamin 1969). In experiments on conditioned suppression in rats Kamin found that animals exposed to a compound CS, consisting of a light and a noise, signalling shock, would normally condition to both elements of the compound. But prior conditioning to one element of the compound alone signalling

Table 3.1 *Design and Results of Blocking Experiments (Kamin, 1969)*

Groups	*Stage 1*	*Stage 2*	*Test* (Suppression Ratio to Light)
Control	—	Noise+Light→Shock	·05
Blocking	Noise→Shock	Noise+Light→Shock	·45
Surprise	Noise→Shock	Noise+Light→Shock+Shock	·08

Note: Conditioning is measured by the extent to which the CS suppresses ongoing lever pressing. This measure, the suppression ratio, will have the value of ·50 when the CS has no effect on lever pressing, and ·00 when it suppresses lever pressing completely. Thus lower ratios indicate more conditioning.

shock would attenuate or block conditioning to the other element. The design and results of one of Kamin's experiments are shown in Table 3.1. Further experiments showed that blocking of conditioning to the light occurred because the light-noise compound signalled the same reinforcer as that signalled by the noise alone; as is shown by the third group in Table 3.1, when an additional (surprising) shock was programmed after each compound trial, substantial conditioning accrued to the light. Subsequent experiments have amply confirmed the conclusion that blocking is a consequence of the added element predicting no change in reinforcement from that signalled by the pre-trained element alone (Rescorla 1971; Wagner 1971; Dickinson, Hall and Mackintosh 1976).

Blocking is, in fact, only one instance of a general phenomenon: conditioning occurs selectively to relatively good predictors of reinforcement at the expense of relatively poor predictors. The effect of prior training with one element is to make it a better predictor of the outcome of a trial. If, however, the elements of a compound CS are differentially correlated with reinforcement from the outset of conditioning, the subject will rapidly come to attribute the occurrence of reinforcement to the better correlated stimulus at the expense of the worse correlated, even though, in the absence of competition from the better predictor, the worse predictor would have conditioned quite adequately (Wagner, Logan, Haberlandt and Price 1968; Luongo 1976). Differences in contiguity have similar effects. A stimulus may be associated with a reinforcer even if there is a long interval between the two, but only provided that there is not another potential signal standing in a closer temporal relation to the occurrence of the reinforcer. An experiment by Revusky (1971) illustrates the point. Rats were given saccharin-flavoured water to drink, and twenty-five minutes later an injection of lithium chloride which made them ill. On a subsequent test, they refused to drink the saccharin-flavoured water, thus showing that they attributed their illness to the consumption of this novel flavour. But if they had drunk another novel substance (vinegar-flavoured water) during this twenty-five-minute interval, they were much readier to drink the saccharin solution. They attributed their illness to the most recently ingested novel substance rather than one tasted earlier. The same principle can be shown to operate in other conditioning paradigms. Rats will show good conditioned suppression to a very long CS signalling occasional shocks, but if each shock is preceded by a brief stimulus, very little conditioning will accrue to the longer CS (Brodigan and Trapold 1974). Pigeons will learn to peck an illuminated key even if there is a delay of nine seconds between pecking and food, but if a second key is illuminated immediately before the delivery of food, they fail to learn to peck the first key (Williams 1975).

Whether or not a particular stimulus or response is associated with a particular reinforcer, therefore, depends not only on its own relationship to that reinforcer, as traditional associative theories have implied, but on whether *other* stimuli or responses are in a more favourable position for the formation of such associations. Thus the reason why even moderate intervals between a particular stimulus or response and a subsequent reinforcer sometimes prevent conditioning is because the occurrence of that reinforcer is attributed to some other event which more closely preceded it.

Rescorla and Wagner (1972) have proposed a formal model of conditioning which explains this central observation by proposing that conditioning depends upon the discrepancy between obtained and expected reinforcement. Perhaps the greatest single virtue of their model is its ability to integrate excitatory and inhibitory conditioning, since it is clear that inhibitory conditioning is produced by a discrepancy between an expectation of reinforcement and the occurrence of no reinforcement (Wagner and Rescorla 1972). Although there is evidence that the symmetry of excitatory and inhibitory conditioning is not as great as the model requires (e.g. Baker 1974; Zimmer-Hart and Rescorla 1974), it remains the most impressive recent attempt to provide a formal theory of simple associative learning.

As an alternative account of selective association in conditioning, Mackintosh (1975, 1977) has suggested that animals may learn to ignore stimuli that predict no change in reinforcement, for example the added element in Kamin's blocking experiment. A possible virtue of this approach is that it relates selective association to another group of experiments. Studies of latent inhibition (Lubow 1973), learned irrelevance (Mackintosh 1973) and learned helplessness (Baker

1976; Maier and Seligman 1976) may all be interpreted as showing that animals find it difficult to associate events which have previously been uncorrelated: they condition only slowly to a stimulus that has in the past signalled no change in reinforcement. In order to handle some of these phenomena, Wagner (1977) has supplemented the Rescorla-Wagner model by allowing that the conditionability of a CS will decline as its novelty wears off. The closest relationship here, of course, is with the phenomenon of habituation.

Whatever the merits of these particular proposals, they should serve to remind us that simple associative learning is simple in name only. Animals do not automatically associate all events that happen to occur together. If they did, they would surely be at the mercy of every chance conjunction of events. In fact, they behave in an altogether more rational manner. By conditioning selectively to good predictors of reinforcement at the expense of poor predictors, and by taking their past experience into account, they succeed in attributing reinforcers to their most probable causes. It is time that psychologists abandoned their outmoded view of conditioning and recognised it as a complex and useful process whereby organisms build an accurate representation of their world.

REFERENCES

Amsel, A., Hug, J. J. and Surridge, C. T. 1969. 'Subject-to-subject trial sequence, odor trails and patterning at 24-hr ITI.' *Psychonom. Sci. 15,* 119-20.

Andrews, E. A. and Braveman, N. S. 1975. 'The combined effects of dosage level and interstimulus interval on the formation of one-trial poison-based aversions in rats.' *Anim. Learn. Behav. 3,* 287-9.

Baker, A. G. 1974. 'Conditioned inhibition is not the symmetrical opposite of conditioned excitation: A rest of the Rescorla-Wagner model.' *Learn. Motiv. 5,* 369-79.

Baker, A. G. 1976. 'Learned irrelevance and learned helplessness: rats learn that stimuli, reinforcers and responses are uncorrelated.' *J. exp. Psychol.: Anim. Behav. Proc. 2,* 130-41.

Bitterman, M. E. 1976. 'Comment.' *Science 192,* 266.

Blackman, D. 1977. 'Conditioned suppression and the effects of classical conditioning on operant behavior.' W. K. Honig and J. E. R. Staddon (eds) *Handbook of operant behaviour*. Englewood Cliffs, N. J.: Prentice Hall.

Brodigan, D. L. and Trapold, M. A. 1974. 'Recovery from conditioned suppression to a partially overlapping compound stimulus.' *Anim. Learn. Behav. 2,* 89-91.

Brown, P. L., and Jenkins, H. M. 1968. 'Auto-shaping of the pigeon's key-peck.' *J. exp. anal. Behav. 11,* 1-8.

Coleman, S. R. 1975. 'Consequences of response-contingent change in unconditioned stimulus intensity upon the rabbit *(Oryctolagus cuniculus)* nictitating membrane response.' *J. comp. physiol. Psychol. 88,* 591-5.

Di Cara, L. V. and Miller, N. E. 1969. 'Transfer of instrumentally learned heart-rate changes from curarized to noncurarized state: implications for a mediational hypothesis.' *J. comp. physiol. Psychol. 68,* 159-62.

Dickinson, A., Hall, G. and Mackintosh, N. J. 1976. 'Surprise and the attenuation of blocking.' *J. exp. Psychol.: Anim. Behav. Proc. 2,* 313-22.

Domjan, M. 1975. 'Poisoned-induced neophobia: role of stimulus generalisation of conditioned taste aversions.' *Anim. Learn. Behav. 3,* 205-11.

Gamzu, E. R. and Williams, D. R. 1973. 'Associative factors underlying the pigeon's key pecking in auto-shaping procedures.' *J. exp. Anal. Behav. 19,* 225-32.

Garcia, J. and Koelling, R. A. 1966. 'Relation of cue to consequence in avoidance learning.' *Psychonom. Sci. 4,* 123-4.

Gormezano, I. and Hiller, G. W. 1972. 'Omission training of the jaw-movement response of the rabbit to a water US.' *Psychonom. Sci. 29,* 276-78.

Gray, J. A. 1975. *Elements of a two-process theory of learning.* London: Academic Press.

Hearst, E. 1975. 'The classical-instrumental distinction: reflexes, voluntary behavior, and categories of associative learning.' In W. K. Estes (ed.) *Handbook of learning and cognitive processes 2,* 181-224. Hillsdale, N. J.: Lawrence Erlbaum Associates.

Hearst, E. 1977. 'Stimulus relationships and feature selection in learning and behavior.' In S. Hulse, H. Fowler and W. K. Honig (eds) *Cognitive processes in animal behavior.* Hillsdale, N. J.: Lawrence Erlbaum Associates.

Hearst, E. and Franklin, S. R. 1977. 'Positive and negative relations between a signal and food: approach-withdrawal behavior.' *J. exp. Psychol.: Anim. Behav. Proc. 3,* 37-52.

Hearst, E. and Jenkins, H. M. 1974. 'Sign tracking: the stimulus-reinforcer relation and directed action.' *Monograph of the Psychonomic Society:* Austin, Texas.

Herendeen, D. L. and Shapiro, M. M. 1975. 'Extinction and food-reinforced inhibition of conditioned salivation in dogs.' *Anim. Learn. Behav. 3,* 103-6.

Jobe, J. B., Mellgren, R. L., Feinberg, R. A., Littlejohn, R. L. and Rigby, R. L. 1977. 'Patterning, partial reinforcement, and N-length effects at spaced trials as a function of reinstatement of retrieval cues.' *Learn. Motiv. 8,* 77-97.

Kamin, L. J. 1969. 'Predictability, surprise, attention and conditioning.' In R. Campbell and R. Church (eds) *Punishment and aversive behavior* 279-96. New York: Appleton-Century-Crofts.

Kimble, G. A. 1961. *Hilgard and Marquis' conditioning and learning* 2nd edn. New York: Appleton-Century-Crofts.

Krane, R. V. and Wagner, A. R. 1975. 'Taste aversion learning with a delayed shock US: implications for the "generality of the laws of learning".' *J. comp. physiol. Psychol. 88,* 882-9.

Leonard, D. W. 1975. 'Partial reinforcement effects in classical aversive conditioning in rabbits and human beings.' *J. comp. physiol. Psychol. 88,* 596-608.

Lett, B. T. 1975. 'Long delay learning in the T-maze.' *Learn Motiv. 6,* 80-90.

Locurto, C., Terrace, H. S. and Gibbon, J. 1976. 'Autoshaping, random control, and omission training in the rat.' *J. exp. anal. Behav. 26,* 451-62.

Lubow, R. E. 1973. 'Latent inhibition.' *Psychol. Bull. 79*, 398-407.

Luongo, A. F. 1976. 'Stimulus selection in discriminative taste-aversion learning in the rat.' *Anim. Learn. Behav. 4*, 225-30.

Mackintosh, N. J. 1973. 'Stimulus selection: learning to ignore stimuli that predict no change in reinforcement.' In R. A. Hinde and J. Stevenson-Hinde (eds) *Constraints on learning*. London: Academic Press.

Mackintosh, N. J. 1974. *The psychology of animal learning*. London: Academic Press.

Mackintosh, N. J. 1975. 'A theory of attention: variations in the associability of stimuli with reinforcement.' *Psychol. Rev. 82*, 276-98.

Mackintosh, N. J. 1977. 'Cognitive or associative theories of conditioning: implications of an analysis of blocking.' In H. Fowler, W. K. Honig and S. H. Hulse (eds.) *Cognitive aspects of animal behaviour*. Hillsdale, N. J.: Lawrence Erlbaum Associates.

Maier, S. F. and Seligman, M. E. P. 1976. 'Learned helplessness: theory and evidence.' *J. exp. Psychol.: Gen. 105*, 3-46.

Miller, N. E. and Dworkin, B. R. 1974. 'Visceral learning: recent difficulties with curarized rates and significant problems for human research.' In P. A. Obrist, A. H. Black, J. Brener and L. V. Di Cara (eds) *Cardiovascular psychophysiology: current issues in response mechanisms, biofeedback and methodology*. Chicago: Aldine Press.

Miller, S. and Konorski, J. 1928. 'Sur une forme particulière des réflexes conditionnels.' *Comptes Rendus des Séances de la Société de Biologie 99*, 1155-7.

Nowlis, G. H. 1974. 'Conditioned stimulus intensity and acquired alimentary aversions in the rat.' *J. comp. physiol. Psychol. 86*, 1173-84.

Rescorla, R. A. 1971. 'Variation in the effectiveness of reinforcement and nonreinforcement following prior inhibitory conditioning.' *Learn. Motiv. 2*, 113-23.

Rescorla, R. A. 1975. 'Pavlovian excitatory and inhibitory conditioning.' In W. K. Estes (ed.) *Handbook of learning and cognitive processes 2*. Hillsdale, N. J.: Lawrence Erlbaum Associates.

Rescorla, R. A. and Wagner, A. R. 1972. 'A theory of Pavlovian conditioning: variations in the effectiveness of reinforcement and nonreinforcement.' In A. H. Black and W. F. Prokasy (eds) *Classical conditioning II: current research and theory*. New York: Appleton-Century-Crofts.

Revusky, S. H. 1968. 'Aversion to sucrose produced by contingent X-irradiation: temporal and dosage parameters.' *J. comp. physiol. Psychol. 65*, 17-22.

Revusky, S. 1971. 'The role of interference in association over a delay.' In W. K. Honig and P. H. R. James (eds) *Animal memory*. New York: Academic Press.

Revusky, S. and Garcia, J. 1970. 'Learned associations over long delays.' In G. H. Bower (ed.) *The psychology of learning and motivation 4*. New York: Academic Press.

Riley, A. L. and Baril, L. L. 1976. 'Conditioned taste aversions: a bibliography.' *Anim. Learn. Behav. 4*, 1S-13S.

Rozin, P. and Kalat, J. W. 1971. 'Specific hungers and poisoning as adaptive specializations of learning.' *Psychol. Rev. 78*, 459-86.

Schwartz, B. 1977. 'Studies of operant and reflexive key pecks in pigeons.' *J. exp. anal. Behav. 27*, 301-13.

Schwartz, B. and Williams, D. R. 1972. 'The role of the response-reinforcer contingency in negative automaintenance.' *J. exp. Anal. Behav. 17*, 351-7.

Seligman, M. E. P. 1970. 'On the generality of the laws of learning.' *Psychol. Rev. 77,* 406-18.

Testa, T. J. 1974. 'Causal relationships and the acquisition of avoidance responses.' *Psychol. Rev. 81,* 491-505.

Wagner, A. R. 1971. 'Elementary association.' In H. H. Kendler and J. T. Spence (eds), *Essays in neobehaviorism: a memorial volume to Kenneth W. Spence* 187-213. New York: Appleton-Century-Crofts.

Wagner, A. R. 1977. 'Priming in STM: an information processing mechanism for self-generated or retrieval-generated depression in performance.' In T. J. Tighe and R. N. Leaton (eds) *Habituation: perspectives from child development, animal behaviour and neurophys.* Hillsdale, N. J.: Lawrence Erlbaum Associates.

Wagner, A. R., Logan, F. A., Haberlandt, K. and Price, T. 1968. 'Stimulus selection in animal discrimination learning.' *J. exp. Psychol. 76,* 171-80.

Wagner, A. R. and Rescorla, R. A. 1972. 'Inhibition in Pavlovian conditioning: application of a theory.' In R. A. Boakes and M. S. Halliday (eds) *Inhibition and learning* 301-36. London: Academic Press.

Wahlsten, D. L. and Cole, M. 1972. 'Classical and avoidance training of leg flexion in the dog.' In A. H. Black and W. F. Prokasy (eds) *Classical conditioning II: current research and theory* 379-408. New York: Appleton-Century-Crofts.

Williams, B. A. 1975. 'The blocking of reinforcement control.' *J. exp. anal. Behav. 24,* 215-25.

Zimmer-Hart, C. L. and Rescorla, R. A. 1974. 'Extinction of Pavlovian conditioned inhibition.' *J. comp. physiol. Psychol. 86,* 837-45.

Chapter 4

Mental Imagery

PETER W. SHEEHAN

It is impossible to come to grips with the phenomena of imagery without adopting a particular philosophical stance. Complex relationships exist between the experience of the person who is imaging, the verbal report of imagery and the behaviour which accompanies it, and the various neurological substrates that underlie the activity in question. A brief glance at the history of imagery indicates something of the shifting assumptions and philosophical positions that have followed the passage of its study through time.

HISTORICAL CONCEPTIONS OF IMAGERY

J. B. Watson almost dealt a death blow to the study of imagery as a genuine phenomenon when he advised Psychology to dispense with consciousness and attempt to translate mentalistic concepts into muscular contractions. Imagery became 'a mental luxury (even if it really exists) without any functional significance whatever' (Watson 1913, p. 174). Viewed in this way, mind was distinct from behaviour in conception, but not realizable in fact. Later, however, under the influence of 'methodological behaviourists' such as Hull and Spence, imagery came to be considered as meaningful and genuine in its own right (a position Watson would not admit) yet scientifically it could only be studied in behaviouristic and physiological terms. The scientific interest engendered in the physical and molecular postulates illustrated by concepts such as $r_g - s_g$ (Spence 1956) indicated, in fact, a subtle aversion to cognitive phenomena. The exponents of this position, still with some influence today, basically asserted that statements concerning cognition ought not to be regarded as genuinely explanatory.

Watson's concern was understandable. The informal meaning of the word 'image' relies heavily on the notion of 'a picture in the mind' and Pylyshyn (1973) suggests that the picture metaphor actually discourages us from debating the fundamental issues. Pylyshyn is careful to note, however, as the methodological behaviourists did, that the existence of the experience of images should not be questioned. The status of imagery, either as an object of study or as scientific evidence, is not in dispute. The point is that because we intuitively know that we see objects in our mind's eye and hear events in our mind's ear we must not assume that the contents of that private knowledge can necessarily be identified in terms of information-processing events that will constitute an appropriate explanatory theory. Imagery phenomena and their neurological substrates are different aspects of a complex total reality (Holt 1972).

In 1964, Holt made an impassioned and exciting plea for people to take up the study of imagery in a paper titled 'Imagery: The return of the ostracized', and soon after, imagery became a fashionable area of cognitive research. The literature saw the emergence of five major texts on imagery in the period 1969-1972 (Richardson 1969; Horowitz 1970; Paivio 1971; Segal 1971; Sheehan 1972a) and the development of a whole new range of sophisticated experimental strategies (see Chase 1973). Within the last decade, research has focussed increasingly on the nature rather than function of imagery, yet today that nature remains elusive, despite the persuasive impact of our intuitive notions concerning what images mean. In 1972, Neisser argued that the study of imagery stood precisely at the intersection of the analysis of memory and perception as the key branches of cognitive psychology – following the 'picture metaphor' to make the same point, perceiving is like looking at pictures and remembering like looking at them another time. Work on the nature of imagery, now, has come to appeal rather specifically to the similarity in structure of perception to imagery, and research has yielded a number of quite distinctive experimental paradigms as a result of this emphasis. Focus has also been placed on *visual* imagery and perception, the importance of seeing apparently reflecting the special adaptive role we normally attribute to vision in everyday waking life.

A SAMPLING OF ISSUES

It is appropriate at this stage to summarize some of the major issues in the field. These raise questions which integrally pertain to the validity of our interpretation of the evidence and hence to the scientific status of data on imagery and its functioning.

Indices of imagery

The concept 'image' is immensely difficult to index in an unequivocal way. Verbal reports, for instance, convey statements about imaging experience rather than index the experience itself, and logically one must distinguish between the experimental task (presumed to arouse imagery), the activity of imaging itself, the subject's report of it, and our belief that imagery has actually been employed. If a person executes a task well (e.g. accurately recalls a list of concrete nouns), we cannot necessarily assume that it is because he has been imaging, even if he reports doing so. The causal implications of the argument are actually quite complex, particularly as they relate to philosophical assumptions about the presence or absence of mental activity.

Mechanism

The most fundamental questions about imagery are clearly those which relate to its defining features and basic underlying structure. Demonstration of effects such as mnemonic aids to memory, facilitation of the recognition of imageable stimuli, and the interfering effects associated with equivalent modality stimulation ultimately raise questions about the reality of imaging as a process which involves mechanisms that are theoretically distinct.

At the outset, the meaning of *functional* and *structural* correspondence has to be sharply outlined. The latter type of correspondence implicates actual physical mechanisms underlying observed effects and assumes the same apparatus is used in imaging and perceiving. Functional correspondence, on the other hand, reflects the regularity of association between external stimulus events, those events manipulated by the experimenter that are assumed to involve the process of imaging, and the behaviour of the subject. On the behavioural side, the test situations may be quite diverse. Testing, for example, may involve the detection of visual or auditory stimuli, reacting to like and unlike stimuli, or manipulating objects in mental space.

Definition

For Richardson (1969), imagery is a quasi-sensory or quasi-perceptual experience which occurs in the absence of those stimulus conditions that are known to produce genuine sensory counterparts. Bugelski

(1970) adopts a much tougher line on the status of experience than Richardson, however, and argues that responses involved in imagery are implicit and internal and are not observable by routine visual inspection; even so, for Bugelski, images are responses which have the capacity to activate some of the same structural mechanisms that occurred on prior occasions when appropriate stimuli were actually present. Hebb (1968) is perhaps most explicit on this point of view, claiming that 'the image is a reinstatement of the perceptual activity' (p. 470) which reflects the operation of hypothesized cell assembly structures in the brain.

This brief sampling of definitions, by no means an exhaustive one, demonstrates both that some theorists weight the role of experience heavily in their attempts to define the nature of imagery, and also that quite differing accounts of imagery are bonded by a common concern for the relatedness of imagery and perception. There are those, however, who reject such an emphasis. Pylyshyn (1973), for example, asserts vigorously that imagery should not be tied to perception. He argues that an adequate characterization of what we know requires that we assert the importance of abstract mental structures to which there is no conscious access and which are basically propositional or conceptual in nature, as opposed to pictorial and sensory. There are other differing viewpoints too (e.g. Piaget and Inhelder 1971; Sarbin 1972). But definitions that are tied to perception have certain distinct advantages (Neisser 1972): they tend to be compatible with the majority of introspective reports and thereby allow us to interpret more easily what is meant when people say that they have an image; and they provide us as well with the opportunity for analyzing imagery in operational fashion.

THE FUNCTION OF IMAGERY

We turn now to review briefly the utility aspects of imagery. The functions actually served by the process are quite ubiquitous. Imagery is a far cry from an 'army of helpers rushing to the mind's assistance' (Betts 1909, p. 53), and extremely vivid imagery can, on occasion, disrupt adaptive problem solving (Richardson 1969), but its effectiveness is perhaps most amply demonstrated in the field of mnemonics. Ross and Lawrence (1968) report the first systematic study of the effectiveness of imagery in this regard, and the extraordinary feats of skilled mnemonists are discussed in depth in the memory literature: Luria's (1968) case, S; Hunt and Love's (1972) case, VP; and Stromeyer's (1970) case, 'Elizabeth'.

Data relating to the impact of stimulus attributes and the effect of the different strategies of recall that subjects may employ are also compelling. There is a strong positive association between the imageability of stimuli and accuracy of recall in a variety of learning test situations (Paivio 1971). Kintsch (1972) found that linguistic complexity accounts for at least some of the effect previously attributed to the 'imageability' of stimuli, however this variable remains as a potent factor (Richardson 1975). Data also point in clear-cut fashion to the effectiveness of imagery instructions, especially when they serve to relate, integrate, or associate together the items to be remembered (Bower 1972). The effects found across the various manipulations designed to arouse or utilize imagery, though, e.g. type of experimental task, instructions, and ability, are not consistent, nor should they be assumed to be so (Anderson 1973; Slee 1976).

It is with respect to the variable of ability that questions concerning functional correspondences are perhaps most strongly debated. Given that individual differences in imaging may relate positively to stimulus encoding and efficiency of subsequent recall (Marks 1973; Sheehan 1972b), it seems important to be able to accurately assess effects in terms of subjects' differentiation in imagery aptitude or skill. We don't really know, for example, that Betts' Questionnaire Upon Mental Imagery (Betts 1909), or its shortened version (QMI, Sheehan 1967), or other tests of imagery function [such as Gordon's test of imagery control (Richardson 1969) and Paivio's (1971) self-report measure of nonverbal thinking] actually oblige subjects to construct mental images. It is disconcerting, for instance, that the intercorrelations among these various tests are not high and their relationships to performance measures of behavioural function far from uniform (White, Sheehan and Ashton 1977). Despite the irregularities in the data, however, the theoretical base for a relationship between ability to image and memory or perceptual function is compelling. If imaging is really effective then it is highly plausible to argue that the strongest indications of that process in action should be evident when performance is related to high (rather than medium or low) aptitude for imagery arousal.

EXAMINING THE NATURE OF IMAGERY

We turn now to consider the nature of imagery, especially as it relates to perception. Specifically, focus will be placed on the different methods that have been used to infer its underlying structure.

Analysis of the relationship of imagery to perception has provided a wide range of sophisticated paradigms of research. These relate primarily to the analysis of (a) illusions, (b) selective interference effects involving modality conflict, (c) reaction times to like and unlike stimuli and (d) mental transformations. There are also other models which focus quite specifically on spatiality and its particular relevance to the structure of imagery.

Analysis of Illusions

If after-effects normally distinctive to perception are associated with the occurrence of imagery, then imagery and perception may be said to be structurally similar. The consequences of imaging, though, must be standard sensory after-effects of perception, and procedures should be instituted to test for genuineness of effect, discounting, for instance, the possible role of demand characteristics and other subtle suggestion effects. The evidence can be considered strong, for example, if subjects report genuine negative after-images to imagined colours. The data on the actual issue are conflicting and it is fair to state that no study to date has unequivocally discounted the potential influence of strong cues existing in test situations to imply appropriate response. Singer and Sheehan (1965), for example, demonstrated that illusory after-effects can be parsimoniously explained by appealing to unverbalized cues associated with routine imagery test procedures.

Analysis of Selective Interference

Assuming that imagery and perception share the same processing features, the argument which this model makes – and it is an influential one – is that images and percepts necessarily conflict with each other when they occur in the same modality (e.g. visual), but not when different modalities are involved (e.g. visual and auditory). Brooks (1967, 1968) first formulated the strategies associated with this model and demonstrated the effects of conflict between visualizing and reading. In the most widely cited extension of Brooks' paradigm, Segal and Fusella (1970) contrasted sensitivity for auditory and visual signals in both a simple detection task and an associated task in which the subjects were specifically instructed to arouse visual and auditory imagery. Their data indicated that visual imagery interfered with the detection of visual signals while auditory imagery interfered with the detection of auditory signals. Analyzed closely, however, Segal and Fusella's (as also Brooks') results demonstrate more about function than the specific nature of imagery. Hypotheses about similarity of function between imaging and perceiving would lead to exactly the same prediction (blocking) given the procedures that were employed. The critical factor may well be the abstract (linguistic versus spatial) structure rather than the particular sensory modality of the internal representations that were being manipulated (Cooper and Shepard 1973). In work employing this paradigm, it is further relevant to note that results do not make it clear that imagery has actually been involved. In a study by Atwood (1971), for example, ultimate appeal seems to have been made to the introspective reports of some subjects who claimed that imaginary scenes had to be temporarily abandoned so that they could perceive and respond to the visual signals that were presented.

Analysis of Reaction Times and Mental Transformations

In an extension of the logic that lies behind the interference paradigm, some researchers have argued that imagery should be best when it occurs in the modality that is most similar to the modality in which stimuli are presented externally. The procedures adopted by Posner (1973), for example, stress the time required to respond discriminatively to some feature of an external stimulus, the logic of this model being that time should be shorter when the subject is more prepared for that stimulus. Subjects, for instance, can more quickly judge whether two successive alphabetic letters have the same name if the letters in question are physically matched (for example A and A versus A and a). Cooper and Shepard (1973), considering that this paradigm did not isolate the role of imagery as unequivocally as it might, accepted the basic conditions of the model and introduced the additional requirement that in order to be fully prepared for the anticipated stimulus, the subject must first perform a transformation upon the internal representation, specifically, one that involves a rotation of the stimulus in mental space. Again, though, it is difficult to know what is the exact nature of the correspondence that is implicated here. The processes involved are clearly complex. Some subjects indicated, for example, that the thing they were mentally rotating was very schematic and their experience was as much kinaesthetic as visual. Overall, data most unambiguously indicated that imagined rotations have a *functionally* distinct component that is distinctively shared with processes that occur when the same person is actually perceiving an external rotation of the stimulus.

The spatial information stored in images and the spatial integration of them with the external stimuli the images are said to represent constitute the most significant features of nonverbal representation processing for a number of researchers in the field (e.g. Byrne 1974; Janssen 1976; Kosslyn 1975; Peterson 1975). Two paradigms in particular (Peterson 1975; Kosslyn 1975) address themselves in ingenious fashion to the spatial attributes of images, both operating on the assumption that there is a structural similarity of imaging and perception. Peterson used spatial matrices in an attempt to measure the locational or 'anchoring' features of imagery and visual perception. The more provocative research, however, comes from Kosslyn who argued that properties on subjectively smaller images ought to take more time to evaluate ('see') than properties on larger images. If images are indeed spatial, then the farther apart one property is from another, the longer it should take to shift attention from that property to the other. Results indicated that people can selectively retrieve information from preset spatial locations on a generative image. Careful experimentation by Kosslyn eliminated several possible alternative hypotheses, yet it would seem that the research – relying perhaps more on one's intuitive knowledge of how images must look than other paradigms we have reviewed – has simply isolated novel functional correspondences between the processes of imaging and perception that have hitherto gone unobserved. Questions can be raised about the data. Neisser (1976), for instance, argues that subjects asked to imagine small details while they are visualizing a far away object reduced in size are basically in an interference situation and that plans for looking at distant or small objects are necessarily distinct from those for examining objects that are large and close.

Other accounts of imagery debate the relationship between the processes of perception and imaging, but have no set of 'representative' proceedures associated with them. One such theory is that proposed by Neisser, who in his most recent statement (Neisser 1976) argues that mental images should be viewed as perceptual anticipations. According to this account, a description of a visual image is a description of what a person is ready or set to see, and images are conceptualized as plans for 'obtaining information from potential environments' (p. 131). For Neisser, imagining and seeing are quite distinct and he rejects the computer model as a framework for understanding imagery in favour of the metaphors of growth and construction. Considered in terms of this framework, selective interference effects become clearly functional. Interference effects are to be expected precisely because the subject is requested to sustain two plans for seeing (or hearing etc.) at the same time. An account such as this demonstrates the point that the hypothesis of structural similarity between imagery and perception is by no means the only explanatory framework into which imagery data may be cast. Explanations that appeal to the processes of perception may be quite viable without any assumptions being made about underlying physiological structure.

The Mechanisms of Imagery

In relation to imagery, questions about structure and mechanism can only really be answered by collecting data on the issue of whether there are specific physiological correlates of imaging which distinguish the phenomenon from other mental events and which overlap with processes known to characterize actual perception. Research has tended to centre on eye movement activity as the most relevant correlate. If structural similarity holds, then one can argue that eye movements associated with imagery should parallel those occurring when the real external stimulus is actually present. In Hebb's (1968) terms, the correlation should be essential rather than adventitious, if imaging is integrally tied to perception. The data indicate that eye movements are neither a necessary nor a sufficient condition for imaging (Bower 1972; Janssen 1976). Imaging a moving stimulus seems to benefit from the chance to make eye movements (Antrobus, Antrobus and Singer 1964), but that appears to be all. As for other measures, the basic problem appears to be that relevant dependent variables (e.g. heart rate, alpha rhythm, respiration rate and eye movement or gaze activity) relate meaningfully to a wide range of mental and cognitive processes. The complexity of the relationship is perhaps most accurately predicted by Neisser's (1976) account of imagery. If images are anticipatory schemata they should be accompanied by some form of anticipatory behaviour. Such a theory predicts that people should move their eyes in ways related to picking up information about imaged stimuli or events, but not necessarily in an all-or-none fashion; which anticipations actually control eye movements will depend on many different factors including overall intentions and the dominance of particular scanning patterns. Features of the visual system also clearly need to be tied not only to the specific sensory features of external stimulation, but also to the properties of their combination (Janssen 1976).

CONCLUSION

A wealth of evidence exists to support the claim that imagery is linked functionally to both remembering and perceiving. Although the paradigms we have reviewed in this chapter raise important implications concerning the nature of imagery and its relationship to perception, the data do not unequivocally establish that link as a structural one. The essential difficulty is that we do not know what ensures the presence or absence of imagery. The variability of the available data is no doubt due, in part, to the fact that manipulations such as mnemonic instruction, ability to image, or the stimulus characteristics of a task do not of themselves guarantee the arousal of imagery. Imagery necessarily reflects the operation of neural activities and they activate physical structures, but, as Bugelski (1970) notes, our knowledge of neurophysiology is not yet adequate enough to allow us to translate imagery into neural terms. The links with perception established by the selective interference and related paradigms merely reflect functional correspondences between external events, experimental manipulations, and subjects' behaviour (as well as their reported experience). These correspondences, for the most part, are consistent with the hypothesis of imaging and its underlying relatedness to perception, but the inference that visual imagery actually utilizes the apparatus of visual perception is too strong.

Newell (1973) has described his reaction to the imagery literature as one of excitement, leaving him 'half distressed and half confused' (p. 283). The field of imagery research abounds with highly sophisticated and elegant methodological paradigms, and many ingenious experiments have been conducted, but, as he laments, the data do not collectively sum or gel together. Research in the future should move toward the integration and organization of the data that currently exist in relation to the analysis of specific research issues. As paradigms alter within the foreseeable future, so will new functional relationships emerge that will be consistent with underlying structure, but likely, as not, unable to provide definitive test of it. As Cooper and Shepard (1973) argue, the problem is to find models or paradigms that specify exactly all of the different subprocesses that mediate between the various stimuli and their resulting responses, particularly since the subprocesses themselves are often related only peripherally to the functions of the imagery involved. The task of defining the nature of imagery is especially elusive for types of imagery not reviewed in this chapter. Considering for a moment the status of eidetic imagery, the nature of which has long been debated in the literature (Gray and Gummerman 1975), the question of its differentiating characteristics raises very important implications for understanding the nature of mental imagery.

In conclusion, the cumulative impact of the research that has been conducted in the last two decades affirms the reality of imagery in quite undeniable fashion. The functional correspondences of imaging to the processes of perception and remembering will no doubt continue to be manifest as new paradigms and test procedures are developed. Although imagery exists, however, it is disappointing that we do not yet know how exactly we should define its nature. In throwing the gauntlet to those who would theorize about its structure, however, it is important that we do not underestimate the value of research which explores its function. Pylyshyn's warnings well in hand, we need to know quite a lot more about the parameters that influence subjects to report (albeit naively) that they see an object 'clearly now, in my mind's eye'.

REFERENCES

Anderson, R. E. 1973. 'Individual differences in the use of imaginal processing.' *Dissert. Abst. Internat. 34,* 887-B.

Antrobus, J. S., Antrobus, J. S. and Singer, J. C. 1964. 'Eye-movements accompanying daydreaming, visual imagery and thought suppression.' *J. Abnorm. soc. Psychol. 69,* 244-52.

Atwood, G. E. 1971. 'An experimental study of visual imagination and memory.' *Cogn. Psychol. 2,* 290-99.

Betts, G. H. 1909. 'The distribution and functions of mental imagery.' *Columbia Univer. Contrib. Educat. Series. 26,* 1-99.

Bower, G. H. 1972. 'Mental imagery and associative learning.' In L. W. Gregg (ed.) *Cognition in learning and memory.* New York: Wiley.

Brooks, L. R. 1967. 'The suppression of visualization in reading.' *Quart. J. exp. Psychol. 19,* 288-99.

Brooks, L. R. 1968. 'Spatial and verbal components of the act of recall.' *Canad. J. Psychol. 22,* 349-368.

Bugelski, B. R. 1970. 'Words and things and images.' *Amer. Psychologist 25,* 1002-12.

Byrne, B. 1974. 'Item concreteness versus spatial organization as predictors of visual imagery.' *Memory and Cognition 2,* 53-9.

Chase, W. G. 1973. *Visual information processing.* New York: Academic Press (Edited Text).

Cooper, L. A. and Shepard, R. N. 1973. 'Chronometric studies of the rotation of mental images.' In W. G. Chase (ed.) *Visual information processing.* New York: Academic Press.

Gray, C. R. and Gummerman, K. 1975. 'The enigmatic eidetic image: a critical examination of methods, data, and theories.' *Psychol. Bull. 82,* 383-407.

Hebb, D. O. 1968. 'Concerning imagery.' *Psychol. Rev. 75,* 466-77.

Holt, R. R. 1964. 'Imagery: the return of the ostracized.' *Amer. Psychologist 12,* 254-64.

Holt, R. R. 1972. 'On the nature and generality of mental imagery.' In P. W. Sheehan (ed.) *The function and nature of imagery.* New York: Academic Press.

Horowitz, M. J. 1970. *Image formation and cognition.* New York: Appleton.

Hunt, E. and Lowe, T. 1972. 'How good can memory be?' In A. W. Melton and E. Martin (eds) *Coding processes in human memory.* Washington, D.C.: V. H. Winston.

Janssen, W. 1976. *On the nature of the mental image.* Soesterberg, The Netherlands: Institute for Perception TNO.

Kintsch, W. 1972. 'Abstract nouns: imagery versus lexical complexity.' *J. verb. Learn. verb Behav. 11,* 59-65.

Kosslyn, S. M. 1975. 'Information representation in visual images.' *Cogn. Psychol. 7,* 341-70.

Luria, A. R. 1968. *The mind of a mnemonist.* New York: Basic Books. (Translated by L. Solotaroff.)

Marks, D. F. 1973. 'Visual imagery differences and eye movements in the recall of pictures.' *Percep. and Psychophys. 14,* 407-12.

Neisser, U. 1972. 'Changing conceptions of imagery.' In P. W. Sheehan (ed.) *The function and nature of imagery.* New York: Academic Press.

Neisser, U. 1976. *Cognition and reality: principles and implications of cognitive psychology.* San Francisco: Freeman.

Newell, A. 1973. 'You can't play Twenty Questions with nature and win: projective comments on the papers of this symposium.' In W. G. Chase (ed.) *Visual information processing.* New York: Academic Press.

Paivio, A. 1971. *Imagery and verbal processes.* New York: Holt, Rhinehart and Winston.

Peterson, M. J. 1975. 'The retention of imagined and seen spatial matrices.' *Cogn. Psychol. 7,* 181-93.

Piaget, J. and Inhelder, B. 1971. *Mental imagery in the child.* New York: Basic Books.

Posner, M. I. 1973. 'Coordination of internal codes.' In W. G. Chase (ed.) *Visual information processing.* New York: Academic Press.

Pylyshyn, Z. W. 1973. 'What the mind's eye tells the mind's brain: a critique of mental imagery.' *Psychol. Bull. 80,* 1-24.

Richardson, A. 1969. *Mental imagery.* New York: Springer.

Richardson, J. T. 1975. 'Imagery, concreteness, and lexical complexity.' *Quart. J. exp. Psychol. 27,* 211-23.

Ross, J. and Lawrence, K. A. 1968. 'Some observations on memory artiface.' *Psychonom. Sci. 13,* 107-8.

Sarbin, T. R. 1972. 'Imagining as muted role-taking: a historical-linguistic analysis.' In P. W. Sheehan (ed.) *The function and nature of imagery.* New York: Academic Press.

Segal, S. J. 1971. *Imagery: current cognitive approaches.* New York: Academic Press. (Edited Text.)

Segal, S. J. and Fusella, V. 1970. 'Influence of imaged pictures and sounds on detection of visual and auditory signals.' *J. exp. Psychol. 83,* 458-64.

Sheehan, P. W. 1967. 'A shortened form of Betts' Questionnaire Upon Mental Imagery.' *J. Clin. Psychol. 23,* 386-9.

Sheehan, P. W. 1972a. *The function and nature of imagery.* New York: Academic Press. (Edited Text.)

Sheehan, P. W. 1972b. 'A functional analysis of the role of visual imagery in unexpected recall.' In P. W. Sheehan (ed.) *The function and nature of imagery.* New York: Academic Press.

Singer, G. and Sheehan, P. W. 1965. 'The effect of demand characteristics on the figural after-effect with real and imaged inducing figures.' *Amer. J. Psychol. 78,* 96-101.

Slee, J. A. 1976. 'The perceptual nature of visual imagery.' Unpublished doctoral dissertation, Australian National University, Canberra, Australia.

Spence, K. W. 1956. *Behavior theory and conditioning*. New Haven: Yale University Press.

Stromeyer, C. F. 1970. 'Eidetic images.' *Psychol. Today Nov.* 76-80.

Watson, J. 1913. 'Psychology as the behaviourist views it.' *Psychol. Rev. 20,* 158-77.

White, K., Sheehan, P. W. and Ashton, R. 1977. 'Imagery assessment: a survey of self-report measures.' *J. Ment. Imagery 1,* 145-69.

Chapter 5

Psychophysiology

MICHAEL G. H. COLES and ANTHONY GALE

INTRODUCTION

What is Psychophysiology?

Psychophysiologists study the relationship between psychological and biological events. The particular flavour of the approach is revealed by the fact that psychophysiologists use techniques and procedures which differ from physiological psychology in a number of ways. Experimental subjects are typically human rather than infra-human; they are studied intact without any attempt to interfere with normal functioning; independent variables are psychological (rather than physiological), and the dependent variables are physiological, behavioural, and experiential. There is great concern with the problem of measurement and data analysis, reflected in a growing dependence on computers and an increasing sophistication in experimental design and statistics. Throughout its history, psychophysiology has been mainly concerned with emotion and motivation, though more recently an interest in cognitive processes has developed. A final defining characteristic of psychophysiology is that its models and theories are couched in psychological language. It follows that the ideal psychophysiologist should have skills in physiology, biochemistry, electronics, computer science and statistics, as well as a working knowledge of psychological theory and methods. Potentially, therefore, psychophysiology is a bridge discipline, drawing together the full range of psychological enquiry, but firmly anchored in biological principles.

Historical Background

Advances in amplifier and galvanometer construction were responsible for the development of objective and reliable psychophysiological *techniques* such as those involved in the measurement the electroencephalogram (Berger) and of electrodermal phenomena (Féré and Tarchanoff). Modern psychophysiological *theory,* relating particularly to the autonomic nervous system, has its origins in the Cannon/James controversy concerning the nature of emotion. The *parallelist* approach (Cannon) sees different physiological systems as functioning in parallel, with peripheral physiological changes occurring as a mere by-product of psychological processes (e.g. Arousal Theory). The *interactionist* approach emphasizes interaction between physiological systems and the functional significance of different reaction patterns. This view is derived from James and is currently exemplified in the Laceys' theory (see below).

Psychophysiology is at present in a state of transition between these two approaches. The turning point came with the publication of the critique of arousal theory by Lacey (1967), who argued that the observed independence of different physiological systems is incompatible with a unitary concept of arousal. Psychophysiologists are slowly beginning to come to terms with the problems raised by Lacey.

Research on cortical activity has different theoretical sources. Studies of the electroencephalogram (EEG) have been closely linked to psychiatry and clinical neurophysiology, while research on event-related potentials (ERPs) is related more to traditional experimental psychology. Because of the physical proximity between electrode sites and the cortex, this research has assumed a relationship between the observed electrical activity and cognitive processes. The question has been to find the key to the relationship.

A recent collection of readings by Porges and Coles (1976) brings together classic papers in the history of psychophysiology.

The Present Chapter

There are few areas of psychology in which psychophysiologists have not been active. Apart from the general areas of emotion and cognitive processes, there is research in pattern perception, language, intelligence, personality, social behaviour, attitudes, memory, pathology, treatment, vigilance, sleep and dreaming.

Psychophysiologists have sometimes been criticized for emphasizing technology at the expense of theory. In selecting the four topics of discussion, we have tried to sample the range of enquiry and to indicate both contemporary *theoretical* controversies and areas of possible advance.

THE PSYCHOLOGICAL SIGNIFICANCE OF CARDIAC ACTIVITY

Few other recent findings in psychophysiology have generated more interest than the observation that decreases in heart rate (HR) occur in situations where other physiological functions (e.g. skin conductance) increase in activity. The Laceys and their co-workers observed this 'directional fractionation' when their subjects were engaged in attentive observation of the environment or 'sensory intake' (Lacey *et al.* 1963). In other tasks involving mental arithmetic and anagram solving, cardiac acceleration occurred. Since the latter tasks seemed to involve cognitive elaboration and environmental 'rejection', their experiments gave rise to the 'intake-rejection' hypothesis relating cardiac activity to the nature of the attentional requirements as perceived by the subject.

Although these original experiments involved *tonic* HR measured over periods of about one minute, recent research has looked at transient, *phasic* changes. For example, during the foreperiods of reaction time tasks there is a beat-by-beat deceleration which reaches its nadir at the imperative stimulus.

The occurrence of cardiac deceleration in certain attention-involving tasks led the Laceys to propose an afferent feedback hypothesis. The hypothesis proposes that decreases in HR are associated with decreases in blood pressure which in turn lead to a reduction in the inhibitory influence exerted by the baroceptors on the cortex. Decreases in HR, therefore, are considered to have *functional* significance because of the positive effects such decreases can have on cortical activity and sensorimotor behaviour.

The intake-rejection and afferent feedback hypotheses have been the subject of much controversy (e.g. Elliott 1972). We shall consider here three classes of research dealing with them.

The Cardiac-somatic Relationship

Cardiac and somatic activity (the activity of the skeletal musculature) are, of course, closely related because of the dependence of muscular activity on cardiac output (and thus on HR). Obrist has consistently argued that it is *this* relationship which provides the key to the understanding of HR changes (Obrist 1976). In particular, the cardiac deceleration which occurs in the foreperiods of reaction time tasks is best understood as a reflection of the reduced metabolic demands which accompany the inhibition of *motor* activity in the foreperiod.

It is the decrease in motor activity, rather than cardiac deceleration *per se,* which has functional significance, for it can serve to reduce 'noise' in the central nervous system so as to enhance those central processes associated with sensorimotor behaviour. The extent of the cardiac-somatic linkage has been evaluated in experiments which show that changes in HR can occur independently of changes in somatic activity (e.g. Coles 1974; Lawler *et al.* 1976). Lawler *et al.* distinguish between task-relevant measures of somatic activity (e.g. in forearm muscle) and task-irrelevant measures (other muscle groups). These measures exhibit different trends in relation to HR as skill in a reaction time task develops.

An interesting and challenging problem for future research will be to establish appropriate procedures for describing concomitance or linkage between physiological functions such as HR and somatic activity.

Cardiac Acceleration

Although research on cardiac activity has tended to focus on deceleration, there has been some research on acceleration and this has yielded three views of its significance. There is evidence to suggest that acceleration is closely related to motor activity (see above). Secondly, it has been considered by many to be the cardiac component of the Sokolovian defensive reflex (Graham and Clifton 1966) which occurs in response to intense stimuli. In this respect, it is believed that acceleration reflects a process associated with raised sensory thresholds (cf rejection). More recently, it has become clear that acceleration occurs in circumstances where explanations in terms of motor activity or the defensive reflex are clearly inappropriate. In these cases (Coles and Duncan-Johnson 1975), the accelerations are associated with information-processing activity. The fact that cardiac acceleration can be influenced by so many different variables suggests that great care should be taken in attributing particular psychological meaning to an observed acceleration. As with other psychophysiological measures, one-to-one relationships between the measure and particular psychological states cannot be assumed.

Cardiac Cycle Time Effects

The duration of a cardiac cycle can be modified by stimuli which occur even within the cycle. The magnitude of this effect is dependent on the temporal placement (cycle time) within the cycle (Lacey and

Lacey 1974). This finding is important, not only because it indicates that the cardiac control system can have a very short response latency, but also because it points to methods for discovering the functional significance of cardiac activity. At present, we do not know much about the variables which influence the effect, nor do we know the degree to which other physiological measures (such as the event-related potentials) are influenced by cycle time.

EVENT-RELATED POTENTIALS

When discrete events occur, potential changes are observed in electrodes placed on the surface of the scalp. The events may be internally or externally generated. The potentials are usually too small to be visible in the EEG record, so several EEG epochs are averaged together, each epoch having the same temporal relationship to the same (repeated) event. As a result of this procedure, which is usually performed by computer, aspects of the EEG which are not 'time-locked' to the event tend to average to zero leaving only those potentials which have a consistent temporal relationship to the event.

Using these techniques, several different event-related potentials (ERPs) have been identified. For the purposes of description and analysis, each potential is characterized by various distinguishing features. These include its polarity (positive or negative), temporal relationship to the event and, in some cases, the distribution pattern of the potential over the surface of the scalp.

Before an event, two classes of potential have been generally identified (see Tecce 1972) – (a) the contingent negative variation (CNV), a slow negative potential which precedes anticipated events, and (b) the motor potential, a faster potential complex with predominant negativity, which precedes voluntary motor responses.

Following an event, there is a series of positive and negative potentials whose morphology and amplitude depend on both the physical and psychological characteristics of the event (see Picton *et al.* 1974). The early potentials (in the first 100 msec) reflect features such as intensity and modality of stimulation, the middle latency potentials (100-200 msec) are enhanced by general changes in attention, while the later components, such as the P_{300}, may be influenced by information processing activity. The P_{300} is a positive potential with latency of about 300 msec.

ERP research is undergoing a period of intense activity. Major new discoveries appear almost monthly, provoking reinterpretation of prevailing views. We have sought to reflect the spirit of contemporary discovery in the topics we have chosen for further discussion.

The P_{300} and Other Positive Potentials

Of all the psychologically relevant components of the ERP which follow the occurrence of events, the P_{300} has received the most attention. The magnitude of the component is dependent on the task-relevance of the eliciting stimulus and its probability (Squires *et al.* 1977). The independence of the P_{300} of the physical properties of stimulation is elegantly revealed by the finding that the P_{300} is observed when an anticipated event *fails* to occur (e.g. Ford *et al.* 1976).

Recently, Squires *et al.* (1976) have shown that the P_{300} (and earlier negative components) are influenced not only by properties of the eliciting stimulus but also by the sequence of events which precedes them. Their subjects had to count the number of times a specific tone (A) occurred within a series of tones in which A and B (another tone) were equiprobable. The P_{300} component following tone A was smaller if, by chance, it was immediately preceded by tones of the same type (e.g. at the end of a sequence like AAAA*A*) than if the preceding tones were of the other type (e.g. following a sequence like BBBB*A*). The authors argue that the experiment shows that the P_{300} is sensitive to subtle changes in expectancy. When ‘expectancy’ was defined mathematically in terms of memory for, and structure of, the preceding event sequence, the correlation between their ERP measure and expectancy was 0.88!

Another interesting positive potential, which may be related to the P_{300}, has recently been identified by Cooper *et al.* (1977). In their task, subjects had to watch a visual display depicting a landscape. From time to time, a vehicle appeared to traverse the landscape and the subject was required to detect the vehicle and later to identify its type (car, truck, etc.). Just before the subject indicated that he had detected a vehicle, a large positive wave occurred. The potential was independent of the precise timing of eye movements and the detection response, and was of sufficient magnitude to be visible even in the raw EEG record. The wave seems to be associated with the psychological process of ‘recognition’ and will certainly be the subject of future research.

Single Trial Analysis

As indicated earlier, the low signal-to-noise ratio of the ERP has made averaging a common practice. While interesting information has been obtained using this technique, the assumption of homogeneity among the events which are grouped for averaging may not always be valid. More discrete questions about the meaning of ERPs can only be answered by looking at single trials.

Recently, Squires and Donchin (1976) used a statistical procedure known as stepwise discriminant analysis (SWDA). The procedure begins with sets of EEG samples, each set being associated with particular events, such as attended (A) and ignored (B) stimuli. SWDA is then used to derive a categorization rule which best discriminates among the sets. The rule is based on some characteristic(s) of the ERP such as the P_{300}. It is then applied to new data sets on a trial by trial basis to determine how each trial is to be categorized (as either A or B). In the case of Squires and Donchin (1976), their rule discriminating between attended and ignored stimuli correctly identified between eighty-one per cent and eighty-nine per cent of a new set of trials. It is likely that at least some of the misidentifications were due to *real* variations in the ERPs rather than to failures of the categorization rule. These variations might be due to sequential effects (see above) or to a failure on the part of the subject to obey instructions. It seems certain that the SWDA procedure will prove to be very important in single trial analysis in the future.

The Dual Nature of the CNV

The experiments which originally identified the CNV as a psychologically interesting measure involved paradigms where a warning stimulus was followed by an imperative stimulus requiring a mental or motor response. During the foreperiod, which was generally quite short (about one sec), the CNV was observed. Recent research, using longer foreperiods, has suggested that the CNV has two components. Thus, Rohrbaugh *et al.* (1976) were able to dissociate an early negativity which followed the warning stimulus from a later negativity which preceded the imperative stimulus. The dissociation was based on two main factors. First, the distribution of the potentials across the cortex was different, with the early wave being maximal over frontal areas and the later potential maximal over areas associated with motor activity. Secondly, only the later potential was related to reaction time. These data suggest that the early component may represent an orientating response, while the late component may be equivalent to the readiness potential and reflect response preparation.

This research is particularly interesting because it indicates the power of distributional analysis in aiding the identification of different ERPs.

BIOFEEDBACK TECHNIQUES

New therapies in medicine and psychiatry share a common life cycle. After initial discovery comes enthusiasm and publicity which leads to overapplication; then there is controversy, laced with 'critical' experiments, followed by systematic investigation, doubt and denial, and finally, limited application to highly specified conditions. Biofeedback techniques are no exception, for they also reflect the apparent need to discover a panacea for complex problems. The biofeedback 'movement' has almost reached the final stage of the life cycle, after much evangelism and commercial exploitation.

The Problem of Measuring Therapeutic Outcome in Psychiatry

Silverstone and Turner (1974) in reviewing 127 studies of drug trials, give these figures for seventy per cent reported improvement after treatment: no controls and not blind, fifty-eight per cent; controls but not blind, forty-six per cent, controls and blind, thirty-three per cent. These dramatic differences show that as rigour increases, so reported efficiency declines. Data for psychotherapeutic treatments reflect similar trends (Eysenck 1960). The following are the accepted proper features of a good test of the outcome of psychological treatment: pre-treatment baseline, pre-treatment wait, no-treatment control, other treatment control, attention-placebo control, spontaneous recovery baseline, treatment level controls, post-treatment assessment, follow-up, and blind rating throughout. The logic underlying these preconditions aims at unequivocal interpretation of outcome. Only a small proportion of biofeedback trials comes near to satisfying these conditions, and the experts are therefore sceptical of all but a few possible applications (Blanchard and Young 1974).

The notion of 'feedback' (providing the person with information concerning his actions) is not new either to psychology in general or to psychotherapy, where there are many methods designed to increase the patient's 'awareness' or 'insight'. The difference here is that the patient is given direct access to autonomic and skeletal activity, which in turn enables him to exercise 'control' over these responses under appropriate conditions. Thus biofeedback techniques are seen to share features which are considered to be generally beneficial in psychotherapy, namely: (i) the patient is taught to relax, a response which is antagonistic to anxiety, (ii) the patient wants to get better and is therefore willing to participate actively in treatment, (iii) the rationale for the treatment is straightforward and easily understood, (iv) both the patient and the therapist have 'faith' in the treatment, (v) the patient receives attention from a sympathetic person, and (vi) responsibility for cure is placed in the patient's own hands and the notion of dependence is replaced by self-help. The key question, to which so far there is no satisfactory answer, is whether biofeedback techniques are so *special,* that over and above these *general* properties of treatment, they can account for a significant proportion of recovery which is specific to the biofeedback procedure *per se*.

The Range of Application

Biofeedback methods have been applied in the following contexts: recovery of muscle control in paralyzed patients, removal of subvocal speech (which disrupts silent reading), muscular control in general relaxation, removal of tension headache, control for cardiac arrhythmias (premature ventricular contractions in particular), blood pressure control in hypertension, reduction of vascular components of phobic responses, circulatory abnormality, abortion of migraine attacks by 'autogenic' adjustment to hand/head temperature ratios, increase of sensorimotor brain rhythms to reduce epileptic seizure, control of muscular spasms and control of secretion of stomach acids in ulcer patients. Blanchard and Young (1974) in a comprehensive review, conclude that treatments involving control of muscle activity are the only biofeedback application supported by strong evidence. It is not the case that other treatments do not work, but rather that the evidence for their efficacy is plagued by poor methodology and design. This conclusion is ironic since the rationale for biofeedback was that it is particularly suited to psychosomatic disorders, which generally involve the autonomic nervous system, and the key controversy over the true nature of the biofeedback phenomena centred upon the mechanisms whereby control over the viscera was achieved.

The Problem of Mediation

Twenty years ago, textbooks claimed that the viscera were not under conscious control. Many accepted a simple distinction between operant conditioning as central, voluntary, conscious and skeletal, and classical conditioning as autonomic and involuntary. Laboratory studies of the operant control of autonomic function have overturned this conception and paved the way for the biofeedback approach. Crucial experiments centred upon the problem of whether use of curare to paralyze non-human experimental subjects, thereby eliminating nervous system circuitry involved in skeletal control ('somatic mediation'), influenced the capacity of the animal to control autonomic functions. A key finding which challenged the somatic view, was that rats trained in heart rate control without curare, subsequently performed better than untrained controls, when both groups were tested under curare. For human subjects, where both somatic *and* cognitive factors may be involved, the question is more complex. The issue of mode of mediation is relevant to treatment since it is important to know whether a patient exercising control over his blood pressure, for example, achieves this by 'thoughts' exclusive to blood pressure *per se* or by increasing overall body tension/relaxation. It seems that under experimental conditions, very specific control of blood pressure can be achieved without affecting other vascular measures (e.g. heart rate, Schwartz 1972). This is encouraging since it means that treatment by biofeedback can be symptom-specific, rather than creating unwanted side effects, as is the case with drug treatments. Finally, as Schwartz (1973) cautions, we must beware of the simple-minded approaches to treatment; the patient may prefer to solve his problems by exercising control over his blood pressure, but the true path to cure may lie with a total reconstruction of his emotional and working environment, which is responsible for precipitating the crises which call for treatment in the first place. At the same time, the reader should be aware that some of the original laboratory findings relating to operant control of autonomic function have not been replicated, even by the authors of the very first published studies (Miller and Dworkin 1974).

PSYCHOPATHOLOGY (ANXIETY AND SCHIZOPHRENIA)

Anxiety

Clinical anxiety is an excellent candidate for psychophysiological research since the behavioural, subjective and physiological symptoms are immediately apparent. The patient reports extreme discomfort and even panic; he is seen to tremble, blush or sweat; he reports extremes of autonomic activity in the form of palpitations, muscular tensions, shortness of breath, lassitude and inability to sleep. If phobias are present, he restricts himself only to familiar surroundings lest he should come into contact with the object of his fears. Yet at the same time, what we observe is an exaggeration of what we ourselves experience in the normal course of living; there is a quantitative rather than qualitative increase in the intensity and frequency of experienced emotion. Therefore, in studying the anxious patient, comparing him with non-anxious persons, or observing changes in autonomic reactivity as therapy takes its effect, we may gain insights into the general physiological mechanisms of normal emotional expression and experience.

Lader, the leading authority in this field, has reviewed psychophysiological studies of anxiety, including research upon both electrophysiological and biochemical aspects of endocrine function, (1975). Observed differences in *tonic* levels of physiological activity between anxious and normal subjects depend very much on the conditions of testing and on the particular measure in question. It is difficult to obtain a true measure of 'resting' activity of someone who is chronically anxious and fearful of new surroundings (Gale 1973). Cardiovascular and electrodermal measures provide a relatively consistent picture of increased activity while cortical and muscular measures are less predictable. For example, in our own research, university students with high neuroticism scores were electrodermally more reactive yet cortically less aroused than normal controls (Coles *et al.* 1971; Gale *et al.* 1971). Exposure to stimulation (*phasic* measures) separates anxious from normal subjects, but here too paradoxes arise since for some measures, like blood pressure, the patient is already so active that additional response could be damaging to the delicate mechanisms of pressure control, and a 'ceiling' effect operates. Therefore, under certain conditions of testing, normals may be more responsive since they are operating well below the optimal or physiologically safe ceiling. Nevertheless, anxious groups typically take longer to *recover* from stimulation, and this is bound up with their inability to adapt to the experimental situation. The classic demonstration both of the general maladaptive nature of anxiety and differential adaptation levels in different anxiety states was provided by Lader (1967). Habituation to repeated stimulation was shown to be fastest for normal subjects and was then systematically ranked for specific phobias, sociophobics, agoraphobics, anxiety states and anxiety with depression; the more general and intense the anxiety, the slower the rate of adaptation. This research followed earlier studies by Lader and Wing (e.g. 1966) showing that within patient groups, rated anxiety correlated with speed of habituation and that treatment with barbiturates shifted the patients' habituation rate towards the normal pattern. Thus we see that a particularly psychophysiological index – the rate of habituation – relates consistently to the intensity of reported anxiety and reflects the effects of successful treatment. Such data emphasise the need in psychophysiology for theoretical models which encompass both physiological and experiential domains.

Schizophrenia

Schizophrenia presents us not with one riddle but with many. The experience of the patient appears to be nothing like our own; he is often socially withdrawn and inaccessible. Language, the normal medium of communication, is typically disrupted. Methodological difficulties abound, for what we observe in the patient is a complex mixture of biological predisposition, environmental precipitators, and the results of drug treatment, social isolation and institutional depression. It is questionable whether 'chronic' patients – hospital residents who for many years have been maintained on major tranquillizers – are still 'schizophrenic'. Drug administration raises both technical and ethical questions for research. Venables (1975) suggests several techniques for statistical control of dosage effects within medicated groups. However he warns that some drugs may act in opposite directions for different sub-groups. One potentially powerful way of overcoming such problems is to study children 'at-risk' both before symptoms appear and before medication and the social consequences of illness obfuscate the picture. Such longitudinal studies will also provide a picture of onset and timecourse of pathology. The most exciting discovery to emerge so far is that the half-recovery time ($\frac{t}{2}$) of the skin conductance response in fifteen-year-old children of schizophrenic mothers predicts breakdown ten years later (Mednick and Schulzinger 1974). An intriguing aspect of $\frac{t}{2}$ is that short recovery is associated with schizophrenia and long recovery with criminality. A nice piece of detective work by Venables (1975) demonstrated that lesions in the limbic system of monkeys have effects which mimic $\frac{t}{2}$ differences in human groups, hippocampal lesions showing fast $\frac{t}{2}$ and amygdaloid lesions showing the reverse. Such findings not only provide a model for the central regulation of electrodermal activity but also suggest possible physiological substrates of schizophrenia. Venables cites evidence showing that schizophrenics, apart from showing short $\frac{t}{2}$, also tend to give cardiac deceleration even when presented with intense stimuli; he then argues using the Lacey hypothesis (see above), that both response patterns indicate an 'openness to stimulation'. Psychopaths on the other hand, in similar circumstances, show cardiac acceleration and longer $\frac{t}{2}$, revealing an insensitivity to 'the nuances of the environment which might otherwise lead to socially acceptable behaviour'. However, other claims have also been made for the psychological significance of $\frac{t}{2}$ (see Edelberg 1972).

Throughout this discussion of schizophrenia we have neglected the fact that traditionally there are many 'schizophrenias'. Has psychophysiology helped in the differentiation of sub-groups? Generally speaking the answer must be negative, although Gruzelier *et al.* (1972) have differentiated paranoid from non-paranoid patients under very specific conditions. Another possibility is that differences in psychophysiological response might themselves provide a basis for differential diagnosis. Thus Gruzelier (1973) has shown that certain patients give no electrodermal response to a neutral stimulus and that they also differ from responding groups on measures of behaviour. He has also demonstrated that there is asymmetry in response, institutionalized right-handers showing reduced response in the left hand. Since central innervation of electrodermal activity is ipsilateral and since the left hemisphere is associated with language, Gruzelier's finding ties in neatly with the work of Flor-Henry (1969) showing EEG abnormality in the left hemisphere for schizophrenia.

Psychophysiological studies of schizophrenia have been confounded by several problems. Diagnosis is unreliable; sampling differs between studies; there are inadequate data from normals under identical testing conditions, and model building often comes *post hoc* in response to complex data. We predict not only a major improvement in methodology but a synthesis and consolidation of these recent findings.

REFERENCES

(Recommendations for further reading are marked with an asterisk)

Blanchard, E. B. and Young, L. D. 1974. 'Clinical applications of biofeedback training: a review of evidence.' *Arch. gen. Psychiat. 30,* 573-89.

*Brown, C. C. (ed.) 1967. *Methods in psychophysiology.* Baltimore: Williams & Wilkins.

Coles, M. G. H. 1974. 'Physiological activity and detection: the effects of attentional and response requirements.' *Biol. psychol. 2,* 113-25.

Coles, M. G. H., and Duncan-Johnson, C. C. 1975. 'Cardiac activity and information-processing: the effects of stimulus significance, and detection and response requirements.' *J. exp. psychol.: Hum. Percep. and Perform. 1,* 418-28.

Coles, M. G. H., Gale, A. and Kline, P. 1971. 'Personality and habituation of the orienting reaction: tonic and response measures of electrodermal activity.' *Psychophysiol. 8,* 54-63.

Cooper, R., McCallum, W. C., Newton, P., Papakostopoulos, D., Pocock, P. V. and Warren, W. J. 1977. 'Cortical potentials associated with the detection of visual events.' *Science 196,* 74-7.

Edelberg, R. 1972. 'Electrodermal recovery rate, goal-orientation and aversion.' *Psychophysiol. 9,* 512-20.

Elliott, R. 1972. 'The significance of heart rate for behavior: a critique of Lacey's hypothesis'. *J. pers. soc. Psychol. 22,* 398-409.

Eysenck, H. J. 1960. 'The effects of psychotherapy.' In Eysenck, H. J. (ed.) *The handbook of abnormal psychology*. London: Pitman.

Flor-Henry, P. 1969. 'Psychosis and temporal lobe epilepsy. A controlled investigation.' *Epilepsia 10,* 363-95.

Ford, J. M., Roth, W. T. and Kopell, B. S. 1976. 'Attention effects on auditory evoked potentials to infrequent events.' *Biol. Psychol. 4,* 65-77.

*Fowles, D. C. (ed.) 1975. *Clinical applications of psychophysiology*. New York: Columbia University Press.

Gale, A. 1973. 'The psychophysiology of individual differences: studies of extraversion and the EEG.' In P. Kline, (ed.) *New approaches in psychological measurement*. London: Wiley.

Gale, A., Coles, M. G. H., Kline, P. and Penfold, V. 1971. 'Extraversion-introversion, neuroticism and the EEG: basal and response measures during habituation of the orienting response.' *Brit. J. Psychol. 62,* 533-43.

Graham, F. K. and Clifton, R. K. 1966. 'Heart-rate change as a component of the orienting response.' *Psychol. Bull. 65,* 305-20.

*Greenfield, N. S., and Sternbach, R. A. (eds) 1972. *Handbook of psychophysiology*. New York: Holt, Rinehart, and Wilson.

Gruzelier, J. H. 1973. 'Bilateral asymmetry of skin conductance orienting activity and levels in schizophrenics.' *Biol. Psychol. 1,* 21-41.

Gruzelier, J. H., Lykken, D. T. and Venables, P. H. 1972. 'Schizophrenia and arousal revisited.' *Arch. gen. Psychiat. 26,* 427-32.

Lacey, B. C., and Lacey, J. I. 1974. 'Studies of heart rate and other bodily processes in sensorimotor behavior.' in P. A. Obrist *et al.* (eds) *Cardiovascular psychophysiology*. Chicago: Aldine.

Lacey, J. I. 1967. 'Somatic response patterning and stress: some revisions of activation theory.' In M. H. Appley and R. Trumbull (eds) *Psychological stress: issues in research,* New York: Appleton-Century-Crofts.

Lacey, J. I., Kagan, J., Lacey, B. C. and Moss, H. A. 1963. 'The visceral level: situational determinants and behavioral correlates of autonomic response patterns.' In P. H. Knapp (ed.) *Expression of emotions in man,* New York: International Universities Press.

Lader, M. H. 1967. 'Palmar skin conductance measures in anxiety and phobic states.' *J. Psychosomat. res. 11,* 271-81.

Lader, M. H. 1975. *The psychophysiology of mental illness*. London: Routledge and Kegan Paul.

Lader, M. H. and Wing, L. 1966. *Physiological measure, sedative drugs and morbid anxiety*. London: Oxford University Press.

Lawler, K. A., Obrist, P. A. and Lawler, J. E. 1976. 'Cardiac and somatic response patterns during a reaction time task in children and adults.' *Psychophysiol. 13,* 448-55.

Mednick, S. A. and Schulzinger, F. 1974. 'Nature-nurture aspects of schizophrenia.' In Lader M. H. (ed.) *Studies of schizophrenia*. London Royal College of Psychiatrists.

Miller, N. E. and Dworkin, B. R. 1974. 'Visceral learning: recent difficulties with curarized rats and significant problems for human research.' In P. A. Obrist *et al.* (eds) *Cardiovascular psychophysiology*. Chicago: Aldine.

*Naatanen, R. 1975. 'Selective attention and evoked potentials in humans – a critical review.' *Biol. Psychol. 2,* 237-307.

Obrist, P. A. 1976. 'The cardiovascular-behavioural interaction – as it appears today.' *Psychophysiol. 13,* 95-107.

*Obrist, P. A., Black, A. H., Brener, J. and Di Cara, L. V. (eds) 1974. *Cardiovascular psychophysiology*. Chicago: Aldine.

Picton, T. W., Hillyard, S. A., Krausz, H. I. and Galambos, R. 1974. 'Human auditory evoked potentials. I: Evaluation of components.' *EEG, clin. neurophysiol. 36,* 179-90.

*Porges, S. W. and Coles, M. G. H. 1976. *Psychophysiology*. Stroudsburg, Pa: Dowden, Hutchinson and Ross.

Rohrbaugh, J. W., Syndulko, K. and Lindsley, D. B. 1976. 'Brain wave components of the contingent negative variation in man.' *Science 191,* 1055-7.

Schwartz, G. E. 1972. 'Voluntary control of human cardiovascular integration through feedback and reward.' *Science 179,* 90-3.

Schwartz, G. E. 1973. 'Biofeedback as therapy: some theoretical and practical issues.' *Amer. psychologist 28,* 666-73.

Silverstone, T. and Turner, P. 1974. *Drug treatment in psychiatry*. London: Routledge and Kegan Paul.

Squires, K. C. and Donchin, E. 1976. 'Beyond averaging: The use of discriminant functions to recognize event related potentials elicited by single auditory stimuli.' *EEG. clin. neurophysiol. 41,* 449-59.

Squires, K. C., Donchin, E., Herning, R. I. and McCarthy, G. 1977. 'On the influence of task relevance and stimulus probability on event-related-potential components.' *EEG. clin. neurophysiol. 42,* 1-14.

Squires, K. C., Wickens, C., Squires, N. K., and Donchin, E. 1976. 'The effect of stimulus sequence on the waveform of the cortical event-related potential.' *Science 193,* 1142-6.

*Sternbach, R. A. 1966. *Principles of psychophysiology*. New York: Academic Press.

Tecce, J. J. 1972. 'Contingent negative variation (CNV) and psychological processes in man.' *Psychol. Bull. 77,* 73-108.

Venables, P. H. 1975. 'Progress in psychophysiology: some applications in the field of abnormal psychology.' In P. H. Venables and M. J. Christie (eds) *Research in psychophysiology*. London: Wiley.

*Venables, P. H. and Christie, M. J. (eds) 1975. *Research in psychophysiology*. New York: Wiley.

*Venables, P. H. and Martin, I. (eds) 1967. *A manual of psychophysiological methods*. Amsterdam: North-Holland.

Chapter 6

Cognitive Effects of Cortical Lesions

JAMES THOMPSON

Whilst the relationship between mind and brain has been a source of speculation for at least two thousand years, the last century has seen a tremendous acceleration of investigation and conjecture on this subject. This interest may have been spurred on by the notion that the fascinating behaviour of brain-damaged patients offered a window into the mind, in which consciousness was thought of as a physical state of the brain. A reductionist spirit inspired the search for 'centres' in the brain, each of which was to be related to a particular deficit, and, by implication, to a particular function in healthy undamaged brains. Another more practical reason for interest in brain function may have been that the century provided a crop of patients who, while young and healthy, had sustained missile wounds of the brain in warfare. These injuries were easier to localize than those caused by diseases, and thus reduced one source of error in drawing inferences about the relationship between brain functions and mental abilities. Precision in the localization of lesions reduced one source of error, but left unresolved another problem – a malfunctioning system was rarely easier to understand than one that was working properly. The damaged brain did not simply give its secrets away, it sometimes produced new odd behaviour, or even seemed to work perfectly well despite extensive damage.

Despite these shortcomings, studies of brain-damaged patients were able to produce an atlas of deficits which was then converted, largely by an act of faith, into a geography of functions for normal brains. To chronicle in full this mapping of deficits is outside the scope of this chapter, and only guidelines and some examples can be given here. Piercy (1964) reviews the field with a clarity which it did not itself possess, and his paper remains a good introduction. Miller (1972) has produced a more up to date textbook, systematizing research results according to the lobe of injury in the brain.

The first finding to emerge from the study of brain injured patients is that conventional intelligence tests show very little deficit, which prompts controversy as to whether the tests are insensitive or whether the brain has the capacity to maintain its functions despite a fair amount of damage. In favour of the insensitivity hypothesis is that brain-damaged patients with intelligence test scores in the average range may be incapable of carrying out particular tasks, or may themselves report deficits which more specialized testing may then confirm. These special tests, as Teuber (1969) put it, can 'make some otherwise silent lesions speak'.

A perplexing point, little discussed, is that although brain damage seems to have little effect on intelligence levels, these levels vary widely in the normal population anyway, and there must be something about brain function to account for the distribution of intelligence. An IQ test may be insensitive to damage, yet it is sensitive enough to rank a population according to intellectual power.

As an example of some of the findings and problems in this area, we will consider the work of Newcombe (1969) who conducted an extensive study of the psychological deficits of 153 patients who had sustained missile wounds of the brain in the second world war, subjecting them to a twenty-three item battery which involved about ten hours of testing.

General intellectual ability seemed unimpaired in the entire group, was no different according to hemisphere of injury and, in those patients for whom data were available, no different from pre-injury scores. Looking at individual subtests, however, some differences emerge. The Similarities Test, a verbal reasoning task (sample question: in what way are a poem and a statue alike?) proved harder for the left hemisphere group as a whole, and also for the frontal group as opposed to the non-frontal group regardless of hemisphere. Newcombe hypothesizes that frontal patients may find it difficult to shift from the concrete and unique impressions evoked by the stimuli to the abstract common property which they share. This subtest illustrates the difficulty which besets the investigator in this field: too often he sets out to learn things about his subjects and ends up only finding out things about his material. The truth is that we do not know what cognitive operations are involved in the similarities task, and this ignorance hinders any explanation for the apparent frontal deficit. Commenting on another finding, that no deficit occurred on a classification task for subjects with left hemisphere injuries despite the fact that these had been reported in the literature, Newcombe remarks, 'These apparently contradictory data illustrate how changes in test material and technique can produce different results, and underline the need to identify the functions embedded in these relatively complex tasks'.

HEMISPHERIC SPECIALIZATION

The fact that the cortex comes in two halves has engendered a body of research into which half does what. The properties originally ascribed to the cortical hemispheres were those of dominance and submission, in which a literate left hemisphere imposed itself on a technical college of the right bank with all the strength of a firm right hand. More recent research has attempted to delineate in more detail which functions are specific to which hemisphere under which circumstances, but the broad outlines remain unchanged.

Newcombe's study, like so many others, confirms that left hemisphere injuries were associated with a mild but consistent deficit in verbal tasks, regardless of the presence or absence of clinically detectable dysphasia. Right hemisphere injuries were associated with visuo-spatial difficulties, notably in this study with deficits in a visually guided maze learning task. Naturally there are differences within hemispheres, the left tempero-parietal group being impaired in tasks requiring immediate registration and verbatim recall while the left parietal and posterior groups were impaired at learning tasks; the right temporal and tempero-parietal being impaired on a visual closure task while the right parietal and posterior groups were most impaired on the image learning task.

The rule 'language left/spatial right' was infringed in Newcombe's study by the finding that the left parietal group experienced difficulty on Block Designs and other orientation tasks. These exceptions to the rule are potentially very revealing, because once again they concentrate attention on the component features of the tasks involved, requiring one to distinguish, for example, between manipulations which are carried out within arm's reach, and action directed to space beyond it, when the person himself, as he walks through a maze, may be a moving reference point.

The strength of this study is that it is a systematic evaluation of a sample of subjects with localized lesions, and it is heartening that, twenty years after their injuries, the majority of the subjects revealed only mild specific deficits, and that the severe deficits of the immediate post injury period receded swiftly over the first few months, and then at a slower but nonetheless sustained pace over the years.

DEVELOPMENTAL WORK

Hebb (1942) outlined the major differences in effect between early and late brain injury, and hypothesized that early injury had a less selective effect than late injury. Using test scores of thirty-two subnormal children for whom there was no direct evidence of brain injury, much less of the location of the presumed injury, Hebb reported that vocabulary scores were lower than performance scores, whilst injuries to the adult brain rarely depressed verbal skills (with the exception of dysphasic subjects). This observation of the greater susceptibility of verbal skills to early brain injury was extended further to form a theory of the development of cortical function. 'An intact cerebrum is necessary for the normal development of certain test abilities, but not for their retention at a nearly normal level. In other words, more cerebral efficiency or more intellectual power is needed for intellectual development than for later functioning at the same level.' The dichotomy presented is between reason and practice, invention and repetition, synthesis and skill. In Hebb's words: 'The contrast is not between intelligence and knowledge, but between capacity to develop new patterns of response and the functioning of those already developed.'

McFie (1961) reported on intelligence test results of fourteen patients with infantile hemiplegia who had undergone hemispherectomy and a further nine who had undergone partial removals of damaged tissue. Those children who had the entire malfunctioning hemi-cortex removed actually gained 8 IQ points post operatively, as compared to the partial removal group who lost 3 points. Those children who had sustained infantile injuries gained 10 points, whereas those injured over the age of one lost 1½ points. There was no significant difference between hemispheres, and the general impression was that either hemisphere could take over the functions of the other if the injury occurred early, and this remaining single hemisphere could in a few cases produce IQ scores in the average range. However, most scores were skewed towards the subnormal range, so this apparent plasticity of function is not without its cost in terms of overall power. It is possible therefore to conceive of the infant brain as constituted of equipotential units, such that early injury to those areas which, for example, are associated with mathematical ability causes other units to take over those functions. On this model, early injury should cause an overall lowering of ability levels without specific deficits, whereas adult injury should leave full scale IQ unimpaired, but deficits of a quite specific nature should result.

Thompson (1977) has provided data which would support this view. Reporting on 282 subjects who had sustained localized cortical injuries in childhood he found a linear relationship between age at injury and full scale IQ, such that those injured before the age of five scored 97, and those injured when fifteen or older had IQs of 106·5, a highly significant difference. When the intelligence subtests were inspected for possible locus of lesion effects, significant differences only really emerged for subjects who had been injured when about thirteen years of age. In those sub-samples where injury occurred earlier, inter-lobe differences were most prominent in the learning tests, such that even children injured at about five years of age showed learning deficits which were in line with the adult pattern. For example, the children with left temporal injuries needed almost twice as many trials as the other groups in order to learn new words.

Other significant findings were that the group as a whole was of average intelligence, and that only those children who had been unconscious for more than three days after their injury, or who had sustained a permanent motor impairment were about one standard deviation below the population mean.

APHASIA

Language disorders subsequent to brain injury have been catalogued and puzzled over until the subject is almost as confused as the patient. Speech production difficulties often follow injuries to the left fronto-parietal region (Broca's aphasics), whilst comprehension of speech is often impaired by left tempero-parietal damage (Wernicke's). The brain is not a piano, and hitting one key does not reliably produce the same note, or any note at all. The range of locations of injuries which have caused language disturbance is pretty wide and it is also typically the case that patients show varying degrees of disturbance across all language functions, perfectly discrete deficits in otherwise normal performance being rare.

Types of asphasia have been proliferated, but it has taken time for neuropsychology to pay much attention to language, and with the advent of the transformational grammarians investigators have been looking more carefully at which aspects of language are affected under which conditions.

Von Stockert and Bader (1976) for example, have looked at some relations of grammar and vocabulary in aphasia. On a sentence order test, Broca's aphasics placed the sentence fragments into a logical string of lexical items, neglecting grammatical errors. Wernicke's aphasics, on the other hand, arranged the units according to grammatical structure, being unaware of the odd lexical meaning. Heilman and Scholes (1976) found that Wernicke's made significantly more lexical errors on a comprehension task than Broca's and conduction aphasics, whilst both these last groups made more syntactic errors than the controls. The Wernicke's aphasics' comprehension of major lexical items was so poor that the investigators felt that they were not testing syntax but rather eliciting random responses.

Blumstein *et al.* (1977) studied phonological factors in auditory comprehension in aphasia, and felt that a deficit in phonemic hearing could not account for the comprehension deficits of Wernicke's aphasics.

Levin *et al.* (1976a) studied patients whose aphasia was a consequence of a closed head injury, and found that the extent of aphasic disturbance was associated with the severity of brain injury as reflected by prolonged coma and injury of the brain-stem. Of the sample who had been injured nearly half had defective scores on tests of naming and/or word association.

Zurif *et al.* (1976), studying the grammatic intuitions of aphasic patients, and in particular their sensitivity to function words, found that Broca's asphasics' difficulties with grammar were far more than an economizing measure to circumvent articulatory problems.

Gallagher and Guildford (1977) found that different forms of wh-questions (what, where, when, etc.) caused different degrees of difficulty to aphasic patients, and that the patients had a limited set of response strategies for the difficult questions which they answered incorrectly.

Bliss *et al.* (1976) got asphasics to repeat grammatical and ungrammatical sentences, and found that they accurately repeated more *grammatical* sentences. They observe: 'Aphasics are to some extent guided by a greater residual knowledge than might be inferred from spontaneous production.'

Shewan (1976) looked at error patterns in auditory comprehension, and her general findings support the notion that, for auditory comprehension of sentences, aphasic patients differ quantitatively from normal adult speakers, but behave qualitatively in a similar manner.

This similarity of form but not power has led Luria (1972) to propose that the injured brain requires stronger and more frequently repeated stimuli to trigger what are now pathologically raised thresholds for word recognition and association. In this view the normal matrix of language is still largely intact but inaccessible and the aim of therapy will be to find those cues and prompts which will facilitate retrieval, and which will permit the rehearsal and retraining of old associations.

Kertesz and McCabe (1977) studied recovery patterns and prognosis in ninety-three aphasics, finding that the greatest recovery was shown by Broca's aphasics, whereas those with global deficits (in all aspects of language) predictably show least. There was no significant differences between those patients who had received therapy and those who had not.

Research in the field is advancing towards a better understanding of the complexities of language, but strong evidence for the efficacy of speech therapy remains elusive.

SPLIT BRAINS

The surgical procedure of cutting the corpus callosum which joins together the two cerebral hemispheres was instituted in the hope that uncontrollable epileptic discharges could be confined to one hemisphere rather than spreading to both. Early examination of these patients revealed surprisingly little deficit, prompting the notion that the sole function of the corpus callosum was to hold the two hemispheres together. Later investigators showed more wit, and were able to devise ways of testing a hemisphere at a time, thus revealing a good deal about the division of mental labour between hemispheres. These investigations have become something of an industry, with a small number of patients doing a large number of intricate and fascinating experimental tasks.

Dimond and Beaumont (1974) have collected together papers in this field, plus work on the hemispheric functions of normal subjects, and this provides a good introduction to the field.

Zaidel and Sperry (1973) administered the Raven's Coloured Progressive Matrices to seven commisurotomy patients, presenting the original printed form of the problem in normal free vision, but requiring subjects to make a choice by touch with one hand only from three metal etched patterns hidden behind a screen. The results showed that the left hand was more successful than the right, an effect which was particularly true of the early part of the test. Hands differed in style as well as accuracy: using their right hands subjects tended to work slowly, giving verbal labels to aspects of the pattern, whereas using their left hand subjects tended to be rapid, confident and silent.

Scores tended to be low for the commisurotomy patients, and higher for the partial commisurotomy patients, supporting the view that the task normally requires considerable interhemispheric integration. This view has been challenged by Le Doux *et al.* (1977) who had the rare opportunity to test a fifteen-year-old boy before and after commisurotomy. This subject gained 11 IQ points post-operatively, improved on memory tasks and performed well enough to make the authors conclude 'cognitive functioning is largely an intra hemispheric process'.

Franco and Sperry (1977) studied hemispheric lateralization for geometry in split brain subjects. As expected the right hemisphere was far superior. Although the left hemisphere was poorer, it was less so for Euclidean geometry, where there are many defining characteristics. On the topological geometry problems, where the defining constraints are lower, the left hemisphere was very poor. This sort of result indicates the barrenness of a mere verbal/non-verbal distinction, and the need to pursue this further so that one can specify what operations must be carried out for each task, and what their level of difficulty is. We cannot hope to learn much about cognitive functions until we can begin to specify the different skills involved in say Euclidean and topological geometry.

Kumar (1977) investigated another non-verbal task, by creating a tactual version of a memory for designs test, and measuring the short term memory of commisurotomy patients. The right hemisphere was markedly superior to the left, which confirms the location of the function, but tells us little about its nature. He also found that subjects with partial commisurotomy (sparing the splenium) performed in the normal range with each hand. This suggests that once tactuo-spatial analysis has been carried out in the right hemisphere, the results can be transmitted across the remaining fibres to the left hemisphere.

Some of the most exciting work with split-brain subjects has related to language function, showing for example that while the right hemisphere could match objects to a visible exemplar (by feeling for them with the left hand behind a screen) it could not name them. New techniques have extended the material that can be used. Zaidel (1976) attempted to measure the auditory vocabulary of subjects who had undergone commisurotomy or hemidecortication. He used an ingenious arrangement which allows one hemisphere at a time to be administered standard picture vocabulary tests, to which it responds by pointing with the contralateral hand. The right hemisphere showed a surprising ability to pick out the pictorial referents of single spoken words, showing a vocabulary level of eleven years seven months, or as Zaidel prefers to put it – 'average aphasic'. Both hemispheres show the same effects of word frequency, though of course the right hemisphere scores are lower than the left hemisphere ones. Zaidel argues that language lateralization to the left hemisphere at or before five years of age is not uniform, in the sense that some language structures such as auditory vocabulary continue to develop in the right hemisphere. He develops a theory in which the right hemisphere supports the left in language, but is dominated by it if the left hemisphere is intact. If injured, the right can perform a rescue function. This theory depends on the assumption that his five patients have not developed a diffuse speech representation because of early injury to the speech areas in the left hemisphere. This is an established phenomenon, yet Zaidel feels he can discount it on the clinical evidence available.

Zaidel (1977) tested these same patients on the Token test, a measure of comprehension in which the subject must manipulate the material in front of him as instructed by the examiner. This test is sensitive to mild asphasic disorders, and it is not surprising that the right hemisphere showed a severe deficit, comparable to the four year level. This is of course much poorer than their right hemisphere vocabulary scores, and leads Zaidel to argue that 'in the normally developing brain distinct language functions exhibit disparate ontogenesis of lateralization in the left hemisphere'. However, in some sense recognition vocabulary is 'easier' than language comprehension, so that if this result is seen in terms of cognitive power rather than cognitive type it may be easier to understand.

Levy and Trevarthen (1977) studied perceptual, semantic and phonetic aspects of elementary language processes in split-brain patients. They found that the right hemisphere was dominant for the visual recognition of words when no semantic or phonetic decoding was required. The left hemisphere, however, assumed control of behaviour when written words had to be matched semantically to pictures, though the right hemisphere was also able to do this task. On tests of rhyming, the left hemisphere was not only dominant but vastly superior to the right, which displayed little, if any ability. These results suggest to the authors that the hemispheres are 'basically differentiated with respect to their generative, constructive capacities in language, as in other functions of intelligence'.

MEMORY

Memory remains as much of a puzzle as it did to Ebbinghaus, and most neuropsychological work distinguishes between short and long-term, verbal and non-verbal and leaves it at that. For an example of a happy marriage between clinical and academic approaches to memory see Shallice and Warrington (1970). Talland (1968) provides an introduction to disorders of memory.

Levin *et al.* (1976b) studied short term recognition memory for random shapes in twenty-four patients who had sustained a head injury. The severity of this injury as measured by duration of coma was closely related to impairment in performance. Memory difficulties were also associated with neurological deficit, aphasic disturbance and signs of brain stem involvement. Brooks (1976) tested eighty-two patients who had suffered severe closed head injuries on the Wechsler Memory Scale. These patients were found to have severe memory difficulties, particularly on Logical Memory and Associative Learning. The duration of post-traumatic amnesia was related to poor memory, as was increasing age, but skull fractures and persisting neurological signs (including dysphasia) in this case were not. Cherlow and Serafetinides (1976) found that when epileptics were tested after surgery on short term verbal and long term 'general knowledge' type tests, deficits were greater among those who had had left hemisphere lobectomies, as opposed to right.

Huppert and Piercy (1976) looked in more detail at the difficulties of amnesic patients, varying both the temporal context and the familiarity of the material. Their findings suggest that the primary deficit in amnesia may implicate contextual memory, rather than memory for the items as such. Brooks (1974) studied the recognition memories of head injured patients, and subjected his results to signal detection analysis, which allowed him to discriminate between accuracy of memory (true positive recognitions) and lack of confidence in memory (false negatives). The head injured subjects showed a significantly impaired memory capacity, and a significantly high degree of caution, being very unwilling to guess.

This sort of approach appears to use error scores in a systematic and informative fashion, and gives some insight into the mental processes which may be occurring in the subject.

OTHER WORK

Houlard *et al.* (1976) tested the effects of the Müller-Lyer and the Ponzo illusions (well known in academic psychology) on patients with unilateral lesions. Those with left sided lesions experienced stronger illusions than normal subjects, but the increases were significant only for the Müller-Lyer. For right hemisphere patients the Ponzo illusion was weakened, and the Müller-Lyer remained equal to control subjects.

Rausch (1977) investigated the cognitive strategies of patients with unilateral temporal lobe excisions on a hypothesis test. The group as a whole were inferior to normals and each hemisphere was as poor as the other. However, though they did not differ in terms of numbers of problems solved, they differed in style. Left hemisphere patients formulated fewer hypotheses than controls, and tended to shift from a given hypothesis even when it was indicated to be correct. Right hemisphere patients tended to retain a given hypothesis even when it was indicated to be incorrect.

Although the work of Harman and Ray (1977) was conducted on normal subjects, their EEG study on hemispheric activity and emotion provides a personal footnote to the otherwise impersonal working lives of the hemispheres. Undergraduates who had unwisely confided in the experimenter were then reminded of emotional events in their past while their brain waves were recorded. Analyzing the power ratios between hemispheres showed that the left hemisphere varied far more with emotionality than the right, which by comparison seemed more stable. The effect may be due to the verbal nature of the stimuli.

CONCLUSION

Neuropsychology has for the most part operated, until relatively recently, in isolation from academic psychology, even as it applies to cognitive processes. It is largely without practical consequences, despite the needs of brain-injured patients requiring rehabilitation. There has been too ready an acceptance of deficits as permanent facts about a person, rather than as difficulties which might possibly be overcome by an energetic application of psychological principles, a fact bemoaned by Meyer (1957) and little heeded in the subsequent twenty years. Stroke patients with speech disorders rarely have a psychologist to assist them, and still receive therapy for which it has proved difficult to find evidence of efficacy. Neuropsychologists have equally been too ready to rely on paper and pencil tests, rather than closely observing the patient under his normal working conditions.

The patient in Newcombe's study who apparently trained himself out of his visuo-spatial deficit by studying and then testing himself on roadmaps did more than many neuropsychologists would have bothered to attempt. More energy must be put into improving function rather than cataloguing dysfunction.

REFERENCES

Bliss, L. S., Tikofsky, R. S. and Guildford, A. M. 1976. 'Aphasic's sentence repetition behaviour as a function of grammaticality.' *Cortex 12,* 113-21.

Blumstein, S. E., Baker E. and Goodglass, H. 1977. 'Phonological factors in auditory comprehension in aphasia.' *Neuropsychol. 15,* 1-18.

Brooks, D. N. 1974. 'Recognition memory after head injury: a signal detection analysis.' *Cortex 10,* 224-30.

Brooks, D. N. 1976. 'Wechsler Memory Scale performance and its relationship to brain damage after severe closed head injury.' *J. neurol. neurosurg. Psychiat. 39,* 593-601.

Cherlow, D. G. and Serafetinides, E. A. 1976. 'Speech and memory assessment in psychomotor epileptics.' *Cortex 12,* 21-6.

Dimond, S. J. and Beaumont, J. G. (eds) 1974. *Hemisphere function in the human brain.* London: *Elek Science.*

Franco, L. and Sperry, R. W. 1977. 'Hemisphere lateralization for cognitive processing of geometry.' *Neuropsychol. 15,* 107-14.

Gallagher, T. M. and Guildford, A. M. 1977. 'Wh-questions: responses by aphasic patients.' *Cortex 13,* 44-54.

Harman, D. W. and Ray, W. J. 1977. 'Hemispheric activity during affective verbal stimuli: an EEG study.' *Neuropsychol. 15,* 457-60.

Hebb, D. O. 1942. 'The effect of early and late brain injury upon test scores, and the nature of normal adult intelligence,' *Proc. Amer. phil. Soc. 85,* 175.

Heilman, K. M. and Scholes, R. J. 1976. 'The nature of comprehension errors in Broca's, conduction, and Wernicke's aphasias.' *Cortex 12,* 258-65.

Houlard, N., Fraisse, P. and Hecaen, H. 1976. 'Effects of unilateral hemispheric lesions on two types of optico-geometric illusions.' *Cortex 12,* 232-40.

Huppert, F. A. and Piercy, M. 1976. 'Recognition memory in amnesic patients: effects of temporal context and familiarity of material.' *Cortex 12,* 3-20.

Kertesz, A. and McCabe, P. 1977. 'Recovery patterns and prognosis in aphasia.' *Brain 100,* 1-18.

Kumar, S. 1977. 'Short term memory for a non-verbal task after cerebral commisurotomy.' *Cortex 13,* 55-61.

Le Doux, J. E., Risse, G. L., Springer, S. P., Wilson, D. H. and Gazzaniga, M.S. 1977. 'Cognition and commisurotomy.' *Brain 100,* 87-104.

Levin, H. S., Grossman, R. G. and Kelly, P. J. 1976a. 'Aphasic disorders in patients with closed head injuries.' *J. Neurol. neurosurg. Psychiat. 24,* 240-9.

Levin, H. S., Grossman, R. G. and Kelly, P. J. 1976b. 'Short-term recognition memory in relation to severity of head injury.' *Cortex 12,* 175-82.

Levy, J. and Trevarthen, C. 1977. 'Perceptual, semantic and photenic aspects of elementary language processes in split-brain patients.' *Brain 100,* 105-18.

Luria, A. R. 1972. 'Aphasia reconsidered.' *Cortex 8,* 34-40.

McFie, J. 1961. 'The effects of hemispherectomy on intellectual functioning in cases of infantile hemiplegia.' *J. neurol. neurosurg. Psychiat. 24,* 240-9.

Meyer, V. 1957. 'Critique of psychological approaches to brain damage.' *J. Ment. Sci. 103,* 80-109.

Miller, E. 1972. *Clinical neuropsychology*. Penguin: London.

Newcombe, F. 1969. *Missile wounds of the brain: a study of psychological deficits*. Oxford University Press.

Piercy, M. F. 1964. 'The effects of cerebral lesions on intellectual functions: a review of recent research trends.' *Brit. J. Psychiat. 110,* 310.

Rausch, R. 1977. 'Cognitive strategies in patients with unilateral temporal lobe excisions.' *Neuropsychologia 15,* 385-95.

Shallice, T. and Warrington, E. K. 1970. 'Independent functioning of verbal memory stores: a neuropsychological study.' *Quart. J. exp. Psychol. 22,* 261.

Shewan, C. M. 1976. 'Error patterns in auditory comprehension of adult aphasics.' *Cortex 12,* 325-36.

Talland, G. 1968. *Disorders of memory and learning*. London: Penguin Books.

Teuber, H. L. 1969. 'Neglected aspects of the post-traumatic syndrome.' In *The late effects of head injury,* Walker, A. E., Caveness, W. F., Critchley, M. (eds) C. C. Thomas, Springfield: Illinois.

Thompson, J. 1977. 'Cognitive effects of cortical lesions sustained in childhood.' Unpublished Ph.D. thesis. University of London.

Von Stockert, T. R. and Bader, L. 1976, 'Some relations of grammar and lexicon in aphasia.' *Cortex 12,* 49-60.

Zaidel, D. and Sperry, R. W. 1973. 'Performance on the Raven's Coloured Progressive Matrices Test by subjects with cerebral commisurotomy.' *Cortex 9,* 34-9.

Zaidel, E. 1976. 'Auditory vocabulary of the right hemisphere following brain bisection or hemidecortication.' *Cortex 12,* 191-211.

Zaidel, E. 1977. 'Unilateral auditory language comprehension on the Token Test following cerebral commisurotomy and hemispherectomy.' *Neuropsychol. 15,* 1-18.

Zurif, E. B., Green, E., Caramazza, A. and Goodenough, C. 1976. 'Grammatic intuitions of aphasic patients: sensitivity to functions.' *Cortex 12,* 183-6.

Chapter 7

Experimental Child Psychology

DUGAL CAMPBELL

The phrase 'experimental child psychology' came into prominence during the 1960's. A new journal *(J. exp. Child Psychol.* 1965) and a new textbook (Reese and Lipsitt 1970) both used the phrase as a title. This review begins by giving some explanation of what was signified by those who adopted and proclaimed the new phrase. The rest of the review aims to illustrate how experimental child psychology has developed during the last decade by describing some experiments in what has become the most characteristic area of the new school of thought: experiments done with infants.

AN HISTORICAL INTRODUCTION

The idea of doing experiments with children is not new: in 1920, for example, Watson and Rayner induced, and later, reduced, fear of a white rabbit in a nine-month boy by classical conditioning. The use of the phrase 'experimental child psychology' was intended to mark the virtues of a return to experimental studies following a period during which other methods had been the dominant form of investigation. The idea represented by 'experimental child psychology' included first, a positive emphasis on some aspects of experimental psychology which, it was argued, could be applied with advantage to the study of children and, second, a critique in reaction against some of the leading features of 'developmental psychology' which until then had been the usual phrase. The positive emphasis was based on carrying into child psychology notions borrowed from general psychology. It should be recalled that, during the fifties and sixties, experimental psychologists had, by and large, abandoned the attempt to explain 'Behaviour' in the grand manner advocated by theoreticians such as Hull and Tolman. Instead they had turned to building models which were avowedly aimed at dealing with specified segments of behaviour, for example, 'pattern recognition', 'short term memory', 'attitude change'. Experiments were designed to test limited but exact hypotheses; using such methods, substantial results had been obtained. A number of psychologists supposed that similar principles could be advantageously applied to studies of children. At first the hypotheses used to devise experiments were borrowed from adult psychology, for example, work was done to see at what age infants could first form conditioned responses; in addition 'experimental' psychology carried with it a connotation of an interest in sensation, perception, learning and cognition and the exclusion of other topics. Later, as this review will show, a number of novel conceptions were developed from experiments done with children which give the field its own peculiar methods and theories.

The reactive aspect of the idea was based on a turn away from traditional developmental psychology which was seen as relying too much upon descriptive studies in which the major analytical device was the correlation coefficient. In addition developmental psychology was suspected of being too much devoted to applied problems and educational studies based on school children over five or six years of age.

A number of other factors should also be noted, each one of which played some part in the revision of ideas that led to the formulation of 'experimental child psychology'. One influence which is readily overlooked is the introduction of new methods of recording behaviour. The advent of electronic recording devices made it possible to record at earlier ages and to measure responses which had not been examined before, for example, eye movements or evoked potentials.

A second important influence was drawn from theoretical proposals made by ethologists. Much of the ethologist's work was originally written in German and had not been accessible to English language workers. After 1950 this line of work became better known in the United Kingdom and the United States (e.g. Tinbergen 1951; Lorenz 1952). The statements of ethologists which particularly attracted psychologists' attention claimed that, early in life, there were critical periods for development. The most conspicuous application of these ideas to the human case is found in the work of Bowlby (1951, 1969); he argued that a young infant deprived of proper experience with his mother will have difficulty in forming attachments in later years. Attachment formation and the early development of emotion have since become major topics in experimental child psychology. It also became plain that, if critical periods work in the way they are said to do, the young must be possessed of well-developed sensory and perceptual systems; for example, in order to obtain a proper experience with the mother the young infant has to be capable, not only of discriminating a face from other objects, but capable too of recognizing the same face when it reappears. The ethologists, in brief, suggested to psychologists that, not only were the events of early life important, but in order to deal with them young children require a more complete information processing capacity than had been generally supposed. Experiments on sensation, perception and memory have in consequence been another staple of experimental child psychology.

This line of thought was reinforced by another influence. Studies of language had been few (but excellent examples of the descriptive methods of developmental psychology) because of the great labour and difficulty in recording, transcribing and analysing infants' speech. Under the impetus supplied by Chomsky (1957) a new line of thought developed. Chomsky's arguments demand that the child, again during the first two years of life, shall possess sensory and cognitive systems that allow him to learn to talk the language he hears around him; he argued that learning to talk a language is an expression of '. . . a ubiquitous process . . . of categorization and extraction of similarities' (Lenneberg 1967), and rejected the notion that learning to talk is an example of a complicated kind of discriminative operant learning. These ideas imply that built into the child is a complicated apparatus which allows a child to seize the linguistic opportunities offered by his environment. The question, 'What evidence is there for such an apparatus?', has also been tackled by experimental child psychologists.

A final dominant influence should also be noticed. The theorists of the thirties and forties had paid little attention to childhood; as a result there was a dearth of hypotheses to use in designing experiments. This lack was abundantly met when the work of Piaget was discovered by English-language psychologists (Piaget 1952, 1954). Piaget had been at work since the 1920s but his work had first appeared in French. His work had led him to think that the child develops apparatus for assimilating new experiences and developing them into the intellectual and cognitive schemata which dominate adult thought. Each schema falls into a progressive sequence (sucking in the new-born is such a schema; so is problem-solving in the adult) each one a '. . . cognitive structure which has reference to a class of similar action sequences . . .' (Flavell 1963). Piaget laid down a definite sequence of schemata to describe the precise order into which fall the tasks the child can successfully do. Although his own work was done with few children his methods lend themselves to the creation of experiments. His experimental methods were seized on to develop a new line of investigation, some of it dominated by the old style (with the purpose of finding out whether the ages at which Piaget estimated certain schemata took hold were in fact the ages at which they did become effective), but much of it intended to test hypotheses by rigorous experiment.

The net result of these different influences was the beginning of a new kind of investigation of children. The new school was experimental (in the sense that it used, so far as possible, manipulative rather than observation methods – ethical considerations prohibit many conceivable experiments with children) and hypothesis testing (in the sense that it used ideas borrowed from models rather than passively observing the changes that take place as children grow older). One result of the new school was that work was directed to younger children than had commonly been examined before.

BRAIN GROWTH, SLEEP STUDIES AND STATE

Psychologists who deal with infants – especially the newborn – find they are not the only specialists in the field. They must share the babies with paediatricians. When experimental psychologists were rediscovering the possibilities of doing experiments with infants, paediatric neurologists and others were revising their impressions of how the brain develops. Much of their discussion has been concerned with the effects of malnutrition, but several points in the neuro-physiological analysis of brain growth have implications for behavioural studies in general (Dobbing and Smart 1973). It seems likely that brain development in humans occurs over a substantially longer period than had formerly been supposed; in humans growth takes place following birth as well as before and developmental changes can be detected during the whole of the first two years of extra-uterine life (Dobbing 1974). During this time the rate of brain growth is not uniform: there are growth spurts – periods in which one kind of development occurs especially quickly – which, in the human, are at a maximum about the time of a term birth. Deprivation – of food or of sensory inputs – can be shown to have effects on the later development of the brain.

Many of the data bearing on these last issues are taken from experiments with animals whose course of brain development and whose growth spurts do not match the human sequence; applications of the model to the human case must be cautious indeed. Yet it seems clear that nutritional deprivation, if it happens during the growth spurt leads to smaller brains, fewer cells, less lipid content, and changed enzyme activity (Dobbing and Smart 1973). From animals there is evidence (Blakemore and Mitchell 1973) that selective visual deprivation leads to alterations in the function of the visual cortex. There is even plausible evidence, obtained from an experiment of nature, that similar events take place in man (Mitchell, Freeman, Millodot and Haegerstrom 1973).

The evidence about brain development and the effects of deprivation suggests that the physiology of development may one day become a source of experimental hypotheses. If the child alters physically during development and if the environment can influence physical development, then some attention needs to be paid to the possibility that developmental changes are due to physiological events.

A close liaison between experimental psychology and neurophysiology has however been made in the study of sleep in infants and children. The discovery of rapid-eye-movement (REM) sleep was, in fact, made in infants (Aserinsky and Kleitman 1955). Since that time, a cyclical pattern of REM and non-REM sleep has been found in adults, too, and in other mammals. Life-long sequential changes in sleep pattern (a decline in the proportion of time spent asleep, and a fall in the proportion of sleep time spent in the REM state) have been observed (Roffwarg, Muzio and Dement 1962). It is now clear that during the period of development in the womb and immediately after birth the rate of change in the sleep pattern is greater than at any other time in life. These changes can be summarized by saying that in the young infant (e.g. in premature infants) the proportion of time spent in the REM state – or something resembling the REM state – is very much higher than in later life. At term something of the order of sixty or seventy per cent of the time spent asleep is REM sleep (Campbell and Raeburn 1973). This proportion falls fairly rapidly following birth as Stage 4 sleep (or non-REM sleep) becomes better organized and takes up a greater and greater proportion of the time spent asleep. Each sleep state becomes easier to distinguish and babies, as they grow older, maintain themselves in one sleep state for longer periods of time. These developmental changes are usually seen as the consequences of a maturing and developing organization of the brain (Parmelee and Sigman 1976).

One implication of the study of infant sleep is a model to account for cot death (sudden infant death syndrome). When the sleep of infants is monitored one sees short intervals of time during which the child stops breathing (sleep apnoea); these are most often seen during

REM sleep. It seems possible that some infants are unable to recover the capacity to breathe following one of these short spells; the question then is: who are these infants and what makes them especially liable to the sudden infant death syndrome (Steinschneider 1975)?

The REM and non-REM sleep states are defined by behaviours which occur consistently together; in REM sleep, for example, one sees irregular respiration, loss of muscle tone, eye movements, small movements of the hands, feet and face, and, if one is making an EEG record, fast, low-voltage waves. Because they occur together it can be supposed that the infant is organized into a particular 'state'. The notion of 'state' has been generalized so that states have been described not only for sleep but also for the waking condition. State scales have been used in a variety of experiments and it can be shown that when the baby is one state reflexes of a particular kind can be elicited whereas when he is in another state the same reflexes cannot be found (Prechtl 1967). For this reason it often makes sense to include babies as subjects in an experiment only if they happen to be in a suitable state – or to postpone the experiment until the baby is in a good state (eg. Friedman 1972).

The most extensive use of the concept of state is to be found in the Brazelton neonatal assessment scale (Brazelton 1973). Brazelton is a paediatrician who has developed a method for examining individual differences between infants. In his examination a large number of behaviours are elicited from the child, each of which is interpreted by taking into account the state of the child at the time the behaviour is elicited. In addition, the test moves the child from one state to another, starting from sleep, then provoking an intense response and finally permitting a return to a quieter final state. An unusual aspect of the test is finding out how the child responds to his own extreme levels of activation; thus one question asked is: can the child calm himself? The Brazelton scale is now being used by a number of investigators to examine the effects of different methods of delivery, to examine the effects on the infant of drugs given to the mother during labour, to find out how the infant contributes to mother-infant interactions, to assess the high-risk infant, and so on. The newborn infant's responses to Brazelton's method provide quick and convincing evidence to the tyro that newly-born infants can organize responses to complex stimuli and, even this early in life, have individual 'styles'.

There is one other type of experimental investigation dealing with the brain which has aroused a great deal of interest. In the adult it is established that speech in right handed people is controlled by the left hemisphere of the brain. Does this hemispheric specialization exist at birth or does it emerge with the development of language (thus representing another possible example of the way in which function might influence organic development)? Some recent evidence favours the notion that the brain is innately constructed to favour lateralization. Structural differences have recently been found in infants' brains in areas which, in adults, are known to be involved with the perception of language (Witelson and Pallie 1973). Behavioural evidence has also been found, for example, by examining auditory evoked potentials to speech sounds and other sounds recorded from the left and right hemispheres of newborns and older infants (Molfese 1975); even turning the head and eyes to voices on either side of the head has been claimed to indicate cerebral asymmetry (Kinsbourne 1972).

SENSATION

A great deal of work has been done to find out what an infant and the newborn can hear, see, or taste. Many of these experiments rely on having the child make a choice between two stimuli shown simultaneously (e.g. Fantz, Ordy and Udelf 1962); if he consistently chooses one over the other then one may conclude he can discriminate between them. Alternatively two stimuli may be shown in such a way that one of the two is put continuously in play so that the child's response to it diminishes and then, when the other stimulus is introduced, the response returns in full (e.g. Friedman, Nagy and Carpenter 1970). This habituation paradigm, in which the recovery of response offered the 'novel' stimulus following the familiarization trials with the 'old' stimulus, allows the conclusion that the child detects a difference between the two stimuli. In other experiments technology has provided a means of obtaining new data; an example is the use of infra-red cinematography to build up a picture of how an infant scans visual fields and targets (Kessen, Salapatek and Haith 1972).

As one might expect many studies are directed to establishing the visual skills of the infant – the ruling idea being to compare them with the visual capability of the adult. It has now been shown that infants from the first days of life direct their gaze towards contours and corners and, further, when no targets are in the field presented to them, they scan by a method in which horizontal saccades predominate. These results have led to concepts which do more than compare infant and adult visual systems. It is possible to deduce a model of infant 'visual competence' from these results (Haith 1976); the model proposes that an infant has an active 'search and hold' system in the brain designed to maximize activity in the visual cortex. In addition one can argue that the combination of visual input and feedback from the eye muscles provides the baby with his first scheme which will prescribe for him the invariant relations between his own activities and the sensory signals derived from the external world.

Given such a system it becomes relatively easy to understand how the infant can detect features of the adult face and appear to be regarding his caretaker in a manner which gratifies her (or him). Contours are provided by borders, such as those of the hair and skin at the forehead, the eyes and the chin.

Obvious questions arise from these studies: for example, how acute is an infant's vision? An answer was provided to this question, for newborn infants, by using optic nystagmus as a measure; moving stripes are shown to an infant – if he can see, the baby will follow the direction of movement by a slow eye sweep, and then, quickly return the eye to a central point before beginning another slow sweep, and so on. If the experimenter makes the stripes in the display narrower and narrower until the nystagmus is no longer evoked then the width of the narrowest stripes which do evoke the optic nystagmus define the threshold for visual acuity. Dayton and others (1964) have shown this width to be an angle of 7.5′ of arc (or 20/150 vision in ophthalmic terms).

Another question which has been often asked is: do infants have colour vision? A longstanding difficulty has held up investigations of colour sensation in infants; in adults the intensity of the stimulus influences judgements of hue. Thus, when different colours are presented to infants it was not possible to say for sure if the infant was able to discriminate hues or if the discrimination was due to a difference in apparent brightness. Nor could one be confident that the adjustments one could make for this confound, using data obtained from adults, were appropriate to infants. The problem has been tackled by a number of extremely ingenious investigations, of which one (Peeples and Teller 1975) can stand as an example. In this experiment the intensity of a colour, red, was deliberately varied very broadly around the intensity of a white standard; the variation in intensity was adjusted in narrow steps so that, at one adjustment, the red light and the white standard would probably be indiscriminable by brightness alone. Discriminations were found across the whole range of the intensity settings; therefore it seems plausible to argue that hue is the critical dimension of discrimination (in infants aged two months).

In other experiments operant learning methods have been used to investigate children's visual skills. If infants aged between one and three months are presented with a pattern that is out of focus (as when one watches a movie which is badly projected onto a screen) it can be shown that they will suck vigorously, if sucking alters the focus so that the pictures comes clearly into view; in addition they look less at the picture when it goes out of focus (Kalnins and Bruner 1973). Thus it seems that as well as having a search and hold pattern for contours the infant will actively work to get a clear contour towards which his fixations may be directed.

Bower (1971), in a striking experiment, has given evidence that infants can see things in relation to space and that they use their knowledge of depth to direct reaching. In his experiment infants four weeks old were seated in front of a screen on which images could be projected from behind; the children wore goggles fitted with two oppositely polarized filters. Sometimes a real object was presented to the infants; when this was done they reached for it and touched it. Sometimes shadows, cast by oppositely polarized beams of light, were projected on the screen in such a way that the infant viewing through the filters saw a different shadow with each eye. When they looked at the rear-projected shadows they reached for the 'imaginary' object created by the ' . . . innate process of stereopsis' and were judged to be surprised (and even to be annoyed) when the apparent object was not to be touched.

When examining auditory sensation the usual stimulus is a sine wave giving a pure tone. This method illustrates some of the problems involved in working with children. A comparison between sine wave tones, presented for a brief time and over a wide frequency range, and more complex white noise suggested that a newborn infant could not discriminate between pure tones. (Turkewitz, Birch and Cooper 1972). But in later studies the state of the infant (at the moment during which the tones were presented) has been much more carefully controlled and in addition the two sounds used were presented continuously. (In studies of vision the infant must have his eyes open at the critical moment of each trial and, in this respect, a control for state is imposed by the eyelids!) Using this second technique it has been shown that infants will learn to suck if it allows them to hear a shift from a familiar to a novel tone (habituation paradigm). (Womuth, Pankhurst and Moffitt 1975).

Some striking experiments in audition have used stimuli which are more complicated than tones. These stimuli embody parts of adult speech: phonemes. These stimuli are generated electronically and comprise small parts of speech output, such as those which distinguish words like bet and get. The 'b' sound and the 'g' sound last for a very short period of time (approximately 250 msec) and it can be shown spectrographically that the difference between them lasts for an even shorter portion of time (approximately the first 50 msec). In a series of experiments it has been shown that infants can discriminate between these sounds. The most sensitive experiments used sucking as the index of the infant's discrimination (Trehub and Rabinovitch 1972). The baby sucks upon a nipple and the pressure within the nipple is recorded. As the baby sucks vigorously high-amplitude pressure changes are found; if these reach a certain criterion one of the two chosen phonemes is presented, through head-phones; infants will suck vigorously to hear the sound for a while, after which their enthusiasm declines (habituation paradigm). When the amplitude has declined beyond a certain preselected point the condition is altered so that when the infant next produces an above-criterion suck he hears the second phoneme; this leads to a return of high amplitude sucking. The initial high amplitude sucking followed by decline and then by a return of high amplitude sucking when the second phoneme is presented is taken as evidence that the child can discriminate the two sounds. This procedure has shown that children can distinguish between consonant phonemes as early as the first four weeks of life. It might be tempting to argue that these findings show that infants' brains are specially designed to take account of sounds which form part of adult speech. One way of testing this idea is to examine if similar results can be obtained in animals which do not talk; chinchillas provide the case in point and they can make the same discrimination (Kuhl and Miller 1975). Perhaps the correct argument is that speech sounds have developed in a way that accommodates auditory perceptual competence.

HABITUATION, ATTENTION AND MEMORY

Once it has been shown that even young infants can hear and see and that they will often prefer to pay attention to such complex stimuli as faces, and that they may have some appreciation of space, then it becomes of interest to enquire how their experience begins to add up. The simplest experiments on this topic usually are described under the heading of attention and turn on the habituation paradigm. If an infant, shown the same object a number of times, will prefer to look at a new object when given a choice between the old and the new the question may be put: why does he look at this new object? Three major notions have been advanced: novelty, discrepancy and complexity. One explanation has been that an infant forms some kind of internal representation or schema of the familiar object and he will look with renewed interest at any object which differs from the schema; the ability to construct such schemata may originate at about two months of age (Jeffrey and Cohen 1971). Another consequence of this view is that the more discrepant the new object is the more likely the baby is to look at it, i.e. there should be a linear relationship between the amount of discrepancy, measured in some fashion, in the new object and the preference that the baby will show towards it (McCall *et al.* 1973).

A rather similar set of ideas is involved in the notion of complexity. It is supposed that as the baby grows up his perceptual skills enable him to deal with stimuli which become progressively more complex. This theory takes account of two sets of factors: the cumulative experience of the baby, not with respect to a particular pair of objects, the novel and the unfamiliar, but with objects in general so that as the baby develops and experiences the everyday world he will develop preferences for more complex objects in general, both new and old. The second facet of this theory is that for any set of objects now being used by the experimenter the baby will prefer the more complex having first been exposed to the less complex. There is a good deal of evidence to support this view. As babies grow up they prefer checker-boards with greater numbers of squares, but a complication here is, as one increases the complexity of a pattern, so one is also increasing other variables, such as the amount of contour; one could perhaps explain the same data in terms of a simpler mechanism, such as an increase in the rate of neural firing caused by crossing more contours (Karmel 1974). At present there is no one account which will cover all the behaviour that we summarize under the heading of attention. Cohen (1972) has suggested that we should think in terms of two ideas: visual stimuli which are attention-getting and other stimuli which one can think of as attention-holding. Attention-getting stimuli operate through things such as movement and colour seen by the periphery of the retinae. The stimuli that maintain fixation may be such factors as novelty and complexity when the object is being steadfastly regarded.

If one supposes that an infant pays attention to objects because he is comparing them with an internal representation of what he has seen or heard in the past, whether this be a current representation of some stimulus encountered recently or some more general schema that can be ascribed to objects in general (such as relative complexity) then we are dealing with memory. At what point can we say that memory exists in the child? In a typical study infants are shown patterns and then are tested for recognition of a familiar pattern at some later time.

It has been shown for example, that six-month-old infants can recognize patterns they have been shown before after delays of up to forty eight hours long (Fagan 1973); photos of faces can be recognized after a two-week delay. In these experiments infants are first familiarized with one stimulus from a set of stimuli and are then tested for their recollection of a familiar stimulus by putting it amongst another similar stimuli. The experimental task requires the baby to recognize – in the form of preferential looking at the novel stimuli in the display.

One particular instance of memory is of particular interest; this is the question of self recognition. Piaget (1954) has discussed the time at which an infant should learn to recognize himself. He argued that as objects become recognized in a manner that is independent of the child's actions the child's own self should become localized as a particular kind of object. Experiments on self-recognition have usually used mirrors (Amsterdam 1972); the child can be shown himself in a mirror and his reactions to the image established, or he can be shown himself in a mirror and some manipulations can be carried out behind him (if he turns around then one must suppose that he recognizes himself in the mirror and in addition that something is going on behind his back) or a mark may be put on his face. There is a progression in the child's treatment of mirror images, from looking at the mirror images as some kind of interesting spectacle, to using the mirror image as a guide to self manipulation, to the final stage when the baby can correctly name himself at about two years of age.

EMOTIONAL DEVELOPMENT

The ideas of self and memory for people have come together in studies of emotional development which have concentrated, under the impetus of Bowlby, on the way in which children develop attachment bonds to particular individuals and get upset when their expectations about other people are falsified. One of the most studied phenomena has been the occurrence of distress to strangers; another commonly studied phenomenon has been the formation of attachment to the mother, although more recently attachment to the father has also been examined (Lynn 1974).

Distress in the presence of strangers is thought to develop in the second half year of life; before that time children generally respond positively to all adults and delay in the development of this 'natural' fear is thought to indicate some abnormal development – such as occurs in institutionalized infants who do not have the opportunity to develop one attachment to any particular caretaker (Tizard and Tizard 1971). The most recent work has suggested that some earlier investigations confused the issues and exaggerated the distress: the occurrence of distress to strangers is perhaps the result of either separation from the parent, being in a strange place, or an unease caused by the stranger's actions. In many experiments, when the stranger was presented, the mother was also absent or the child was in a strange place (cf. Cox and Campbell 1968). When these variables are more carefully controlled there does still seem to be a response to strangers. Younger infants show cardiac changes in the presence of strangers and older ones show what are called defensive reactions – cardiac acceleration as well as wary facial expressions (Provost and Decarie 1974). Despite all this, stranger distress does not seem to be as universal a phenomenon as once was thought. An interesting study has suggested that the fear shown to strangers is a consequence of the experimental technique which often has obliged the stranger to act in an unfamiliar manner; when the adult brought into the experiment behaves like the mother then the negative reaction is cut down (Decarie 1974). Reactions to strangers are explained either in terms of incongruity or discrepancy; incongruous, strange or discrepant new stimuli attract attention but also alert a defensive reaction (as, for example, the remarkably upsetting effect that people with deformities often have on children). An alternative view, due to Piaget, is that, as children develop their sensory-motor intelligence, they can develop notions of a particular individual; it becomes possible for them to recognize the mother as one individual and to know then that she is absent and that they are dealing with somebody who is not the mother. This other person may be a source of distress. However, measures of development using tests of Piaget's concepts do not link the development of ideas about permanent objects to the onset of stranger distress (Decarie 1974).

There are also positive emotions. The most important of these is attachment to the mother and it is assumed that under ordinary family circumstances a child will develop an attachment to the person who looks after him, usually the mother. Earlier studies have shown that the attachment may form to the person who provides the greatest amount of stimulation and interest (Schaffer and Emerson 1964). This can in fact be somebody other than the mother. However, when one looks at variations in attachment one discovers that mothers who provide greater quantities of stimulation to the infant and who are more attentive to the baby seem to provoke a greater amount of attachment (Schaffer 1971).

There is another side to attachment: what causes the mother to be attached to the child? It appears that if mothers are given more opportunity to play with their children early in life, shortly after birth, then attachment is more firmly rooted and differences resulting from this early experience have been reported as late as two years in life. These results may be practically important because there are a number of circumstances, such as premature delivery, when the baby often stays in hospital and the mother goes home, which break the early association between mother and child (Kennell, Trause and Klaus 1975).

CONCLUSION

Experimental child psychology has accomplished a remarkable amount during the past decade; this is best shown by the remarkable quantity of interesting and competent work (which is only partially illustrated by the sample of work cited in this review). The general tendency of the work can be summarized in three propositions:

i) studies of infants have shown that behavior in early life is more complexly organized than had been imagined and that the infant is more competent than he had been given credit for by earlier psychologists and paediatricians;
ii) workers in this field have brought experimental techniques to bear on issues which had earlier been topics of speculation; and
iii) models have been proposed whch give an account of psychological development during early childhood based upon experimentally established data derived from a wide range of investigations.

By developing models in this way experimental child psychology has adopted the modes of general experimental psychology and, in this sense, expectations of the 1960s have been fulfilled. One might say the experimental child psychology has come of age.

REFERENCES

Amsterdam, B. 1972. 'Mirror self-image reactions before age two.' *Developmental Psychobiology 5*, 297-305.

Aserinsky, E. and Kleitman, N. 1955. 'A motility cycle in sleeping infants as manifested by ocular and gross bodily activity.' *J. appl. Physiol. 8*, 11-18.

Blakemore, C. and Mitchell, D. E. 1973. 'Environmental modification of the visual cortex and the neural basis of learning and memory.' *Nature 241*, 467-8.

Bowlby, J. 1969. *Attachment and loss: 1, Attachment.* London: Hogarth Press.

Bowlby, J. 1951. 'Maternal care and mental health.' *Bull, W.H.O.3,* 355-534.

Bower, T. R. G. 1971. 'The object in the world of the infant.' *Sci. Am. 225,* 30-8.

Brazelton, T. B. 1973. *'Neonatal behavioural assessment scale.'* London: Heinemann. (Clinics in Developmental Medicine No. 50).

Campbell, D. and Raeburn, J. 1973. 'Patterns of sleep in the newborn.' In T. J. Boag and D. Campbell (eds). *A triune concept of the brain and behaviour* by Paul D. MacLean. Toronto: University Press.

Chomsky, N. 1957. *Syntactic structures.* The Hague: Mouton.

Cohen, L. B. 1972. 'Attention-getting and attention-holding processes of infant visual processes.' *Child Development 43,* 869-79.

Cox, F. N., and Campbell, D. 1968. 'Young children in a new situation with and without their mothers.' *Child Development 39,* 123-31.

Dayton, G. O., Gones, M. H., Aiu, P., Rawson, R. A., Steele, B. and Rose, N. 1964. 'Developmental study of co-ordinated eye-movement in the human infant. I. Visual acuity in the human newborn: a study based on induced optokinetic nystagmus recorded by electro-oculography.' *Arch. Ophthalmol. 71,* 865-70.

Decarie, T. G. 1974. *The infant's reaction to strangers.* New York: International Universities Press.

Dobbing, J. 1974. 'The later growth of the brain and its vulnerability.' *Pediatrics 53,* 2-6.

Dobbing, J. and Smart, J. L. 1973. 'Early undernutrition, brain development and behaviour.' In: S. A. Barnett (ed.) *Ethology and development.* London: Heinemann Medical Books (Clinics in Developmental Medicine No. 47).

Fagan, J. F. 1973. 'Infant's delayed recognition memory and forgetting.' *J. expt. Child Psychol. 16,* 424-50.

Fantz, R. L., Ordy, J. M. and Udelf, M. S. 1962. 'Maturation of pattern vision in infants during the first six months.' *J. comp. physiol. Psychol. 55,* 907-17.

Flavell, J. H. 1963. *The developmental psychology of Jean Piaget.* Princeton, N. J.: van Nostrand.

Friedman, S. 1972. 'Habituation and recovery of visual response in the alert human newborn.' *J. exp. Child Psychol. 13,* 339-349.

Friedman, S., Nagy, A. N. and Carpenter, G. C. 1970. 'Newborn attention: differential response decrement to visual stimuli.' *J. exp. Child Psychol. 10, 10,* 44-54.

Haith, M. M. 1976. 'Visual competence in early infancy.' In R. Held, H. Leibowitz and H. L. Teuber (eds) *Handbook of sensory physiology 8.*

Jeffrey, W. E. and Cohen, L. B. 1971. 'Habituation in the human infant.' In H. Reese (ed.) *Advances in child development and behaviour. 6,* 63-97. New York: Academic Press.

Kalnins, I. V. and Bruner, J. 1973. 'The coordination of visual observation and instrumental behavior in early infancy.' *Perception. 2,* 307-14.

Karmel, B. Z. 1974. 'Contour effects and pattern preferences in infants: a reply to Greenberg and O'Donnell.' *Child Development 45,* 196-99.

Kennell, J. Trause, M. and Klaus, M. 1975. 'Evidence for a sensitive period in the human mother.' In T. B. Brazelton (ed.) *Parent-infant interaction.* New York: Elsevier.

Kessen, W., Salapatek, P. and Haith, M. M. 1972. 'The visual response of the human newborn to linear contour.' *J. exp. Child Psychol. 13,* 9-20.

Kinsbourne, M. 1972. 'Eye and head turning indicates cerebral dominance.' *Science 176,* 539-541.

Kuhl, P. and Miller, J. 1975. 'Speech perception by the chinchilla: voiced-voiceless distinction in alveolar plosive consonants.' *Science 190,* 69-72.

Lenneberg, E. 1967. *Biological foundations of language.* New York: Wiley.

Lorenz, K. 1952. *King Solomon's ring.* London: Methuen.

Lynn, D. 1974. *The father, his role in child development.* Monterey, California: Brooks-Cole.

McCall, R. B., Hogarty, P. S., Hamilton, J. S. and Vincent, J. H. 1973. 'Habituation rate and the infant's response to visual discrepancies.' *Child Development. 44,* 280-7.

Mitchell, D. E., Freeman, R. D., Millodot, M. and Hagerstrom, G. 1973. 'Meridional amblyopia: evidence for modification of the human visual system by early visual experience.' *Vision Research. 13,* 535-58.

Molfese, D. 1975. 'The ontogeny of brain lateralisation for speech and non-speech stimuli.' *Brain and Language 2,* 356-68.

Parmelee, A. H. and Sigman, M. 1976. 'Development of visual behaviour and neurological organisation in pre-term and full-term infants.' In A. D. Pick (ed.) *Minnesota symposia on child development 10.* Minneapolis: University of Minnesota Press.

Peeples, D. R. and Teller, D. Y. 1975. 'Colour vision and brightness discrimination in two-month-old human infants.' *Science 189,* 1102-3.

Piaget, J. 1954. *The construction of reality in the child.* New York: Basic Books.

Paiget, J. 1952. *The origins of intelligence in children.* New York: International Universities Press.

Prechtl, H. F. R. 1967. 'Enteroceptive and tendon reflexes in various behavioural states in the newborn infant.' *Biol. Neonat. 11,* 159-75.

Provost, M. and Decarie, T. G. 1974. 'Modifications du rhythme cardiaque chez des enfants de 9-12 mois au cours de la rencontre avec la personne étrangère.' *Canad. J. Behav. Sci. 6,* 154-68.

Reese, H. W. and Lipsitt, L. P. 1970. *Experimental child psychology.* New York: Academic Press.

Roffwarg, H. P., Muzio, J. N. and Dement, W. C. 1966. 'Ontogeny of the human sleep-dream cycle.' *Science 152.* 604-19.

Schaffer, H. R. 1971. *The growth of sociability.* London: Penguin Books.

Schaffer, H. R. and Emerson, P. E. 1964. 'The development of social attachments in infancy.' *Monogr. soc. res. Child Develop. 29,* No. 94.

Steinschneider, A. 1975. 'Implications of the sudden infant death syndrome for the study of sleep in infancy.' In A. D. Pick (ed.) *Minnesota symposia in child development 9.* Minneapolis: University of Minnesota Press.

Tindbergen, N. 1951. *The study of instinct.* Oxford: Clarendon Press.

Tizard, J. and Tizard, B. 1971. 'The social development of two-year-old children in residential nurseries.' In H. R. Schaffer (ed.) *The origins of human social relations.* London: Academic Press.

Trehub, S. E. and Rabinovitch, M. S. 1972. 'Auditory-linguistic sensitivity in early infancy.' *Devel. Psychol. 6,* 74-7.

Turkewitz, G., Birch, H. G. and Cooper, K. K. 1972. 'Responsiveness to simple and complex auditory stimuli in the human newborn.' *Developmental Psychobiology 5,* 7-19.

Watson, J. B. and Rayner, R. 1920. 'Conditioned emotional reactions.' *J. exp. Psychol. 3,* 1-14.

Witelson, S. and Pallie, W. 1973. 'Left hemisphere specialisation for language in the newborn.' *Brain, 96,* 641-6.

Womuth, S. J., Pankhurst, D. and Moffitt, A. R. 1975. 'Frequency discrimination by young infants.' *Child Development 46,* 272-5.

FURTHER READING

Journals

Current work can be found in a number of journals: *Child Development; Journal Experimental Child Psychology; Developmental Medicine and Child Neurology; Development Psychobiology; Journal of Child Psychology and Psychiatry; Merrill-Palmer Quarterly* (which often carries review articles); *Monographs of the Society for Research in Child Development; Developmental Psychology*. Some medical journals have reports of interest to psychologists: *Pediatrics; J. of Pediatrics.*

Reviews

Developmental psychology has been well-served by authors and editors who publish review papers. These often provide the easiest way to discover the course of one line of work. Reviews may be found in: *Annual Review of Psychology; Annual Review of Physiology; Annual Review of Medicine; Advances in Child Development and Behaviour; Minnesota Symposia on Child Psychology; Review of Child Development Research.* There is a useful compilation of recent papers in: *Annual Progress in Child Psychiatry and Child Development.*

Books

There are a number of recent books which include introductions to leading topics of investigation or provide useful background information:

Brown, Roger. 1973. *A first language*. Cambridge, Mass.: Harvard University Press.

Foss, B. M. (ed.) 1975. *New perspectives in child development.* Harmondsworth: Penguin Books.

Illingworth, R. S. 1972. *The normal child.* London: Churchill Livingstone.

Newton, G. and Levine, S. 1968. *Early experience and behaviour.* Springfield, Ill.: C. C. Thomas.

Phillips, J. L. 1969. *The origins of intellect: Piaget's theory.* San Francisco: W. H. Freeman.

Rutter, M. 1972. *Maternal deprivation reassessed.* London: Penguin Books.

Schaffer, H. R. 1971. *The growth of sociability*. London: Penguin Books.

Vernon, P. E. 1969. *Intelligence and cultural environment*. London: Methuen.

The most complete collection of data and thinking about child development is to be found in Mussen, P. H. (ed.) 1970. *Carmichael's manual of child psychology.* New York: Wiley.

Chapter 8

Sex Differences

C. H. SINGLETON

The wise psychologist of today prides himself or herself in the adoption of an interactionist position in nature-nurture debates, yet with rare exceptions, psychologists studying sex differences have tended in recent years to polarize into biological and environmental camps. In the former the emphasis has been upon the biological inevitability of various differences between the sexes (Hutt 1972), while those in the latter have stressed that in general sex differences are so intertwined with socialization pressures and cultural norms and expectations that very little can be regarded as inevitable (Maccoby and Jacklin 1975).

SOME PERSPECTIVES ON THE BIOLOGICAL VIEWPOINT

In fact, those in the biological camp are not fundamentally interested in sex differences *per se,* for these researchers regard sex differences more as a key with which to unlock some of the mysteries of genetic, neural, and hormonal determinants of behaviour. However, in order to serve this purpose, sex differences must first be demonstrably clear and consistent. Unfortunately, this is rarely, if ever, the case. Even the most powerful example the biological protagonists can cite, namely the sex difference in aggressive behaviour, is not entirely unequivocal. Although there is evidence that in all mammalian species other than man the males are more aggressive than the females, aggressive behaviour is relatively easy to assess in animals, whereas in humans the expression of aggression can take many subtle forms and measurement is not at all easy. The continuity of the animal evidence is undeniably suggestive of a biological substrate to aggressive behaviour, and experimental manipulation of hormones in animals furnishes further support for this view, since androgens (male sex hormones) have the effect of increasing aggression and estrogens (female sex hormones) have the opposite effect. In humans, however, the relationship between androgens and aggressive behaviour is far from clear, although clinical studies indicate that drugs with estrogenic qualities can be used to control aggressive tendencies. (For reviews see chapters by Rogers in Lloyd and Archer 1976, and by Moyer in Friedman *et al.* 1974.)

Observational studies of children generally report a higher frequency of rough and tumble play and of physical conflict episodes between boys than between girls or between boys and girls (Serbin *et al.* 1973; Smith and Green 1975). Thus it is not a simple matter of biology, since boys learn at an early age to direct their aggression towards other boys and not towards girls. Moreover, Sandidge and Friedland (1975) found that both boys and girls showed more antisocial aggression when taking male roles than when taking female roles.

Other behaviours with which the biological protagonists are chiefly concerned are emotional, maternal and nurturant behaviour, sensory capacities, and cognitive abilities such as perception, language, and spatial, mathematical and motor skills. The evidence for biological inevitability of sex differences in these areas is far weaker than that concerning aggression (Fairweather 1976; Maccoby and Jacklin 1975). Nevertheless, the biological viewpoint requires a strong belief in biological determinism of these characteristics because without this assumption sex differences can no longer be regarded as a key to understanding biological mechanisms underlying behaviour. Thus there is an implicit circularity in the rationale behind the biological approach.

Of course, it is highly probable that all behaviour has a biological basis to some extent. However, no serious genetic mechanisms have been proposed to account for sex differences in any cognitive ability other than spatial ability, and although there has been much work on hormonal determinants of gender identity (Money and Ehrhardt 1972) hormonal influences on other human behavioural characteristics are highly conjectural at the present time. Hormonal theories which have been put forward to explain sex differences in temperament and cognitive ability have been reviewed by Archer (in Lloyd and Archer 1976). He points out that many studies have misinterpreted basic hormonal evidence, and he strongly criticizes inferences made from animals to humans. Manipulation of hormones in animals is relatively simple; in humans it is dangerous, although nature's manipulation of hormones in the menstrual cycle affords opportunities for safe research.

It has been found that female volunteers for psychological experiments tend to be in the ovulatory stage of their menstrual cycle (Doty and Silverthorne 1975); this bias could possibly affect findings of behavioural differences between the sexes, for there is evidence that the menstrual cycle is associated with changes in mood and concentration. However, contrary to previous beliefs, recent studies employing objective measures have failed to reveal any significant cognitive decrement during the premenstrual period (Golub 1976).

The pattern of family intercorrelations for spatial ability suggests transmission from mother to son and from father to daughter, but not from father to son, which implies a sex-linked genetic mechanism. However, a number of anomalies call for some qualification of this hypothesis (Eliot and Salkind 1975; Yen 1975). On average males are superior to females on most, but by no means all, spatial tasks, but there is evidence that this difference is accentuated in cultures where females play a very submissive role (India, for example) and absent altogether in cultures where women are not submissive (among the Eskimo, for example). Of course, this does not entirely rule out genetic mechanisms since the lack of sex differences in spatial ability among the Eskimo might be the result of genetic adaptation to life in a featureless landscape where poor direction-finding ability might prove fatal. Moreover, sex differences in spatial ability are not found until middle childhood or later (Maccoby and Jacklin 1975) which suggests either a maturational component in genetic determination, or some interplay with hormonal factors, or some environmental influence. Waber (1977) reports that late maturing adolescents of both sexes performed better than early maturers on spatial tests, but not on verbal tests, which she suggests is indicative of hormonal involvement in spatial skills. The problem is that some sex differences in spatial ability have been demonstrated well before increases in hormone secretions during puberty (Salkind 1976), and high spatial ability seems to be associated with high masculinity in females but with *low* masculinity in males (Petersen 1976). It has occasionally been contended that the spatial superiority of males could stem from differential play experiences encouraged by cultural pressures (boys playing more frequently with blocks and constructional toys, for example). Although this hypothesis has never been properly investigated there is evidence that the spatial ability of girls can be improved by instruction (Maxwell *et al.* 1975) or diminished by an upbringing which amplifies sex-role differences (Domash and Balter 1976).

In recent years there has been an increasing research focus on lateralization of brain function, which some postulate as the fundamental causal mechanism behind cognitive sex differences in general, and verbal and spatial ability differences in particular. Many studies find that, on average, females are superior to males on tests of verbal ability from adolescence onwards, but some investigations have reported no significant differences. Clinical and experimental studies indicate that in most right-handed individuals the left hemisphere of the brain governs language functions, while visuo-spatial information is processed by the right hemisphere (Nebes 1974; see also the chapter by Harris in Eliot and Salkind 1975). The position on cerebral dominance for mixed-handed and left-handed persons is still far from clear (Lishman and McMeekan 1977). It has been argued that lateralization of language function in the left hemisphere occurs somewhat earlier for girls (although the evidence for this has been disputed), and if this is the case it is possible that girls could develop an early advantage in verbal activities (which could actually inhibit further development of nonverbal thought), while boys continue to develop facility in visuo-spatial thought processes. A prediction from this hypothesis is that children who develop superior verbal skills relatively early should be inferior in spatial ability to those somewhat slower in verbal development. This prediction remains to be tested. There has also been some controversy as to whether spatial functioning might benefit from a bilateral cerebral representation, but clinical and experimental evidence at the present time suggests that this is doubtful (Fairweather 1976).

Despite a powerful folklore to the contrary, the empirical evidence for female superiority in verbal skills during childhood is rather weak, although girls are generally superior in reading attainment up to age ten (Thompson 1975). However, there are strong indications that this difference could be largely because school reading materials are of less interest to boys (for whom content appears to be more important than for girls) and because boys regard reading as a feminine activity (Asher and Markell 1974; Dwyer 1974). Since lateralization of brain function is assumed to occur well before the appearance of sex differences in verbal ability, some alternative or additional mechanisms need to be postulated to account for such differences.

That female superiority in language could be the cumulative product of practice and experience arising from the child's upbringing and relations with siblings and peers, is a view rarely considered, perhaps because those in the environmental camp generally feel that cognitive abilities are more the province of the biological opposition. Yet there is evidence that such a view could be correct, which in turn suggests a fundamental misplacement of biological emphasis; the true biological basis of the phenomenon may well turn out to lie in subtle behavioural differences between the sexes at birth which elicit different responses from the mother. Further sex differences can then emerge as a result of reciprocal interactions in which feedback is the key feature (Archer and Lloyd 1974). The interactionist position does not focus exclusively on biology nor on environment but on the ways in which both continuously modify each other.

CHILD REARING AND THE BEGINNINGS OF INTERACTION

The network of potential influences upon the child in the family situation is very complex indeed, and the isolation of mechanisms by which sex differences emerge from socialization and child rearing processes is an intricate problem. Not only must we consider independent parental influences on children (e.g. encouraging boys and girls to exhibit behaviour which the parents consider to be sex-appropriate), but we must also take into account the differential treatment of boys and girls which is elicited *by the children themselves* (e.g. if boys are less conforming than girls they may experience more intense discipline). Furthermore, the children in a family may influence each other, so that the sex(es) of a child's sibling(s) may have different consequences for his cognitive and personality development. Sibling influence may be either direct (for example, the boy with older brothers having more powerful models for masculine behaviour than the boy with older sisters) or mediated by the parents (for example, the lone boy with several sisters might receive stronger parental encouragement for masculine behaviour than the boy in a family with more equal sex distribution).

A fascinating sex difference in child rearing which emerges very early in the child's life is that parents handle their male infants more vigorously than their female infants, the latter being treated as though they were more fragile (Fagot 1974; Lewis 1972; see also the chapter by Moss in Friedman *et al.* 1974). Could this be because parents base their behaviour on some preconception of the characteristics they are trying to shape in their sons and daughters? Alternatively, do parents believe that boys and girls are behaviourally different from birth and allow for such differences in their handling? Or could the reason be that male infants somehow *elicit* more vigorous stimulation than female infants? Males are generally regarded as the more vigorous sex: their basal metabolic rate is higher than that of females, and most relevant studies find that throughout childhood boys typically have a higher physical activity level than girls (Goggin 1975). The child who is active will also afford himself different learning experiences compared to the relatively passive child. However, in neonates (Korner 1973) and during the first year or so of life (Clarke-Stewart 1973) no consistent sex differences in overall activity level have been detected, thus it cannot be the activity level which elicits the differential parental treatment of male and female infants.

However, male infants tend to exhibit a greater frequency of irritable behaviour (i.e. they tend to be more 'fussy' but not actually to cry more than girls), and have generally been found more difficult to calm. Consequently, the mother tends to cuddle her male infant more in order to quieten him, while the female infant is more likely to be left to settle herself if possible (see the chapter by Môss in Friedman *et al.* 1974). Newborn females also have greater cutaneous and oral sensitivity than males (Korner 1973), thus they may need less intense stimulation in order to be quietened or to be aroused. Thus it could be hypothesized that the general style of physical interaction between parents and their infants is a function of the child's relative irritability and response to pacification; the more frequent and more stimulating handling of boy babies, initially in order to quieten them, generalizes to the overall interaction pattern hallmarked by vigour.

Another sex difference in child rearing which has been reasonably well established is that mothers of baby girls generally talk more to them than to baby boys (Lewis 1972), and also, reciprocal vocalization with the mother tends to be a more frequent occurrence for girls. There is, however, evidence that these effects interact in a complex manner with social class and situation (Lewis and Freedle 1973) and with the experience of the mother (Thoman 1974). Since there are no basic differences between boys and girls in amount of vocalization in early infancy (Maccoby and Jacklin 1975) we must look elsewhere for an explanation of the sex difference in maternal vocalization. Whether the origin of this phenomenon lies in subtle differences of response to social stimuli very early in life, remains to be seen.

By the time children get to the age of two there is evidence that in spontaneous play mothers of girls are talking more to their daughters, asking more questions of them, repeating their daughters' utterances more often and using longer utterances compared with mothers of boys, who by contrast tend to use more directives with their sons (Cherry and Lewis 1976). Not surprisingly, girls of this age talk to their mothers more than boys do, and over the preschool period, at least, talk more to other children than boys do (Smith and Connolly 1972). The greater verbal interaction between mother and daughter could result from the fact that the attachment behaviour of girls is characterized by a higher frequency of proximity-seeking than boys. If mothers and daughters spend more time in close proximity they may be more likely to develop a relationship in which a high frequency of verbal interchange is the norm. The closer and more intimate peer relationships of females in later childhood and adulthood could to some extent be a product of this early experience of proximity to the mother, and could also further enhance verbal skills.

Vocalizing is one type of distal expression of attachment in young children, whereas proximal expression of attachment includes touching and maintaining physical closeness. Proximity-seeking has been regarded as an important aspect of dependency, but 'dependency' is a very diffuse concept and not a cluster of highly correlated behaviours. Research by Lewis and his associates (see Lamb 1976, for review) has revealed that in free-play episodes at twelve months, girls show greater proximal attachment than boys, providing the observation sessions are long enough. Duration of observation appears to be a crucial variable which explains the many negative findings in the literature. Over the period from twelve to twenty-four months of age, girls show a transformation from proximal to distal expression of attachment with their fathers, but do not show this transformation with their mothers; boys, on the other hand, exhibit this transformation for both parents (see the chapter by Lewis and Weinraub in Friedman *et al.* 1974). It would seem that the societal taboo on all except female-female proximal relations is the most likely explanation of this phenomenon, although maternal attitudes to dependency and the child's opportunities for proximal relations would also seem to be operative factors (Cornelius and Denney 1975).

It has been widely assumed that boys develop greater independence than girls as a result of differential socialization pressures (Mischel 1970). The evidence on this issue has been equivocal, partly because of the difficulty of definition and measurement, and partly because the majority of studies have been concerned with the preschool period when differences in parental treatment of boys and girls may be minimal, or at least too subtle to be detected by the relatively crude measures employed. The Newsons' longitudinal study of child rearing in Nottingham found sex differences relating to independence at age seven. Boys were found to be more likely to spend a high proportion of their time away from the home and vicinity of the parents, and had fewer restrictions placed upon their movements. The girls were found to be much more likely to lead a sheltered and protected life, possibly because parents worry about the dangers of molestation. However, the developmental implications of girls being more chaperoned than boys are enormous. The authors comment: '. . . children who are kept under closer and more continuous surveillance must inevitably come under consistently greater pressure towards comformity with adult standards and values.' (Newson, J. and E. 1976, p. 101).

The question of whether females *are* more conforming than males is a vexed one. The evidence indicates that girls are more obedient to adults, especially in early childhood (Serbin *et al.* 1973), but experimental studies of susceptibility to group norms and pressures from peers have generally found no significant sex differences in conformity, although there is evidence that females show behavioural and attitudinal conformity to the ideas of a member of the opposite sex, particularly if they regard him as attractive (Cantor 1975; Zanna and Pack 1975). The greater reluctance on the part of boys to comply with adult standards and directives could be because boys are somehow *expected* to be less compliant – 'boys will be boys' – but it could also be the result of the nature of male affiliative relations with peers. Boys tend to have *extensive* peer relations (i.e. they usually play in groups or gangs), while girls tend to have *intensive* peer relations (i.e. they usually play with only one or two other girls (Waldrop and Halverson 1975). Since a larger social group inevitably tends to evolve a dominance hierarchy, it could be that boys orientate their behaviour predominantly towards peers and girls orientate their behaviour more towards adults and towards more intimate relations with 'best friends', thus avoiding competition for position in a hierarchy. The pattern of children's anxieties supports this view, for girls show greater concern about doing well at school (Morris *et al.* 1976) and greater anxiety for acceptance by adults, while boys show greater anxiety for acceptance by other children (Davie 1973). On the other hand there is experimental evidence that under certain circumstances reinforcement from adults is more important for boys than for girls (Altshuler and Kassinove 1975; Dweck and Bush 1976), thus the issue is obviously a very complex one.

In the nursery school girls have been found to show greater proximity-seeking to a nurturant adult (Serbin *et al.* 1973). This could be because they like to talk with the teacher, or it could be a function of dependency or security needs. An interesting hypothesis would be that the greater amount of cuddling the male receives in infancy could create a somewhat more secure and confident personality, which under normal circumstances can be subsequently expressed in greater adventurousness and less proximity-seeking.

Most research on child rearing considers only mothers and ignores fathers, which is particularly regrettable for the study of sex differences since there is accumulating evidence that mothers and fathers differ in many aspects of child rearing. For example, mothers seem to be more interpersonally orientated than fathers when fostering their children's development, whereas fathers concentrate their attention more towards direct development of their children's skills (Osofsky and O'Connell 1972). Furthermore, behavioural differences have been shown to be subject to cross-sex effects, i.e. sex of child interacts with sex of parent. Such cross-sex effects have already been noted with respect to attachment behaviour, and have also been found with respect to dependency and aggressive behaviours, fathers being more permissive of these behaviours in their daughters, and mothers showing more indulgence of such behaviours in their sons (Maccoby and Jacklin 1975). In fact, there is a fair amount of evidence that adults generally tend to behave more leniently towards children of the opposite sex (Dion 1974; Gurwitz and Dodge 1975). The occurrence of these cross-sex effects within the family should not be regarded as surprising, for we would naturally expect to find sibling influence effects interacting with the sex of the siblings, and parents are in one sense only 'super siblings'; in some cases siblings even act as parents.

SIBLING INFLUENCE

It has frequently been reported that ordinal position of birth is negatively correlated with mental ability, yet most studies of birth order neglect to take the variables of sex and age-spacing between siblings into account. There is, however, evidence that these variables are essential to an understanding of the complexities of intra-family effects on intellectual ability (Cicirelli 1976). In the two-child family it has been found that the young child with a male sibling tends to be superior in achievement and ability, particularly verbal ability, to the child with a female sibling. The reason often suggested for these findings is that the more vigorous, aggressive, and competitive male stimulates his sibling to a greater extent than does the relatively more passive female. With adolescents and students of college age, however, brothers seem to have an enhancing effect solely on their siblings' quantitative ability, whereas verbal ability seems to be enhanced by female siblings. There is also evidence that fairly close age-spacings between siblings are disadvantageous for boys, probably because sibling rivalry is intensified. (See Sutton-Smith and Rosenberg 1970, for a general review on sibling studies.) Sibling rivalry may be partly resolved by 'deidentification' (i.e. regarding one's sibling as entirely different from oneself). Schachter *et al.* (1976) found that same-sex siblings deidentify significantly more than do opposite-sex siblings, and that first sibling pairs (first and second born) deidentify more than second pairs (second and third born) or jump pairs (first and third born).

It would seem reasonable that older siblings should exert a greater influence upon younger siblings than vice versa. This has been demonstrated using various indices of social and personality development: younger siblings of both sexes become more maculine if they have an older brother and more feminine if they have an older sister; this effect is not found for the influence of the younger sibling on the older (Sutton-Smith and Rosenberg 1970). A similar effect has been reported for verbal ability by Singleton (1978): in this study a large sample of fourteen- and fifteen-year-olds were tested on three measures of verbal ability. As might be expected, females had significantly higher mean scores than males, but also, both males and females with older sisters performed significantly better than those with older brothers. This sibling influence effect was not found for children with only younger siblings. It is argued that interaction with the more verbally skilled older sister enhances the verbal development of the younger siblings.

A number of studies by Cicirelli have focussed on the teaching influence of the older sibling on the younger (see Cicirelli 1975, for review). He demonstrated that older sisters were more effective than older brothers as teachers of younger siblings on a concept learning task; for older boys and girls as teachers of *unrelated* younger children, however, there was no difference in teaching effectiveness. The older sisters tended to make particular use of deductive teaching methods (explaining, describing, demonstrating and illustrating), which may stem from being accustomed to telling their younger siblings what to do. The ineffectiveness of older brothers as teachers may be due to more intense sibling rivalry, resulting in the younger siblings' rejection of help. This latter hypothesis was given further support by subsequent research in which a categorization task was employed. Although older sisters were not found to be better teachers with this less structured task, the data suggest that girls tend to interact with an older sibling in terms of receiving direct instruction, while for boys the older sibling acts more as a model for behaviour and a source of feedback on performance.

In yet another task, this time involving problem solving, Cicirelli found that children with older brothers performed as well alone as after aid by the sibling or the mother, whereas children with older sisters showed more advanced problem solving after aid by the sibling or by the mother. Children with same-sex siblings tended to press for a more rapid solution of the problem, again, perhaps, because of greater rivalry between same-sex siblings. It appears that the child with an older sister learns to accept help and direction more, both from her and from the mother, while the child with an older brother has had to learn to be more independent in order to cope with the power and rivalry of the older brother. This view is consistent with the findings of Bigner (1974) that children with an older male sibling assigned more high-power actions to the sibling than did children with an older female sibling. Cicirelli's discovery that the differential characteristics of children with older brothers and older sisters transfers to a situation in which the sibling is absent and the *mother* is offering help, is particularly important since it implies an indirect effect of sibling-sibling interactions on the mother-child relationship.

CONCLUSIONS

The view that certain behavioural differences between the sexes are biologically inevitable in humans is more a premise than a valid conclusion of the biological approach. Nevertheless, there is evidence for the involvement of genetic, hormonal, and brain maturational factors in such differences, particularly in the areas of cognitive ability and aggressive and nurturant behaviour. In all cases, however, there are anomalies which suggest the importance of environmental factors also. A critical but easily overlooked issue is that scientific journals typically eschew publication of negative findings, thus there may be countless results which do not reveal any significant differences between the sexes of which we are totally unaware.

The assumption of biological inevitability, that culture and society can neither create nor eradicate sex differences but merely reflect and modulate within certain limits those predetermined by biology, has two main foundations. Firstly, the continuity of given sex differences across various species and across various human cultures, and secondly, the early appearance of certain differences between the sexes. Both these considerations have superficial appeal but they do not withstand closer examination. The variation of behaviours between species calls into question the assertion that the same trait is being assessed across those species; this problem is particularly acute when inferences are made from animals to humans. Moreover, in humans the variability of any given trait within either gender group is greater than the variation between males and females. In general, however, males show somewhat more psychological variability than females, and boys are statistically over-represented in virtually all psychopathological conditions of childhood, which together imply that males are more susceptible to environmental influence. There is indeed some evidence for this (Rutter 1976) although the mechanism is unclear. It has been suggested that psychological vulnerability could in some cases arise because boys are developmentally immature in comparison with girls and yet still expected to jump the same educational hurdles at the same chronological age. However, while there is evidence that boys lag behind girls in skeletal maturity it is debatable whether this implies a comparable lag in brain maturation.

The assumption of biological inevitability based on early appearance of sex differences in childhood is a seductive view, yet boys and girls experience differential parental treatment and socialization pressures almost from the very beginning, so that only those differences in infant behaviours which appear in the first few weeks of life can really be considered in this context. However, the biological argument also has a theoretical foundation derived from speculations on the evolutionary adaptation of *Homo sapiens* to the requirements of hunting and nurturing infants (Hutt 1972), but, as Archer has pointed out (in Lloyd and Archer 1976), it is unwarranted to argue that because a characteristic may have an evolutionary adaptive basis it is therefore inflexible in every individual. In any case, the contemporary environment is radically different from that for which traditional sex roles were originally adapted.

The environmental view is that sex differences emerge largely as a result of cultural norms and expectations expressed principally through differential socialization practices. The biological counter to this is that social conventions usually have some rational basis; for example, *why should* parents encourage their daughters to be nurturant and tolerate greater boisterousness in their sons unless there was some biological basis for doing so? An environmentalist's retort is likely to be that a biological basis for such behaviours might have been important in enabling *Homo sapiens* to evolve a social organisation founded on division of labour, but that biology has since been overwritten by at least half-a-million years of cultural evolution. Our culture is now as much a part of us as our biology.

The interactionist position provides an alternative conceptual framework for studying this problem. Subtle differences between boys and girls at birth can initiate differential parental treatment which amplifies differences in the offspring, which in turn can bring about further modification of parental behaviour, and so on. Early sex differences in infant behaviour and parental handling thus became increasingly refined and differentiated as the child grows older and can have far-reaching consequences for other behaviours. The emphasis of this approach is on the two-way nature of the process, and on the complex patterns of influence within the family situation, the result of which is that the only real inevitability is the continuous environmental modification of our biology.

REFERENCES

Altshuler, R. and Kassinove, H. 1975. 'The effects of skill and chance instructional sets, schedule of reinforcement, and sex on children's temporal persistence.' *Child Development 46,* 258-62.

Archer, J. and Lloyd, B. 1974. 'Sex roles: biological and social interactions.' *New Scientist 64,* 582-4.

Asher, S. R. and Markell, R. A. 1974. 'Sex differences in comprehension of high- and low-interest reading materials.' *J. educ. Psychol. 66,* 680-7.

Bigner, J. J. 1974. 'Second borns' discrimination of sibling role concepts.' *Devel. Psychol. 10,* 564-73.

Cantor, G. N. 1975. 'Sex and race effects in the conformity behaviour of upper-elementary school-aged children.' *Devel. Psychol. 11,* 661-2.

Cherry, L. and Lewis, M. 1976. 'Mothers and two-year-olds: a study of sex-differentiated aspects of verbal interaction.' *Devel. Psychol. 12,* 278-82.

Cicirelli, V. G., 1975. 'Effects of mother and older sibling on the problem-solving behaviour of the younger child.' *Devel. Psychol. 11,* 749-56.

Cicirelli, V. G. 1976. 'Sibling structure and intellectual ability.' *Devel. Psychol. 12,* 369-70.

Clarke-Stewart, K. A. 1973. 'Interactions between mothers and their young children: characteristics and consequences.' *Monogr. soc. res. Child Develop. 38,* No. 153.

Cornelius, S. W. and Denney, N. W. 1975. 'Dependency in day-care and home-care children.' *Devel. Psychol. 11,* 575-82.

Davie, R. 1973. 'The behaviour and adjustment in school of seven-year-olds: sex and social class differences.' *Early Child devel. and Care. 2,* 39-47.

Dion, K. K. 1974. 'Children's physical attractiveness and sex as determinants of adult punitiveness.' *Devel. Psychol. 10,* 772-8.

Domash, L. and Balter, L. 1976. 'Sex and psychological differentiation in preschoolers.' *J. genet. Psychol. 128,* 77-84.

Doty, R. L. and Silverthorne, C. 1975. 'Influence of the menstrual cycle on volunteering behaviour.' *Nature 254,* 139-40.

Dweck, C. S. and Bush, E. S. 1976. 'Sex differences in learned helplessness: 1. Differential debilitation with peer and adult evaluators.' *Devel. Psychol. 12,* 147-56.

Dwyer, C. A. 1974. 'Influence of children's sex role standards on reading and arithmetic achievement.' *J. educ. Psychol. 66,* 811-6.

Eliot, J. and Salkind, N. J. (eds.) 1975. *Children's spatial development.* Springfield, Illinois: Charles C. Thomas.

Fagot, B. I. 1974. 'Sex differences in toddler's behaviour and parental reaction.' *Devel. Psychol. 10,* 554-8.

Fairweather, H. 1976. 'Sex differences in cognition.' *Cognition 4,* 231-80.

Friedman, R. C., Richart, R. M. and Vande Wiele, R. L. (eds) 1974. *Sex differences in behaviour.* New York: Wiley.

Goggin, J. E. 1975. 'Sex differences in the activity level of preschool children as a possible precursor of hyperactivity.' *J. genet. Psychol. 127,* 75-81.

Golub, S. 1976. 'The effect of premenstrual anxiety and depression on cognitive function.' *J. pers. soc. Psychol.* 34, 99-104.

Gurwitz, S. B. and Dodge, K. A. 1975. 'Adults' evaluations of a child as a function of sex of adult and sex of child.' *J. pers. soc. Psychol. 32,* 822-8.

Hutt, C. 1972. *Males and females.* Harmondsworth: Penguin Books.

Korner, A. F. 1973. 'Sex differences in newborns with special reference to differences in the organisation of oral behaviour.' *J. Child psychol. Psychiatr. 14,* 19-29.

Lamb, M. E. 1976. 'Proximity-seeking attachment behaviours: a critical review of the literature.' *Genet. psychol. Monogr. 93,* 63-89.

Lewis, M. 1972. 'State as an infant-environment interaction: an analysis of mother-infant behaviour as a function of sex.' *Merrill-Palmer Quarterly 18,* 95-121.

Lewis, M. and Freedle, R. 1973. 'Mother-infant dyad: the cradle of meaning.' In P. Pliner, L. Krames, and T. Alloway (eds) *Communication and affect: language and thought.* New York: Academic Press.

Lishman, W. A. and McMeekan, E. R. L. 1977. 'Handedness in relation to direction and degree of cerebral dominance for language.' *Cortex 13,* 30-43.

Lloyd, B. and Archer, J. (eds) 1976. *Exploring sex differences.* London: Academic Press.

Maccoby, E. E. and Jacklin, C. N. 1975. *The psychology of sex differences.* London: Oxford University Press.

Maxwell, J. W., Croake, J. W. and Biddle, A. P. 1975. 'Sex differences in the comprehension of spatial orientation.' *J. Psychol. 91,* 127-31.

Mischel, W. 1970. 'Sex-typing and socialization.' In P. H. Mussen (ed.) *Manual of child psychology. Vol. II.* New York: Wiley.

Money, J. and Ehrhardt, A. A. 1972. *Man and woman, boy and girl.* Baltimore: Johns Hopkins Univ. Press.

Morris, L. W., Finkelstein, C. S. and Fisher, W. R. 1976. 'Components of school anxiety: developmental trends and sex differences.' *J. genet. Psychol. 128,* 49-57.

Nebes, R. D. 1974. 'Hemispheric specialization to commissurotomized man.' *Psychol. Bull. 81,* 1-14.

Newson, J. and Newson, E. 1976. *Seven years old in the home environment.* London: George Allen and Unwin.

Osofsky, J. D. and O'Connell, E. J. 1972. 'Parent-child interactions: daughters' effects upon mothers' and fathers' behaviours.' *Devel. Psychol. 7,* 157-68.

Petersen, A. C. 1976. 'Physical androgyny and cognitive functioning in adolescence.' *Devel. Psychol. 12,* 524-33.

Rutter, M. 1976. 'Parent-child separation: psychological effects on the children.' In A. M. Clarke and A. D. B. Clarke (eds) *Early experience: myth and evidence.* London: Open Books.

Salkind, N. J. 1976. 'A cross-dimensional study of spatial visualization in young children.' *J. genet. Psychol. 129,* 339-40.

Sandidge, S. and Friedland, S. J. 1975. 'Sex-role-taking and aggressive behaviour in children.' *J. genet. Psychol. 126,* 227-31.

Schachter, F. F., Shore, E., Feldman-Rotman, S., Marquis, R. E. and Campbell, S. 1976. 'Sibling deidentification.' *Devel. Psychol. 12,* 418-27.

Serbin, L. A., O'Leary, K. D., Kent, R. N. and Tonick, I. J. A. 1973. 'A comparison of teacher response to the pre-academic and problem behaviour of boys and girls.' *Child Development 44,* 796-804.

Singleton, C. H. 1978. 'Sex differences in sibling influence on verbal ability of adolescents.' *Brit. J. educ. Psychol.* In press.

Smith, P. K. and Connolly, K. 1972. 'Patterns of play and social interaction in pre-school children.' In N. Blurton Jones (ed.) *Ethological studies of child behaviour*. London: Cambridge University Press.

Smith, P. K. and Green, M. 1975. 'Aggressive behaviour in English nurseries and play groups: sex differences and response of adult.' *Child Development 46,* 211-4.

Sutton-Smith, B. and Rosenberg, B. G. 1970. *The sibling*. New York: Holt, Rhinehart and Winston.

Thoman, E. B. 1974. 'Some consequences of early mother-infant interaction.' *Early child devel. and Care 3,* 249-61.

Thompson, G. B. 1975. 'Sex differences in reading attainments.' *Educ. Res. 18,* 16-23.

Waber, D. P. 1977. 'Sex differences in mental abilities, hemispheric laterisation, and rate of physical growth at adolescence.' *Devel. Psychol. 13,* 29-38.

Waldrop. M. F. and Halverson, C. F. 1975. 'Intensive and extensive peer behaviour: longitudinal and cross-sectional analyses.' *Child Development 46,* 19-26.

Yen, W. M. 1975. 'Sex linked major-gene influence on selected types of spatial performance.' *Behav. Genet. 5,* 281-98.

Zanna, M. P. and Pack, S. J. 1975. 'On the self-fulfilling nature of apparent sex differences in behaviour.' *J. exp. soc. Psychol. 11,* 583-91.

FURTHER READING

Fairweather, H. 1976. 'Sex difference in cognition.' *Cognition 4,* 231-80.

Friedman, R. C., Richart, R. M. and Vande Wiele, R. L. (eds) 1974. *Sex differences in behaviour*. New York: Wiley.

Lloyd, B. and Archer, J. (eds) 1976. *Exploring sex differences*. London: Academic Press.

Maccoby, E. E. and Jacklin, C. N. 1975. *The psychology of sex differences*. London: Oxford Univ. Press.

Chapter 9

Behaviour Modification

CHRIS KIERNAN

In this chapter we will consider developments in behaviour modification and behaviour therapy. Behaviour modification is a term which has been much misunderstood in academic and in popular psychology. The basic ideas stem from the work of Skinner (1938, 1953). The characteristic axioms are that behaviour represents the central datum of psychology and that behaviour is controlled by environmental consequences, rewards and punishments. Underlying these principles is an optimism very much like that at the basis of all science. If we can find out what variables control behaviour then we will be able to predict and control the outcome of behavioural interactions.

The origins of behaviour therapy were in the Hullian tradition as incorporated in the work of Wolpe (1958). Behaviour therapy also represented an attempt to derive explanations and solutions to human problems, largely neuroses, from laboratory studies of learning in infra-human organisms.

The progress of the behavioural approach has been similar in many ways to that of psychoanalysis. The approach has been introduced into one area of human concern after another. Phobic responses, chronic schizophrenia and mental handicap were the starting points. The progress into nursing, medicine, clinical and educational psychology, teaching, service administration, social work and more recently architecture and environmental design has paralleled the dissemination of psychoanalytic ideas. Development has stemmed from the attempt to meet new problems and to assimilate the best of existing skills and attitudes in each area.

Taken on their own behaviour modification techniques like reward, satiation and flooding are undoubtedly powerful but do not explain or account for anything. In order to be meaningful the techniques need to be seen within the framework of behaviour theory. In fact it is only when this is done that some techniques can be used effectively. For example time-out, the withdrawal of reward following undesirable behaviour, *must* be used against a background of substantial reward for alternative behaviour or it will be ineffective (Kiernan 1975). Sadly time-out is often used without reward for other behaviour with the consequence that the technique fails.

The behavioural approach does not dictate what behaviour should be taught or should be removed from the person's repertoire. All that it tells us is *how* behaviour might be changed. It is for society or other branches of psychology or education to suggest the content of behaviour change programmes.

The behavioural approach has developed its own characteristic methodology. There is a tendency to rely on single subject designs using the reversal or multiple baseline techniques (Baer, Wolf and Risley 1968). Single subject designs can demonstrate 'causal' relations rather like those shown in much physiological experimentation. Group designs and Fisher's statistics may be used to compare the effectiveness of different programmes.

In this section we will describe recent studies which exemplify important trends.

TEACHING SELF-HELP

Teaching Mentally Handicapped People to Dress

Behaviour modification has revolutionized the teaching of the mentally handicapped. New and effective techniques for teaching self-help skills and eliminating problem behaviours have been devised and put into practice. These developments have substantially eased the lot of the handicapped *and* the people who care for them. One of the main contributors to the change has been Nathan Azrin (cf. Azrin and Armstrong 1973; Azrin and Foxx 1971; Azrin, Sneed and Foxx 1973; Foxx and Azrin 1972, 1973; Webster and Azrin 1973).

Azrin's dressing programme represents a good example of increasing the effectiveness of teaching. The overall goal is 'to teach dressing . . . within a few days and in a very enjoyable atmosphere' (Azrin, Schaeffer and Wesolowski 1976). The report describes results from seven 'students' with an average CA of thirty-one years but average Social Age of 1·6 years and Mental Age of 1·5 years.

The programme is typical of many behaviour modification programmes. The first step was to test, on two occasions, whether the person could dress or undress. This test was also repeated at the start of each training day and at the end of training to give a measure of progress. The second step was to identify three types of reward: some, like praise, which could be given all the time without disrupting activity; some, like snacks, which disrupted dressing but took only a short time to give (these were given after each trial), and some which took a long time, like going for a walk. These were used after each dressing session.

The training sequence is described in detail, a necessary prerequisite if the method is to be used by others. The student was seated to eliminate unsteadiness when standing. He was taught to use both hands in handling each garment, so competing out undesirable responses with either hand. Early success was guaranteed. Five 'easy' garments, all without laces, buttons or snaps were used at first and training began with garments which were two sizes too big. The correct size was introduced as training progressed. Undressing was taught first, the whole sequence being gone through rather than the more usual garment-by-garment teaching. Azrin ignores a traditional formula in behaviour modification, backward chaining, by using a forward sequence of steps in teaching. It is normally assumed that the soundest teaching method is backward chaining. This involves teaching the last step first, then the penultimate step, etc. This allows the student always to work towards a defined reward which always occurs at the same time. Forward chaining involves teaching the first step first and then, in effect, putting the student on extinction for that behaviour by requiring him to perform another step before getting reward. This can often lead to frustration and very slow learning. In order to avoid this Azrin used both verbal prompts, instructions and manual guidance for the new steps in any sequence.

Sessions were very long by usual standards, two three-hour sessions being run in the course of each day. Azrin attributes the success of these three hour sessions to the intensive reinforcement procedures used.

All seven students learned to dress and undress themselves. One person took only four hours (less than one training day), the two slowest took twenty training hours; the median time was ten training hours or under two training days.

The Azrin method questions 'accepted thinking' in several ways. The assumption that dressing takes a long time to teach, that the mentally handicapped learn slowly, that they can only take very short training sessions, are all questioned. So are the more technical assumptions about backward chaining. In practical terms the programme represents a considerable improvement on anything available before.

GENERALIZATION OF LEARNED RESPONSES

A dominating concern of behaviour modification is with the generalization of learned responses. There may be little point in modifying behaviour in one setting if the change does not generalize to other settings. This concern has led behaviour modifiers to experiment in order to throw light on controlling stimuli but more commonly to try to intervene in the natural environment in order to change the behaviour of parents or professionals dealing with the person in need of help.

The next three studies illustrate these trends.

Stimulus Control in Autistic Children

Arnold Rincover and Robert Koegel (1975) analyze transfer of a learned response from a 'therapy' to a 'real life' setting. Their study was based on laboratory investigations which had shown that autistic children might well learn to respond to one element of a complex stimulus and that the element might not be one which the therapist would be able to predict. They analyzed stimulus control of learned responses in four children who failed to transfer from a training room where they had been taught by one therapist to an outdoor setting where they were tested by a stranger. The children were taught to imitate simple responses like touching or moving a body part.

Various stimuli present in the training room were systematically introduced outside and responses tested in their presence. A reversal design was used, the initial transfer test being alternated with the new stimulus situation so as to make sure that any responding to the new stimuli could be attributed to them and not simply to some process of gradual generalization from the training setting. Once an effective stimulus had been isolated its effects were tested in between three and six test sessions.

An effective stimulus was isolated for each of the four children. With one child the therapist had shown the child his reward, a sweet, by holding it up before giving him his task instruction 'touch your chin'. It emerged that the hand movement, without the sweet, was the effective cue. When the stranger used this the child responded on twenty-five out of forty transfer trials. For a second child the therapist's response of holding the child's hand before modelling a response proved to be the controlling stimulus, for the third child it was a touch on the elbow on the first trial of a sequence.

The fourth child, Cliff, failed to transfer responding even when the therapist tested him outside. Bringing the chairs and tables from the training room produced 100 per cent responding, the chairs alone zero. Cliff was responding only in the presence of the tables and chairs.

The study begins to analyze the types of irrelevant stimuli which may control the child's behaviour. It also makes the important point that failure to transfer is not a failure that should be attributed to the child's condition or disability; it is more due to the teacher failing to analyze controlling stimuli.

Working with Parents

An axiom of the behavioural model is the assumption that, if behaviour is to change, the people in immediate contact with the client may well have to change how they behave.

This orientation, coupled with requests for help from parents, has led to a plethora of studies with parents of handicapped and behaviourally disturbed children (Johnson and Katz 1973; O'Dell 1974). Many reported studies make rather naive assumptions about carry-over from instructions and verbal behaviour when the parents are with the therapist to behaviour with the child. In general little attention has been paid to changes in parent behaviour.

Awareness of this has led to a number of studies in which 'treatment' is carried out in the setting where problem behaviours occur. For example Barnard, Christopherson and Wolf (1977) have recently reported a study in which children were taught 'appropriate shopping behaviour' in supermarkets. The children, two six-year olds and one five-year old, ran off from their mothers and disturbed goods on the shelves in a way that resulted in 'embarrassment, frustration, raised voices and spanking'. With the co-operation of supermarket managers the behaviour was 'treated' *in the supermarkets.* A points system, already used at home, was extended to the supermarket. The study used a typical multiple baseline technique. First there were between four and eight visits to the store with no intervention. These were designed to record the 'normal' behaviour of mother and child. Then points were given to the child for staying close and deducted for moving away. The basis for giving and deducting points was explained to the child. After between six and eight visits under this condition points were awarded also for not touching goods on the shelves, again on a points system. Points were 'backed up' by exchange for more tangible rewards at home.

The intervention was successful in keeping the children closer to the mother and in preventing children touching the products on shelves. Measures of parent satisfaction increased and measures of one child-mother interaction showed a substantial change in the quality of talk between them. During baseline eight per cent of mother's talk was positive, thirty-three per cent negative. During treatment positive talk rose to sixty-six per cent, negative fell to seven. At follow-up only twenty-eight per cent was positive, but there was no negative talk. The amount of talk remained about the same throughout.

Disruptive Behaviour in Normal Preschool Children

A second example of intervention in the natural environment comes in a paper from Todd Risley's research group at the University of Kansas. Porterfield, Herbert-Jackson and Risley (1976) report the development of a method for controlling the disruptive behaviour of toddlers in a day-care centre. The problem faced by the group was that, although effective in reducing disruption, conventional time-out techniques were unacceptable to the day-care staff and therefore unlikely to be used in practice. This is a very common problem in practical settings. In order to be adopted techniques must harmonize with the climate of thinking of the staff who are to use the techniques. Simple demonstrations of laboratory effectiveness are not enough. We need experimentation which shows that techniques will be used by staff.

In their report the authors describe a reversal study in which two techniques were used. The first was the traditional 'Redirection' procedure. Under this condition disruptive behaviour was interrupted, the teacher explained to the child that his play was inappropriate and he was distracted or redirected by being given another toy. The problem with this technique was the likelihood that adult attention and being given a new toy were both rewards for disruptive behaviour. (Data from the study support this idea.) The alternative procedure, 'Sit and Watch,' involved explaining to the child what he or she had done wrong, separating him from the group and having him sit and watch for up to a minute and then to say that he understood what he had done wrong or describe appropriate play. The child was then praised for appropriate play. This procedure involves an acceptable form of 'time out', sitting and watching, with verbal prompting, self-instruction and reward for appropriate play.

Porterfield's study shows the effectiveness of the 'Sit and Watch' technique in reducing disruptive behaviour and improving ratings of the pleasantness of the sound of the centre. The technique was introduced gradually to the staff through description, modelling and direct feedback on use. At the end of the study three of the five staff preferred sit and watch, the other two did not like either technique but in general preferred redirection. Interestingly enough parents did not object at all to 'sit and watch', indeed some said that their only criticism was that it was not strict enough.

This study is interesting and characteristic of behaviour modification studies in the use of several measurement techniques and in the complex picture which their use reveals.

TEACHING PROGRAMMES WITHIN THE BEHAVIOURAL TRADITION

The last two studies to be described illustrate the development of teaching programmes or packages within the behavioural tradition. Programmes have been devised with the idea that clients with different problems or levels of development can be 'plugged in' to an already tested teaching sequence.

Programmes for Language Development

The Skinner-Chomsky 'controversy' about verbal behaviour has, to a large extent, been by-passed by those concerned with the teaching of language. They have relied more on examining what concepts and strategies the person needs to acquire in order to learn language (Snyder and McLean 1976; Yule and Berger 1975). One laboratory researcher, David Premack, was interested in whether infra-human organisms could learn to use language. Premack avoided the use of auditory means of communication since many earlier studies on chimpanzees had suggested that even with great efforts they were not going to learn to speak. Premack argued that, nonetheless, the chimpanzee could be taught to use propositional language. In a now famous series of studies Premack showed that his animals could learn to communicate using plastic plaques to represent words. He has recently drawn together his arguments in book form (Premack 1976).

As a result of Premack's work John Hollis and Joe Carrier began experimenting with the use of the non-speech system with mentally retarded children. What emerged was that children who had hitherto been unable to communicate could learn to do so using the plastic 'words'. They learned to 'name' objects and identify them by 'name', to follow and to give simple instructions, to use simple, and in some cases, complex syntax.

Carrier's work represents an attempt to develop a programme which can be field-tested for effectiveness when used by relevant professionals with appropriate clients.

Carrier (1976) describes results from an extensive trial of his programme, the Non-Speech Language Initiation Program (Non-SLIP) (Carrier 1974; Carrier and Peak 1975). Carrier reports that the programme has been used with 180 children nearly all of whom were non-verbal at the start of training. Of these only three were unable to complete the early phases of training. Eventually vocal speech was included in the training of fifty-seven children and of these fifty-six 'moved on to successful training in conventional speech and language therapy'. Twenty-one were known to be using speech outside the trainingroom environments. Carrier provides data on such things as the average time taken to progress through various sections and error rates on subprogrammes.

How effective Non-SLIP will be in the long run remains to be seen. What is impressive is the embodiment of research findings in programmes and the attempt to apply measurements to the success of these programmes (See Snyder, Lovitt and Smith 1976; Lloyd 1976 for reviews).

The Testing of 'Packages'

Once packages have been developed it is necessary to test them for their viability against other procedures. There is a long tradition of testing behaviourally-based programmes against psychotherapy or other dynamically orientated approaches.

A good recent example of this continuing tradition comes from the field of weight control.

Hall, Hall, DeBoer and O'Kulitch (1977) report a study which compares the outcome of several different programmes. Their study illustrates the self-critical approach of many behaviour modifiers and the attempt to analyze the components of treatment through group designs. Hall and her colleagues used three behaviourally based programmes. These were 1) a reinforcement programme in which the therapist provided reward for weight loss, 2) a self-management procedure (Hall, Hall, Hanson and Bordon 1974) designed to allow the subject to provide herself with rewards for weightloss, 3) a combined self and therapist managed procedure, 4) a psychotherapy group and 5) a no contact control.

The thinking behind the study was that slow weight loss is normally shown in self-management training but external management produces rapid loss. However external management does not produce carry-over effects after contact has ceased whereas self-management is specifically designed to be used without external support. Unfortunately Hall had found self-management techniques were not used adequately in the long term. Hall argues that this is due to the low level of reward for using the technique because weight loss is slow. Consequently she suggests that *combining* self and external management should provide a blend of rapid weight loss and development of self management: this should lead to rapid weight loss which will reward self-management and lead to better carry over.

The design can make several predictions on outcome over a short period of treatment (ten weeks) and for the twenty-two week and thirty-four week follow-up periods. Seventy-four subjects from a weight reduction club took part in the study. All had to be persuaded to participate, to be 'treated' and finally followed-up. This type of time-consuming and effortful exercise is typical of many behaviour modification studies. However it is necessary to invest this amount of effort if realistic data are to be gathered. Similarly the therapists in this study had to be skilled in group psychotherapy and behaviour modification as well as to hold carefully the requirements of research.

The outcome of the study showed a significant advantage to behavioural as opposed to psychotherapeutic technique over the treatment period. This is a typical result in most fields where outcome studies are performed. The specific predictions about follow up were not upheld. Not only were the differences between the three behavioural groups not significant but the differences between psychotherapy and behavioural groups diminished to statistical insignificance. This trend was confirmed at the six month follow-up.

Obviously not all programmes fail to transfer to follow-up, but this example is instructive. One thing which the advent of behavioural approaches seems to have done in therapy is to make people increasingly aware of the importance of evaluation. This emphasis often produces the kind of result exemplified by Hall's work thereby focussing attention on the need to find out why programmes fail and leading to more sophisticated analyses and a greater knowledge of potentially powerful variables.

CONCLUSION

The papers selected for discussion reflect the author's biasses and interests. Another author might well have chosen to emphasize entirely different trends. From this author's viewpoint the dominating trend in behaviour modification is the concern with identifying ways in which behaviour can be modified in the settings in which people live. The concern is with techniques which are effective in promoting and maintaining change. In this context the use of the behavioural approach in analyzing contingencies operating in organizations needs mentioning (Kushlick 1975; Rothman, Erlich and Teresa 1975). This is likely to become a crucial feature of the approach as we come to grips with the influence of organisational variables in retarding development. The other persisting feature of behaviour modification is the fundamental concern with objective measurement and evaluation. It is probably this central concern which most clearly distinguishes the behavioural approach from others and which leaves behaviour modification and behaviour therapy mature, alive and exciting in the late 1970s.

REFERENCES

Azrin, N. H. and Armstrong, P. M. 1973. 'The "mini-meal" – A method for teaching eating skills to the profoundly retarded.' *Ment. Ret. 11,* 9-11.

Azrin, N. H. and Foxx, R. M. 1971. 'A rapid method of training the institutionalised retarded.' *J. appl. Behav. Anal. 4,* 89-99.

Azrin, N. H., Schaeffer, R. M. and Wesolowski, M. D. 1976. 'A rapid method of teaching profoundly retarded persons to dress.' *Ment. Ret. 14,* 29-33.

Azrin, N. H., Sneed, T. J. and Foxx, R. N. 1973. 'Autism reversal: eliminating stereotyped self stimulation of retarded individuals.' *Amer. J. ment. Def. 78,* 241-8.

Baer, D. M., Wolf, M. M. and Risley, T. R. 1968. 'Some current dimensions of applied behaviour analysis.' *J. appl. Behav. Anal. 1,* 91-7.

Bandura, A. 1968. *Principles of behaviour modification.* New York: Holt Rhinehart and Winston.

Barnard, J. D., Christopherson, E. R. and Wolf, M. M. 1977. 'Teaching children appropriate shopping behaviour through parent training in the supermarket setting.' *J. appl. Behav. Anal. 10,* 49-59.

Carrier, J. K. 1974. 'Application of functional analysis and a non-speech response mode to language teaching.' In L. V. McReynolds (ed.) *Developing systematic procedures for training children's language,* A.S.H.A. Monograph No. 18.

Carrier, J. K. 1976. 'Application of a non-speech language system with the severely language handicapped.' In L. L. Lloyd (ed.) *Communication assessment and intervention strategies.* Baltimore: University Park Press.

Carrier, J. K. and Peak, T. 1975. *Non-speech language initiation program.* Lawrence, Kansas: H and H Enterprises.

Foxx, R. M. and Azrin, N. H. 1972. 'Restitution: a method of eliminating aggressive disruptive behaviour of retarded and brain damaged patients.' *Behav. Res. Ther. 10,* 15-27.

Foxx, R. M. and Azrin, N. H. 1973. *Toilet training the retarded: a rapid program for day and night-time independent toileting.* Champaign, Illinois: Research Press.

Gardner, W. I. 1971. *Behaviour modification in mental retardation.* Chicago: Aldine, Atherton.

Hall, S. M., Hall, R. G., De Boer, G. and O'Kulitch, P. 1977. 'Self and external management as compared with psychotherapy in the control of obesity.' *Behav. Res. Ther. 15,* 89-96.

Hall, S. M., Hall, R. G., Hanson, R. M. and Bordon, B. L. 1974. 'Permanence of two self-managed treatments of overweight in university and community populations.' *Consult. clin. Psychol. 42,* 781-6.

Johnson, C. A. and Katz, R. C. 1973. 'Using parents as change agents for their children: a review.' *J. child psychol. Psychiat. 14,* 181-200.

Kiernan, C. C. 1975. 'Behaviour modification.' In A. M. Clarke and A. D. B. Clarke (eds) *Mental deficiency: the changing outlook*. London: Methuen.

Krasner, L. and Ullman, L. P. 1973. *Behaviour influence and personality.* New York: Holt, Rhinehart and Winston.

Kushlick, A. 1975. 'Improving services for the mentally handicapped.' In C. C. Kiernan and F. P. Woodford (eds) *Behaviour modification with the severely retarded.* London: Associated Scientific Press.

Lloyd, L. L. 1976. *Communication assessment and intervention strategies.* Baltimore: University Park Press.

O'Dell, S. 1974. 'Training parents in behaviour modification: a review.' *Psychol. Bull. 81,* 418-33.

Porterfield, J. K., Herbert-Jackson, E. and Risley, T. R. 1976. 'Contingent observation: an effective and acceptable procedure for reducing disruptive behaviour of young children in a group setting.' *J. appl. Behav. Anal. 9,* 55-64.

Premack, D. 1976. *Intelligence in ape and man.* New York: Wiley.

Rincover, A. and Koegel, R. L. 1975. 'Setting generality and stimulus control in autistic children.' *J. appl. Behav. Anal. 8,* 23546.

Rothman, J., Erlich, J. L. and Teresa, J. G. 1975. *Promoting innovation and change in organizations and communities: a planning manual.* New York: Wiley.

Skinner, B. F. 1938. *The behaviour of organisms.* New York: Appleton, Century-Crofts.

Snyder, L. K., Lovitt, T. C. and Smith, J. O. 1976. 'Language training for the severely retarded: five years of behaviour analysis research.' *Except. Children. 42,* 7-15.

Snyder, L. K. and McLean, J. E. 1976. 'Deficient acquisition strategies: a proposed conceptual framework for analyzing severe language deficiency.' *Amer. J. Ment. Def. 81,* 338-49.

Webster, D. R. and Azrin, N. H. 1973. 'Required relaxation: a method of inhibiting agitative-disruptive behaviour of retardates.' *Behav. Res. Ther., 11,* 67-78.

Wolpe, J. 1958. *Psychotherapy by reciprocal inhibition.* Stanford: Stanford University Press.

Yule, W. and Berger, M. 1975. 'Communication, language and behaviour modification.' In C. C. Kiernan and F. P. Woodford (eds) *Behaviour modification with the severely retarded.* London: Associated Scientific Press.

FURTHER READING

Behaviour modification and behaviour therapy has maintained its identity in terms of publication of specific journals and textbooks. Central amongst these are the *Journal of Applied Behaviour Analysis*, the main journal of behaviour modification and *Behaviour Research and Therapy*, *Behaviour Therapy* and *Journal of Behaviour Therapy and Experimental Psychiatry* all publishing outlets for the behaviour therapists. Significant reviews and texts appear frequently in book form. In behaviour modification Gardner (1971) remains a central and authoritative reference covering much of the earlier work in the field. Krasner and Ullman (1973) incorporate not only behaviour modification and behaviour therapy approaches but also material and ideas from other fields within a general behavioural framework. Their work represents an excellent example of the integration of differing approaches within a general behavioural framework (c.f. Bandura 1968). Two annual review series have been established in the behaviour therapy field. *Advances in Behaviour Therapy* is a well established series published by Academic Press. *The Annual Review of Behaviour Therapy, Theory and Practice* is published by Brunner/Mazel (New York).

Chapter 10

Human Learning

MICHAEL J. A. HOWE

INTRODUCTION

Numerous reports of investigations into human learning are published each year, but there is no clearly defined field of human learning research and no widely accepted detailed theoretical account of human learning processes. Researchers studying the different kinds of human learning share few common assumptions, do not to a marked extent read or publish in the same journals and do not manifest the shared identifications with an area of study that is apparent in some branches of experimental psychology. This may be inevitable in view of the sheer diversity of both the varied forms of learning and of the circumstances in which learning occurs, and in view of the widely differing backgrounds of those who conduct research into human learning.

Few specific statements can be made that broadly apply to contemporary research into all kinds of human learning. Some of the research has highly theoretical aspects, but the theories are customarily about the cognitive processes that underly retention and retrieval of information, or about the structural organization of knowledge, rather than being about learning processes as such, in the sense of ones directly involved in acquisition of knowledge or skills. A notable exception is the recent article by Bransford and Franks (1976), in which the authors attempt to account for the manner in which the individual's past experience sets the stage for acquiring new knowledge. The continuing failure of attempts to specify particular physiological changes that have a broadly causative influence on every kind of learning (Thompson 1976) is indicative of the difficulty of identifying common factors that are basic to learning in its different forms. The titles of recent book-length publications demonstrate that the psychology of human learning is typically regarded as being closely interdependent with memory (e.g. Crowder 1976), cognitive processes in general (Estes 1975, being the first volume of a new series), motivation (the series edited by G. H. Bower – e.g. 1976 – now having reached double figures) and development (e.g. Sheppard and Willoughby 1975; Howe 1975a).

The amount and diversity of human learning research necessitate a highly selective approach in a brief survey of recent developments. I have chosen to draw attention to research in five topic areas where my impression is that significant progress is being made. It is hoped that the following topics, which are largely unrelated and selected somewhat arbitrarily, will provide a broadly representative cross-sample of recent research into adult and child learning.

INFANT LEARNING

Psychologists have become sharply aware of the difficulties of conducting research into infant learning and of establishing whether an observed change in an infant's responses is clearly indicative of learning rather than the various additional determinants of infant behaviour. As well as the frequent and unpredictable variations in aspects of the infant's state that influence both sensitivity and responsiveness (Ashton 1973) there exist various difficulties associated with attempting to observe learning in an immature organism, in whom the schemas that are to be used in demonstrations of learning are themselves incompletely differentiated, and in whom the transfer from the predominantly physiological modes of functioning which are dominant in the prenatal infant to the psychological forms of adaptation necessary for survival after birth is still incomplete (Sameroff 1972; Fitzgerald and Brackbill 1976). So far as infant learning is concerned, any hard separation between learning research as such and the investigation of developmental changes is out of the question.

Much research into infant learning continues to take the form of studies of classical and operant conditioning. Infant classical conditioning research remains somewhat isolated from the larger body of theory and research into animal conditioning, a fact that is lamented by Fitzgerald and Brackbill (1976). However, the growing tendency in animal research to question the generality of any laws or principles that concern learning has not been unnoticed by researchers studying human conditioning. Fitzgerald and Brackbill have observed that there no longer appear to be straightforward relationships between age and ease of conditioning, although it remains clear that conditioning is especially unstable in the youngest infants and that young babies require relatively lengthy inter-stimulus intervals during conditioning sessions.

In research into operant control of infant behaviour, recent findings by Bloom and Esposito (1975) and Bloom (1975) indicate that the often-cited finding by Rheingold, Gewirtz and Ross (1959) that social conditioning can produce increases in vocalization in three-month-old infants may need revision. It appears likely that the observed increases in vocalizing were due to an eliciting rather than a reinforcing effect of the social events which were provided as reinforcement for vocalization in the study by Rheingold, Gewirtz and Ross. Bloom and Esposito incorporated experimental controls in which social events were provided by the experimenter, but were not contingent upon vocalizations by the infant subjects. The amount of vocalization observed in infants who received non-contingent vocalization was as large as that occurring in experimental group infants for whom vocalizations were immediately succeeded by adult social stimulation, intended to have a reinforcing function. It thus appears that the findings of Rheingold, Gewirtz and Ross may not be due to social conditioning. Millar (1976) has pointed out that the necessary control conditions that were absent from the experiments of Rheingold, Gewirtz and Ross were also absent in other studies apparently demonstrating conditioning of different social behaviours, such as smiling. However, Millar also notes that social conditioning of infants slightly older than three months has been observed in circumstances whereby the experimental control procedures adopted rule out the possibility that an elicitating effect of non-contingent social events was the real cause of apparently conditioned responses.

YOUNG CHILDREN'S SOCIAL LEARNING FROM TELEVISION

Much social learning is based upon observation, which is often followed by imitation. Bandura (1976) summarizes the social learning analysis, according to which observational learning is governed by, first, attentional processes, second, retention of information about observed activities, third, the ability to convert symbolic representations into appropriate actions, and fourth, adjustments on the basis of informative feedback. It is apparent that the ability to imitate is crucial for social learning, and is normally learned early in life (Parton 1976).

The social environment directly experienced by the young child is augmented by the mass media, especially television, which provides a kind of window on a large range of events and lifestyles outside the child's immediate experience. Since the young child does not possess the adult's factual knowledge against which the accuracy of what is depicted on the television can be checked, the child is frequently misled by distorted views of life shown on this medium (Howe 1977a; Liebert, Neale and Davidson 1973). Thus a child may learn that violence, which is typically depicted in a glamorous or exciting context, is very common, often successful in the short run, and apparently regarded as a legitimate means of gaining one's ends by large numbers of people. Recent social learning research on the effects upon children of observing violence has included a number of ingenious experiments which have aimed to avoid the evident artificiality of many studies conducted in the 1960s. After watching televised violence children who have been carefully led to believe they were in a 'real life' situation have been shown to be more tolerant of aggression in others than children in a control group (Drabman and Thomas 1974; Thomas and Drabman 1975).

A number of recent studies have investigated social learning from non-violent television contents. Galst and White (1976) examined the effects of television advertising on American children's purchase-influencing behaviour in a supermarket. It was found that children most frequently requested those items which were most often advertized in television commercials directed at children. The fact that the children requested heavily sweetened foods that are much advertized was regarded by the authors as a cause for concern, since heavy consumption of sugar has been shown to contribute to diabetes and tooth-decay.

Some experiments have investigated the effects on child viewers of depicting positive or helpful forms of social behaviour. In a study by Sprafkin, Liebert and Poulos (1975) six-year-olds watched a programme from a *Lassie* series which included a dramatic example of a boy risking his life to save a puppy. Subsequently the children played a game during which they were made to believe they had to choose between helping some distressed puppies and earning points from the game, towards a prize. Those children who had watched the *Lassie* programme that had included the helping episode were significantly more helpful in this situation than children in two control groups, who either watched a different *Lassie* episode or another popular programme. The authors conclude that it is possible to produce television programming that includes action and adventure and has a salutary rather than a negative social influence on young viewers. Rushton (1975) found that whereas simply preaching about the virtues of being generous had little effect on children's behaviour the decay rate of positive social behaviour were accompanied with positive statements. However, Rushton and Owen (1975) obtained the surprising finding that after watching generous television models who also preached generosity, children reacted by acting less generously than children who saw a selfish television model who preached selfishness.

The results of an impressive American field study by Coates, Pusser and Goodman (1976) showed that children aged three to six years who initially had relatively few social contacts with others interacted with other children to a greater extent following a one-week period during which they regularly watched two television programmes, *Sesame Street* and *Mister Rogers' Neighborhood.* Watching the latter programme also led to increased social contacts among children who obtained high initial scores on a measure of social interaction. A social learning effect is also indicated by the finding of Gorn, Goldberg and Kanungo (1976) that white Canadian children, aged between three and five years, who were exposed to twelve-minute films depicting non-white children, subsequently showed a strong preference for playing with non-whites. As one might expect, up to the age of four years there are age-related increases in attention to television (Anderson and Levin 1976).

VERBAL LEARNING AND VERBAL KNOWLEDGE

Recent years have witnessed an increasing willingness to admit that learning, knowing and remembering are highly interdependent. Rather than characterizing learning as a process that primarily involves the acquisition of information received from the environment, it is more satisfactorily regarded as involving transactions whereby the individual, who has a highly active mental life that is largely based on the activities of the cognitive structures he possesses, becomes involved in transactions that enable him to make use of environmental data. Thus in trying to understand why older children can retain a larger number of perceived items than younger children it is necessary to extend the investigation beyond considering the properties of learning processes and memory systems as such, and consider the broader cognitive characteristics that contribute to the child's knowledge, in particular to his knowledge of the semantic attributes of list items. Verbal learning is influenced by the manner in which the materials to be learned are encoded by the individual learner. A number of processes contribute to the strategies through which learners bring to bear their existing knowledge and intellectual skills in order to minimize the amount of entirely new associative learning required to deal with a particular task.

Efficient learning of verbal materials depends upon organization, and results obtained by Bellezza, Richards and Geiselman (1976) make it clear that such organization cannot take place in the absence of encoding. Younger children are especially hindered by their lack of knowledge of the semantic features of verbal items (Perlmutter and Myers 1966), whereas it has been shown by Waters and Waters (1976) that older children spontaneously draw upon their semantic knowledge in order to encode items to be retained. Geis and Hall (1976) have found that when younger children are able to encode items semantically the younger subjects retain as many items as older children. Findings by Chi (1977), who provides a review of evidence on the issue, support this result, but she reports age-related differences in both the time taken to encode items and in the amount of time required to recognize words. Furthermore, in experiments by Worden (1976) and Ceci and Howe (1977) it was observed that older children were more effective at searching for and retrieving items they had retained.

Ceci and Howe (1977) observed that younger children were sometimes *more* successful at recalling word items than older subjects, if retrieval cues were provided. Young children out-performed their elders when, due to differences in semantic knowledge, for the older subjects cues were incompatible with codings used in acquiring items, but the cues were not perceived by the younger subjects as being incompatible. The assumption that differences in the amount of rehearsal account for age-related improvements in performance at verbal learning tasks is thrown into question by findings of Naus, Ornstein and Aivano (1977). They observed that the quality of rehearsal is at least equally crucial as the actual amount. Certainly, however, the use of rehearsal and other strategies that reflect the individual's intentionality do increase with age, and contribute to developmental improvements in performance (Wellman, 1977). Taken as a whole, the recent findings make it clear that a person's ability to learn word lists is highly dependent upon his existing body of knowledge and on the forms of encoding that this permits.

It appears likely that those individuals who obtain high scores in tests of intelligence tend to be people who possess effective intellectual skills, appropriate semantic knowledge, and who make extensive use of the strategies that are found to be effective in tasks that involve learning. Differences between learners who are more and less successful appear to lie not so much in the possession of any particular quality or strategy, but in the effective learners being in a better position to call upon a range of effective procedures or strategies to facilitate learning. The successful learner tends to be an individual who has acquired an extensive set of intellectual skills, varying in function and complexity. When faced with a new task in which learning is demanded he will be in a position to bring into operation procedures that are appropriate to the new situation (Howe 1976). Until recently there has been relatively little interchange between researchers in the fields of intelligence-testing, whose aims have been primarily practical and psychometric, and researchers studying learning. However, investigations focussing upon the interdependence of learning and general intellectual abilities are becoming more common. For instance, Hunt and Lansman (1975) have described a variety of ways in which individual differences in performance at intellectual tasks can be related to the processes and systems investigated in experimental psychology.

IMAGERY AND HUMAN LEARNING

The output of articles describing investigations into imagery processes in learning has declined somewhat since the early 1970s, but there continues to be controversy on certain basic issues. Further evidence has been obtained both for and against Paivio's dual-trace hypotheses, whereby distinct systems are said to exist for coding linguistic and sequential information, on the one hand, and for pictorial and spatial information processing, on the other hand. Anderson (1976) noted that the dual code hypothesis predicts that with word items temporal structures should be retained better than spatial structures, whilst one would expect the opposite to be true in the case of pictures. A series of experiments indicated that temporal and spatial structures were coded independently, with linguistic materials being associated with temporal superiority. Anderson interpreted her findings as supporting the dual code account. Pellegrino, Siegel and Dhawan (1975) also found support for the dual coding hypothesis, which postulates independent systems. They found that dual memory cues facilitated retention of pictorial stimuli in a task that introduced auditory distraction. However, Hasher, Riebman and Wren (1976) reported results that provide no support for the dual process account. They observed that although imagery facilitated acquisition it did not improve long-term retention. Instructions to use imagery had no positive effects, and there were no differences in long-term performance between individuals who reported using imagery and those who reported not doing so.

There have been some interesting recent developments in research into the possible functions of imagery in practical everyday learning. Imagery appears to be important in reading performance (Jorm 1977), memory for objects in real scenes (Dirks and Neisser 1977) and sentence retention (Andre and Sola 1976). As Morris (1977) indicates, a variety of mnemonic systems that make use of visual imagery have been shown to facilitate learning. However, as Morris points out, despite the potential value of mnemonic systems most people make relatively little use of them. Morris suggests that two reasons for reluctance to extend the use of such systems are that some effort is involved in learning the systems and that they can only assist in the learning of certain kinds of items, such as lists of concrete, unrelated words. For other kinds of learning tasks they appear to be less useful.

One kind of learning for which systems that make use of imagery can be helpful is second-language acquisition. Findings reported by Atkinson (1975) and Raugh and Atkinson (1975) indicate that the systematic use of a learning system that depends heavily upon the learner using visual imagery can lead to very marked increases in the vocabulary-learning aspect of acquiring a foreign language. An ingenious method was devised, involving, first, an acoustic link stage, whereby the spoken English word was associated to an English 'keyword' that sounded similar to part of the foreign word. For example, the English word *pot* was used as the keyword for the Spanish word meaning duck *(pato),* which is pronounced, roughly, *pot-o*. Next, there was a second, imagery link stage, in which the learner formed a mental image of the keyword interacting with the English translation. For instance, one might form a vivid image of a duck trying to hide under an overturned flower pot. Cumbersome as this two-stage vocabulary acquisition process may appear to be, a series of experiments have shown it to be highly effective, and students who learned Spanish words using the keyword method obtained substantially higher learning scores than subjects in control groups. It is possible, that this method, based upon visual imagery, may provide a useful practical breakthrough, facilitating the difficult and arduous vocabulary learning requirement that forms a necessary part of the learning of any foreign language.

THE EFFECTS ON LEARNING OF NOTE-TAKING AND RELATED ACTIVITIES

The work by Atkinson (1975) that was described in the previous section illustrates the fact that practical problems of student learners have continued to attract the attention of some investigators. Some research into practical issues has been fairly closely tied to developments of a more theoretical nature in cognitive psychology. Thus Walter Kintsch, who has been prominent in research investigating verbal memory and the structure of knowledge, has described an experiment (Kintsch and Bates 1977) in which students were tested for their recognition of the contents of a normal lecture. On tests administered two days after the lecture the students were not only able to discriminate successfully between sentences that had occurred in the lecture and entirely new sentences, but they could also discriminate between sentences taken from the lecture and paraphrases of them, thus demonstrating verbatim retention in addition to memory for meaning. After five days verbatim memory was considerably reduced, but extraneous remarks such as jokes, comments and announcements were very frequently recognised, presumably because they stood out from the main lecture contents. Surprisingly, students were no more likely to recognize the sentences that described the main topics of the lecture than materials describing specific details.

A persistent difficulty in research on student learning has been that of providing measures of meaningful learning and retention that are both sensitive and reliable. Carver (1975) has extended his earlier work of the development of a 'Reading Storage' test, in which learners are required to attempt to identify the phrases that have been altered in a prose passage. Carver's findings indicate that this test does consistently provide more reliable measures of comprehension and retention than alternative procedures currently available.

Student learning from prose texts is clearly influenced by the design of instructional materials, and Hartley and Burnhill (1977a, 1977b) have provided a number of guidelines intended to help writers produce clear and comprehensible texts. The guidelines they list all have some empirical backing in the form of research findings on learning or comprehension. They include statements about the effects upon learning of different kinds of questions, a matter which has been systematically examined in recent research (e.g. Frase and Schwartz 1975; Howe and Colley 1976; Rickards 1976; Taylor 1977) about the use of space, headings, sentence construction, typographical design details and the use of illustrations.

Note-taking activities have a number of outcomes that can influence learning. The apparently simple activity of underlining the sentence in each paragraph which the reader considers to be the most important can improve recall of the whole passage (Rickards and August 1975). Taking notes does appear to help some individuals attend to information they are trying to learn (Howe 1975b, 1977b). The findings of a series of studies by Hartley (1976) indicate that providing students with brief handouts that may be used in conjunction with their own note-taking activities can help students understand the basic structure of the information presented in a lecture. However, note-taking activities did not necessarily produce increased learning. The relative effectiveness of different learner activities may depend to a large extent upon the manner in which the information has been presented (Howe and Singer 1975; Howe 1977b). It was found that learners who listened to information presented at a normal speaking rate retained considerably more of the passage if they were not required to record the information in writing. This was also so for students who read the information, but not for those individuals who heard it presented at dictation speed. Requiring note-taking or copying by students may sometimes impose a degree of rigidity in the learning situation, disrupting the tendency of able students to make use of learning strategies they know to be effective.

REFERENCES

Anderson, D. R. and Levin, S. R. 1976. 'Young children's attention to "Sesame Street".' *Child Development 47*, 806-11.

Anderson, R. E. 1976. 'Short-term retention of the where and when of pictures and words.' *J. exp. Psychol. Gen. 105*, 378-402.

Andre, T. and Sola, J. 1976. 'Imagery, verbatim and paraphrased sentences, and retention of meaningful sentences.' *J. educ. Psychol. 68*, 661-9.

Ashton, R. 1973. 'The state variable in neonatal research.' *Merrill-Palmer Quarterly 19*, 3-20.

Atkinson, R. L. 1975. 'Mnemotechnics in second-language learning.' *Amer. Psychologist 30*, 821-8.

Bandura, A. 1976. 'Observational learning.' *XIIth International Congress of Psychology, Paris.*

Bellezza, F. S., Richards, D. L. and Geiselman, R. E. 1976. 'Semantic processing and organization in free recall.' *Memory and Cognition 4*, 415-521.

Bloom, K. 1975. 'Social elecitation of infant vocal behavior.' *J. of exp. Child Psychol. 20*, 51-8.

Bloom, K. and Esposito, A. 1975. 'Social conditioning and its proper control procedures.' *J. exp. Child Psychol. 19*, 209-22.

Bower, G. H. 1976. *The psychology of learning and motivation, 10*. New York: Academic Press.

Bransford, J. D. and Franks, J. J. 1976. 'Toward a framework for understanding learning.' In G. H. Bower (ed.) *The psychology of learning and motivation, 10*. New York: Academic Press.

Carver, R. P. 1975. 'Comparing the Reading-Storage Test to the Paraphrase Test as measures of the primary effect of prose reading.' *J. of educ. Psychol. 67*, 274-84.

Ceci, S. J. and Howe, M. J. A. 1977. 'Semantic knowledge as a determinant of developmental differences in recall.' Unpublished manuscript, University of Exeter.

Chi, M. T. H. 1977. 'Age differences in memory span.' *J. exp. Child Psychol. 23,* 266-81.

Coates, B., Pusser, H. E. and Goodman, I. 1976. 'The influence of "Sesame Street" and "Mister Rogers' Neighborhood" on children's social behavior in the preschool period.' *Child Development 47,* 138-44.

Crowder, R. G. 1976. *Principles of learning and memory.* Hillsdale, New Jersey: Lawrence Erlbaum Associates.

Dirks, J. and Neisser, U. 1977. 'Memory for objects in real sciences: the development of recognition and recall.' *J. of exp. Child Psychol. 23,* 315-28.

Drabman, R. S. and Thomas, M. H. 1974. 'Does media violence increase children's tolerance of real-life aggressiveness?' *Developmental Psychol. 10,* 418-21.

Estes, W. K. (ed.) 1975. *Handbook of learning and cognitive processes, 1.* New York: Wiley.

Fitzgerald, H. E. and Brackbill, Y. 1976. 'Classical conditioning in infancy: development and constraints.' *Psychol. Bull. 83,* 353-76.

Frase, L. T. and Schwartz, B. J. 1975. 'Effect of question production and answering on prose recall.' *J. educ. Psychol. 67,* 628-35.

Galst, J. P. and White, M. A. 1976. 'The unhealthy persuader: the reinforcing value of television and children's purchase-influencing attempts at the supermarket.' *Child Development 47,* 1089-96.

Geis, M. F. and Hall, D. 1976. 'Encoding and incidental memory in children.' *J. exp. Child Psychol. 22,* 58-66.

Gorn, G. J., Goldberg, M. E. and Kanungo, R. N. 1976. 'The role of educational television in changing the intergroup attitudes of children.' *Child Development 47,* 277-80.

Hartley, J. 1976. 'Lecture handouts and students note-taking.' *Programmed learning and Educational Technology 13,* 58-64.

Hartley, J. and Burnhill, P. 1977a. 'Understanding instructional text: typography, layout and design.' 233-47. In M. J. A. Howe (ed.) *Adult learning: psychological research and applications.* London: Wiley.

Hartley, J. and Burnhill, P. 1977b. Fifty guidelines for improving instructional text.' *Programmed Learning and Educational Technology 14,* 65-73.

Hasher, L., Riebman, B. and Wren, F. 1976. 'Imagery and retention of free-recall learning.' *J. exp. Psychol. Hum. Learn. Mem. 2,* 172-81.

Howe, M. J. A. 1975a. *Learning in infants and young children.* London: Macmillan.

Howe, M. J. A. 1975b. 'Taking notes and human learning.' Bulletin of the British Psychological Society 28, 158-61.

Howe, M. J. A. 1976. 'Good learners and poor learners.' *Bulletin of the British Psychological Society 29,* 16-9.

Howe, M. J. A. 1977a. *Television and children.* London: New University Education.

Howe, M. J. A. 1977b. 'Learning and the acquisition of knowledge by students, some experimental investigations.' In M. J. A. Howe (ed.) *Adult learning: psychological research and applications* 145-60. London: Wiley.

Howe, M. J. A. and Colley, L. 1976. 'The influence of questions encountered earlier on learning from prose.' *Brit. J. educ. Psychol. 46,* 149-54.

Howe, M. J. A. and Singer, L. 1975. 'Presentation variables and students' activities in meaningful learning.' *Brit. J. educ. Psychol. 45,* 52-61.

Hunt, E. and Lansman, M. 1975. 'Cognitive theory applied to individual differences.' In W. K. Estes (ed.) *Handbook of learning and cognitive processes, 1.* New York: Wiley.

Jorm, A. F. 1977. 'Effect of word imagery on reading performance as a function of reader ability.' *J. of educ. Psych. 69,* 46-54.

Kintsch, W. and Bates, E. 1977. 'Recognition memory for statements from a classroom lecture.' *J. exp. Psychol.: Hum. Learn. Mem. 3,* 150-9.

Liebert, R. M., Neale, J. M. and Davidson, E. S. 1973. *The early window.* New York: Pergamon Press.

Millar, W. S. 1976. 'Operant acquisition of social behaviors in infancy: basic problems and constraints.' 107-40. In H. W. Reese (ed.) *Advances in child development and behaviour, 11.* New York: Academic Press.

Morris, P. 1977. 'Practical strategies for human learning and remembering.' 125-44. In M. J. A. Howe (ed.) *Adult learning: psychological research and applications.* London: Wiley.

Naus, M. J., Ornstein, P. A. and Aivano, S. 1977. 'Developmental changes in memory: the effects of processing time and rehearsal instructions.' *J. exp. Child Psychol. 23,* 237-51.

Parton, D. A. 1976. 'Learning to imitate in infancy.' *Child Development 47,* 14-31.

Pellegrino, J. W., Siegel, A. W. and Dhawan, M. 1975. 'Short-term retention of pictures and words: evidence for dual coding systems.' *J. exp. Psychol.: Hum. Learn. Mem. 1,* 95-102.

Perlmutter, J. and Myers, N. A. 1976. 'A developmental study of semantic effects on recognition memory.' *J. exp. Child Psychol. 22,* 438-53.

Raugh, M. R. and Atkinson, R. L. 1975. 'A mnemonic method for learning a second language vocabulary.' *J. educ. Psychol. 67,* 1-16.

Rheingold, H., Gewirtz, J. L. and Ross, H. W. 1959. 'Social conditioning of vocalization in the infant.' *J. comp. Physiol. Psychol. 52,* 68-73.

Rickards, J. P. 1976. 'Interaction of position and conceptual level of adjunct questions on immediate and delayed retention of text.' *J. educ. Psychol. 68,* 210-7.

Rickards, J. P. and August, G. J. 1975. 'Generative underlining strategies in prose recall.' *J. educ. Psychol. 67,* 860-5.

Rushton, J. P. 1975. 'Generosity in children: immediate and long term effects of modelling, preaching and moral judgement.' *J. pers. soc. Psychol. 31,* 459-64.

Rushton, J. P. and Owen, D. 1975. 'Immediate and delayed effects of T.V modelling and preaching on children's generosity.' *Brit. soc. Clin. Psychol. 14,* 309-10.

Sameroff, A. J. 1972. 'Learning and adaptation in infancy: a comparison of models.' In H. W. Reese (ed.) *Advances in child development and behavior. 7.* New York: Academic Press.

Sheppard, W. L. and Willoughby, R. H. 1975. *Child behavior; learning and development.* Chicago: Rand McNally.

Sprafkin, J. N., Liebert, R. M. and Poulos, R. W. 1975. 'Effects of a prosocial televised example on children's helping.' *J. exp. Child Psychol. 20,* 119-26.

Taylor, F. J. 1977. 'Acquiring knowledge from prose and continuous discourse.' 107-23. In M. J. A. Howe (ed.) *Adult learning: psychological research and applications.* London: Wiley.

Thomas, M. H. and Drabman, R. S. 1975. 'Toleration of real life aggression as a function of exposure to televised violence and age of subject.' *Merrill-Palmer Quarterly 21, 227-32.*

Thompson, R. E. 1976. 'The search for the engram.' *Amer. Psychologist 31,* 209-27.

Waters, H. S. and Waters, E. 1976. 'Semantic processing in children's free recall: evidence for the importance of attentional factors and encoding variability.' *J. of exp. Psychol.: Hum. Learn. Mem. 2,* 370-80.

Wellman, H. M. 1977. 'The early development of intentional memory behavior.' *Human Development 20,* 86-101.

Worden, P. E. 1976. 'The effects of classification structure on organized free recall in children.' *J. of exp. Child Psychol. 22,* 519-29.

Chapter 11

Cross-Cultural Studies

GUSTAV JAHODA

There are at least two ways in which cross-cultural psychology differs substantially from most of the other areas dealt with in this *Survey*. First, it concerns a mode of approach rather than a specific topic, and therefore spans a great many different areas of psychology. Secondly, it is not usually given much attention in undergraduate courses, so that an appropriate background cannot be taken for granted. Hence the aim of the present chapter can only be to provide unavoidably selective glimpses of the field, in the hope of inspiring readers to follow these up in more depth. Since most of the literature is widely scattered across journals* the framework adopted here consists of books (or chapters within them) published after 1970, which are more readily accessible. It should also be mentioned that a number of useful introductory texts are now available, which are listed at the end.

TESTING GROUND FOR THEORIES

Practically all of modern scientific psychology had its origin in western industrial societies. Much of it, from Binet onwards, was developed in relation to the particular needs of these societies; and a moment's reflection will show that the major fields of application such as educational, clinical or occupational psychology are closely tied to the institutions of modern industrial society. It might be thought that this does not apply to the more theoretical aspects of psychology, and this has in fact long been tacitly assumed. However, as soon as this assumption is examined it becomes evident that it is open to challenge. The overwhelming majority of subjects on whose behaviour psy-

*There are two journals specially devoted to cross-cultural studies: *International Journal of Psychology* and *Journal of Cross-Cultural Psychology*.

chological theories are based were college students or school children, hardly a representative sample of humanity at large. The implication is that their behaviour was unaffected by their specific cultural background, which is highly unlikely. One of the important, though extremely difficult, tasks of cross-cultural work is therefore to assess the range of applicability of psychological theories or generalizations by testing them with subjects of divergent cultural backgrounds. Two illustrations of such attempts will be given.

Piagetian theory

When Piaget carried out his studies with Genevan children he remained long convinced that the imposing theoretical edifice built on this foundation was essentially biological in character and therefore valid for the human species at large. When he gradually changed his position, it was as a result of a series of cross-cultural studies of cognitive development from the 1950s onwards. In an article originally published in 1966 and reprinted in Berry and Dasen (1974) he had come to adopt a very different standpoint: '. . . the main advantage of cross-cultural studies is to allow a dissociation of the sociocultural and individual factors in development.' (p. 300.)

Since Piaget wrote this there has been a further burgeoning of research, and there are probably more cross-cultural psychologists working in this field than in any other. Yet, as frequently happens, we do not have any simple answers, instead, further complexities have been uncovered. Most of the research has been concentrated on the single theme of conservation, and the methods used have not always been comparable. There clearly are many common trends in the findings; thus no researcher has reported an inability to identify the main stages postulated by Piaget. However, there appear to be wide variations in the sequence in which different kinds of conservation are achieved; and similarly the ages of their emergence seem to diverge widely. Moreover, there is the controversial claim that a substantial proportion of people in some cultures do not get beyond concrete operations. While the particular cultural features responsible for such variations remain to be specified, there is one important conclusion to be drawn: the sociocultural factors play a much larger part in cognitive development than Piaget had envisaged; and it is likely that his theory will have to be revised so as to take this into account.

Theories of Intergroup Relations

In social psychology there is an abundance of such theories, based in the main on artificial laboratory and less frequently natural groups, mainly in America or Europe. Most of the studies have involved pairs of groups and larger numbers are very rare. Moreover, where natural groups are involved, studies tend to concentrate on one group's attitudes to the other and reciprocal relations are less often examined. The reason is that it is difficult to find a variety of groups, each with a well-defined identity, in mutual contact; hence in the U.S. the black-white dichotomy is usually the dominant theme. Under these circumstances the testing of theories yielding conflicting predictions tends to be difficult and largely inconclusive.

Brewer and Campbell (1976) decided to take advantage of the fact that one can find a wide range of culturally varied tribal groups with a strong sense of their identity within confined geographical areas in Africa. Their design was fairly simple in principle, though of course considerable practical problems had to be overcome. They devised a survey interview dealing essentially with interethnic contacts and attitudes, including own-group attitudes. The interviews were conducted with members of thirty different groups in a region where Kenya, Uganda and Tanzania border on each other. The questions always concerned thirteen different outgroups and their own group. The analysis of this material was complex, and the results are probably unique, in as much as significance tests were based on groups consisting of ten to thirty groups.

A brief example of the findings may be cited, concerning the effect of physical distance. Frustration-aggression theory would hold that displacement of aggression takes place towards available outgroups, neighbouring ones being most appropriate for this purpose. Therefore proximity should be inversely related to attraction. On the other hand functional theories of interpersonal relations such as those of Homans or Newcomb stress the positive rewards of interaction, predicting that proximity makes for liking (other more elaborate formulations predicting curvilinear relationships will be ignored here). At any rate, the outcome of the Brewer and Campbell study showed a positive linear relationship between proximity and attraction. The unprecedented strength of this conclusion lies in the fact that it held up for data averaged across ten groups in each of the three countries considered separately.

THE SEARCH FOR UNIVERSALS

Human behaviour is always a function of nature and culture in varying proportions. When cross-cultural studies seek to test the validity of theories in different settings, the question at issue is whether the theory has perhaps underrated the cultural component in the behaviour under consideration. There are other kinds of cross-cultural studies, however, which tackle the opposite problem. In other words, their aim is to probe the extent to which deeper uniformities underlie the surface cultural diversity of certain behaviours.

Facial Expression

The problem of the inherited versus learned origin of human facial expression of emotion was first raised by Darwin, who also suggested what we would now call cross-cultural studies as a means of resolving the issue. Darwin himself decided, on the basis of somewhat questionable evidence, that facial expression was innate and universal. Subsequent writers such as Klinberg and La Barre rejected Darwin's view, proposing instead that the expression of emotions is learnt and culture-specific. The whole controversy is fully discussed by Ekman (1973), who himself carried out a series of careful and ingenious cross-cultural studies. These led him to the view that some facial expressions of emotion are universally present in the human species. Whilst universality as such is not conclusive proof of an evolutionary origin and thereby innateness, it does make such an inference more plausible. Ekman also demonstrated that the 'natural' expression is in certain situations masked by so-called display rules which are culturally determined.

Subjective Culture

This term was first coined by Osgood, and later taken up by Triandis and used in a somewhat different sense. Triandis (1972) in a book which deals also with general issues of cross-cultural psychology, regards 'subjective culture' as the manner in which people perceive their social environment. The object of the series of studies reported there was to isolate certain general patterns of response to these environments which underlie the bewildering variety of social behaviour encountered in different cultures.

Osgood was concerned with a somewhat similar problem, but focussing entirely on language. Most languages differ in phonology, grammar and semantics in a way which makes them mutually unintelligible. Yet Osgood believed that at a deeper level certain universal features could be extracted. Specifically, he was concerned to test the hypothesis that irrespective of culture and language people everywhere will use the same descriptive framework in allocating the affective meaning of concepts;

and he is referring to the three dimensions of Evaluation, Potency, and Activity. This seemingly simple hypothesis was tested in the course of a massive volume of studies conducted all over the globe and employing highly sophisticated methods. The outcome, reported in Osgood, May and Miron (1975), was a confirmation of the hypothesis. In fact, Osgood argued that what he called the E-P-A system is biologically functional, since people in any situation have to make judgements as to whether an organism or object in the environment is good or bad *for them,* and whether it is strong or weak and active or passive *in relation to them.*

PERCEPTION AND COGNITION

During the nineteenth century there were numerous reports from travellers, missionaries and ethnographers to the effect that what were then described as 'primitive' people differ from the 'civilized' both in the way they see the world and how they think about it. The first systematic psychological study was the famous Cambridge expedition to the Torres Straits at the turn of the century, in which McDougall, Myers and Rivers took part. Whilst exploding some myths, e.g. that 'savages' have extraordinary acuity of vision, they did establish some important perceptual differences. Neglected for over half a century, their findings were taken up again in what has become an active field of research. McDougall *et al.* did not concern themselves with cognition as such. It has been studied more recently in three distinct approaches. The earliest were the studies of 'race' differences in intelligence, now largely discredited; much later came the cross-cultural work on cognitive development, already mentioned in a different context; lastly, there are experimental studies, which will be considered here.

From a more general perspective, work in this area has consisted first of all in ascertaining what cultural differences actually exist; and this is methodologically often a difficult problem in itself. The next step is to formulate hypotheses which could account for these differences, which in turn have to be tested.

Perception

Three major lines of research are prominent here, the earliest one being the study of geometric illusions initiated in the Torres Straits by Rivers who demonstrated differences in susceptibility. His work was taken up again by Segall, Campbell and Herskovits (1966) who stimulated renewed interest in this problem so that a great deal of new information has been collected which has a bearing not only within the cross-cultural sphere, but also on theories of geometric illusions in general. It must be admitted, however, that the problems are far from being solved.

The second field was opened up by Hudson who noted the difficulties experienced by people in African cultures in interpreting two-dimensional representation of three-dimensional objects or scenes. An extensive review of the issues involved is provided by Hagen and Jones (1977).

The third topic relates to the perception of pictures, and this will be used for a more detailed illustration. For over a century it has been reported from various parts of the world that there are people unable to make sense of pictures. Deregowski (1973), whose work will be discussed, quotes a Scottish missionary:

'Take a picture in black and white, and the natives cannot see it. You may tell the natives, "This is a picture of an ox and a dog," and the people will look at it and look at you, and that look says that they consider you a liar.'

Other more recent accounts, including some by anthropologists, tend to confirm that there is a real and very puzzling problem here. On the basis of this kind of material it has been suggested that the understanding of pictures depends on prior learning within a pictorial environment such as that in western cultures; but there is other evidence, i.e. from young children and even animals, which throws serious doubts on such an interpretation. Much of the early evidence is anecdotal, and carefully designed psychological studies are required to establish the facts. Unfortunately pictureless environments are rapidly disappearing all over the world, but Deregowski managed to find one in a remote part of Ethiopia. While it is not possible to describe the details of this fascinating study, it was clear from the responses of the Me'en when presented with pictures of familiar animals that on the whole they were neither completely meaningless or fully apprehended by them at once. It would appear that they gradually, and in some cases very laboriously, extracted meaning from the pictures.

Cognition – Experimental Anthropology

Nineteenth-century ethnographers shared with laymen the belief that 'savages' were incapable of logical thinking. Anthropologists have long abandoned such notions, and after being misled by the early studies of 'racial' intelligence psychologists have followed suit. However, there remain some important problems to be resolved in this sphere, since there is no shirking the fact that children and adults in pre-literate cultures do exhibit differences from Europeans in the way they respond to cognitive tasks. Whilst cross-cultural psychologists are in general extremely reluctant to resort to genetic interpretations of such differences, there is some disagreement as to how they might be explained. One view is that in the absence of appropriate environmental stimulation certain mental structures fail to develop, so that the differences in performance actually reflect a difference in the underlying cognitive processes. An alternative view is that any environment capable of supporting human life is sufficient for the development of cognitive structures shared by all humans, and all that is needed for these to become manifest is suitable transposition of the cognitive tasks into a more familiar idiom. The latter view is strongly espoused by Michael Cole (Cole, Gay, Glick and Sharp 1971), who has advocated what he calls 'experimental anthropology'; by this he means experiments based on a thorough knowledge of the cultural background of the subjects. One of his numerous studies employing such a strategy will serve as an example.

Working among the Kpelle of Liberia, he was interested in their inferential behaviour. At the outset he employed a gadget devised by the Kendlers for American children. This consisted of a box with several compartments, which required the subject to learn a series of button-pressing responses and the dropping of an object into a hole, which led to a reward. Non-literate children and adolescents did very poorly on this task, but can one conclude from this that they are incapable of making the necessary inferences? Cole and his associates thought not, and proceeding on this assumption they constructed a task which was formally equivalent to the original Kendler one, but consisted only of familiar materials. Under these conditions, as anticipated, the Kpelle generally performed just as well as the American subjects.

This was a relatively straightforward instance where it was possible to demonstrate a basic similarity in cognitive functions once the problem had been presented in a manner which took account of the culturally determined experience of the subjects. However, there are many other cases where it is either much more difficult to find culturally equivalent tasks or where, even if they are found, differences persist. The question then remains whether one is faced with some fundamental differences in cognitive processes, or whether it is merely that the culture has not provided adequate opportunities for the acquisition of particular cognitive skills. While this issue remains unresolved, Cole and his associates have certainly made a substantial contribution by introducing the research strategy now known as 'experimental anthropology'.

EFFECTS OF SOCIO-CULTURAL CHANGE

As far as cognitive processes are concerned, one way of throwing further light on the problem would be by means of extended training studies. Unfortunately these require such large resources that they have seldom been attempted on a large scale. What has been done extensively is to compare illiterate people with others who have experienced varying periods of formal schooling. The general finding has been that schooling, however poor and inadequate it may be, appears to have a powerful impact. Not only does it impart a number of cognitive skills which remain undeveloped within traditional cultures, but it also seems to modify attitudes and motivations. Thus schooling constitutes one of the main agents of socio-cultural change, though it is of course by no means the only one: changes in occupational roles, urbanization and associated alterations in the structure of the family and other institutions all play their part. Hence the assessment of the effects of social change has been a key theme in cross-cultural studies.

Social Change and Cognition

In 1931 a team of Russian psychologists went to the remoter regions of Uzbekistan in Central Asia. This was an ancient Islamic culture, but in the rural areas especially backward and illiterate. Upon this sleepy backwater burst the revolution which sought to improve education, introduce a collectivist economy and generally propagate the new socialist principles. The aim of the team was to observe the psychological consequences of this radical change, and in particular its effects on the structure of cognitive processes. It was the first study of its kind, remarkable for its originality and range. The inspiration for it came from Vygotsky, and it was Luria who carried out the fieldwork; curiously enough, it remained unpublished for more than forty years (Luria 1976) and Cole, in his foreword, suggests some political reasons for this.

The methods employed in this pioneering work are unlike those of later cross-cultural studies, with the possible exception of some Piagetian researches. Luria is a master of his own version of the 'clinical' method, which he applied with superb effect to the people of Uzbekistan. The basic design involved a comparison of the behaviour of those who had remained relatively unaffected by social change with that of people who had received some training within the framework of revolutionary cadres. The scope of his inquiry ranged widely over such areas as perception, various aspects of thinking and imagination, including also people's self-images.

In order to illustrate the approach, the study of reasoning and problem-solving will be briefly indicated. Two different strategies were adopted in an effort to probe the subjects' reasoning powers. In one version, they were given a problem that was directly related to their own personal experience and could therefore be solved either by directly relying on that experience or by formal logic; in both cases the outcome would be the same, but the paths to the solution different ones. In the alternative version the problem content was in direct conflict with personal experience, so that only people employing formal reasoning would be capable of arriving at the solution. Here is an extract from the protocol of an illiterate farm worker:

E.: 'It is four hours on foot to Vuadil, and eleven hours to Fergana. How much more of a trip is it to Fergana?' (Does not conform to the real distances.)

S. 'Vuadil is halfway there. It's three hours from here to Vuadil, and another three from Vuadil to Fergana.'

E. 'But what is it according to the problem?' (The conditions of the problem are repeated.)

S.: 'Three hours farther'.

E.: 'How did you know?'

S.: 'I tell you, Vuadil is halfway, and then the road from Vuadil to Shakhimardan is poor and beyond that it's good.'

It will be evident from this that the subject was incapable of apprehending the hypothetical nature of the problem, and in spite of insistent probing clung to the answer rooted in personal experience. By contrast, a student who had attended the village school for a mere few months had no trouble whatsoever with a problem of this type. There were consistent differences between people according to the extent to which they had been affected by social change, and it was shown that this applied also to their self-awareness, the way they saw themselves in relation to others in their environment.

Social Change and 'Modernity'

The general direction of social change in Soviet Central Asia, the

Far East, Africa or South America is always away from traditional cultures towards something new. While the precise nature of the mix between old and new is somewhat controversial, there is wide consensus that there are a number of common elements in the mentality which comes to be acquired, and these have been extensively studied. Foremost in this field is the work of Inkeles and Smith (1974) who have identified a number of traits which together make up what they call 'modernity'. Their perspective is basically an economic one, and they describe as 'modern' what they consider the personal qualities which relate to large-scale productive enterprise – and it is of course true that most developing countries aspire to this. Their extensive list of such qualities includes openness to new experience, growth of opinions on a variety of issues, increase in information about the world, new attitudes to time, an enhanced feeling of control over one's fate and several others.

They developed scales to measure these characteristics, and applied them in six different cultures in three continents. Their aim was not merely descriptive, since they had produced a theoretical model about the syndrome of modernity, which they wished to test. Using an elaborate design together with path analysis and multiple regression techniques, they came to the conclusion that the three factors which accounted for some ninety per cent of the variance in modernity were education, exposure to mass media and factory experience. One of their most significant findings was that very substantial changes in attitudes, motives and outlook can and do occur after adolescence; and it should be noted that this conflicts somewhat with other views about the early childhood determination of personality.

SOCIALIZATION, PERSONALITY AND THE ECO-SYSTEM

The idea that personality is closely related to, if not determined by culture is one which goes back to the anthropological writing of Benedict and Mead during the inter-war period. This led to a surge of activity in culture-personality studies pioneered by Kardiner and inspired largely by psychoanalysis. While much of this work provided rich and fascinating detail about growing up in a large variety of different cultures, and offered more or less plausible speculative interpretations about cultural determinants of personality, the outcome was on the whole disappointing. This is because the whole massive effort failed to yield any general principles capable of being applied to cultures other than those specifically studied. Hence the gradual demise of the old 'culture-and-personality' school, and a shift towards rather different research strategies; and two of the major ones will now be outlined.

Culture and Socialization

The 'new look' in culture and personality began in the 1950s with the work of John Whiting, who remains a dominant figure in this sphere. He saw the need to collect information from a wider range of cultures, and for this purpose resorted to the Human Relations Area Files which consist of categorized extracts from ethnographic field reports from all over the world. He generated a series of hypotheses, eclectically derived from psychoanalysis and behaviour theory, which were tested with data from the cross-cultural files. Many of the hypotheses were ingenious and 'non-obvious'; for instance, he predicted an inverse relationship between general indulgence during infancy and fear of ghosts at funerals, which was confirmed.

In spite of these successes the cross-cultural files had some serious drawbacks, especially the fact that relevant information was not always available or often unduly dated. Therefore he set about organizing a vast project whereby material and child behaviour was collected by teams of researchers in six different cultures. The project has been in existence for over twenty years, constituting the largest single effort of its kind. Its original aim was the ambitious one of arriving at generalizations about the relationships between culture, socialization and personality. After some years it became evident, however, that the complexity of the global problem is such that even the powerful resources at Whiting's disposal were not equal to the task. Hence there came a shift to a more limited objective, namely an exploration of the cultural factors influencing socialization and child behaviour. The results of this extensive project are concisely presented in Whiting and Whiting (1975).

In addition to obtaining detailed information about the cultural background and child rearing, the chief method consisted of collecting five-minute behaviour samples of children aged three to six and seven to eleven over a period of about a year. The approach was not strictly ethological, however, in as much as the analysis went beyond factual description; taking account of the context of any interactions, the material was categorized in psychological terms such as 'offers or seeks help', 'reprimands', or 'seeks attention'. The resulting data were subjected to multidimensional scaling, and two independent dimensions emerged: nurturance and responsibility versus dependence and dominance (Dimension A); and sociable-intimate behaviour versus authoritarian-aggressive behaviour (Dimension B). These dimensions varied across cultures, and an effort was made to discover which features of the cultural backgrounds were responsible for particular types of behaviour. On further analysis it was found that two fundamental characteristics were associated with dimensions A and B respectively. One was cultural complexity (in terms of hierarchy of authority and multiplicity of roles), which governed dimension A; the other was the nature of the household structure, influencing dimension B. Since the cultures varied on both these characteristics, the neat fit between cultural features and the social behaviour of the children is convincing. The authors have therefore largely succeeded in uncovering some general principles underlying cultural uniformities and variations in behaviour.

Cognitive Style and the Eco-system

During the past decade or so a novel and highly promising approach has been developed in cross-cultural studies, based on Witkin's theory of psychological differentiation. The theory holds that differentiation is a global organismic phenomenon, so that field-dependent or field-independent cognitive styles manifest themselves throughout all areas of psychological functioning. It has the great advantage from the cross-cultural point of view that its mode of assessment is not tied to any particular content, and can therefore be adapted to the backgrounds of particular cultures.

First employed by Dawson in Sierra Leone, psychological differentiation has now been widely adopted as a conceptual tool in cross-cultural research. The boldest use of it has been made by Berry (1976) who built upon this foundation a theoretical model linking ecology, culture and behaviour. Starting from previous research about the child-rearing antecedents of cognitive style, which indicated that it develops adaptively in response to the requirements of a particular ecological niche (e.g. hunters/gatherers tend to be field-independent, agriculturalists and pastoralists field-dependent), he developed an elaborate model of eco-cultural and behaviour systems. This concerns not merely behaviour in traditional cultures, but also attempts to take into account modernizing influences of the kind previously discussed.

It must not be thought that this was a mere theoretical exercise. Berry not only made predictions about quantitative relationships within various parts of his model, but he himself collected data from a variety of cultural samples in different parts of the world to test them, ranging from Africa to the Arctic. The usual outcome of the testing of such a complex model tends to be indecisive, but a majority of Berry's predictions were confirmed with a remarkable degree of accuracy.

CONCLUSION

It will have become all too evident from this sketch of recent advances in cross-cultural studies that the field is a very heterogeneous one, held together mainly by the fact that it involves empirical research in different cultures. This means that it has certain difficult methodological problems in common, which it was not possible to discuss; perhaps it might just be mentioned that these are over and above the problems inherent in any psychological work. It will have become apparent from the presentation that cross-cultural studies can be roughly divided into two major types. The first is ancillary to other fields of psychology, serving as a testing-ground for theories; as such almost any topic in psychology lends itself to cross-cultural study. It is held by some that this aspect of cross-cultural studies will in due course bring about its own extinction, through being absorbed by the specialism to which it currently remains subsidiary; thus for example developmental psychology should in future involve as an integral part appropriate cross-cultural studies.

There is another type, however, which also has been illustrated, and this is unlikely to suffer such a fate. This concerns studies on the psychological effects of social change, or the work of Berry on eco-systems, where cross-cultural theories *sui generis* are being created. There is reason to hope on the basis of recent substantial progress that this type of cross-cultural work will become more firmly established as a specialism in its own right. In any case, types of cross-cultural work provide an exciting challenge for those who believe that psychology should not be confined to western parochialism.

INTRODUCTORY TEXTBOOKS

Cole, M. and Scribner, S. 1974. *Culture and thought*. New York: Wiley.

Lloyd, B. 1972. *Perception and cognition*. Harmondsworth: Penguin.

Munroe, R. L. and R. H. 1975. *Cross-cultural human development*. Monterey, Calif.: Brooks/Cole.

Price-Williams, D. R. (ed.) 1969. *Readings in cross-cultural studies*. Harmondsworth: Penguin.

Serpell, R. 1976. *Culture's influence on behaviour*. London: Methuen.

REFERENCES

Berry, J. W. 1976. *Human ecology and cognitive style*. New York: Wiley.

Berry, J. W. and Dasen, P. R. (eds) 1974. *Culture and cognition*. London: Methuen.

Brewer, M. B. and Campbell, D. T. 1976. *Ethnocentrism and intergroup attitudes*. New York: Wiley.

Cole, M., Gay, J., Glick, J. A. and Sharp, D. W. 1971. *The cultural context of learning and thinking*. New York: Basic Books.

Deregowski, J. B. 1973. 'Illusion and culture.' In R. L. Gregory and E. H. Gombrich (eds). *Illusion in nature and art*. London: Duckworth.

Ekman, P. (ed.) 1973. *Darwin and facial expression*. New York: Academic Press.

Hagen, M. A. and Jones, R. F. (in press). 'Cultural effects on pictorial perception.' In H. Pick and R. Walk (eds) *Perception and experience*. New York: Plenum Press.

Inkeles, S. A. and Smith, D. H. 1974. *Becoming modern*. London: Heinemann.

Luria, A. R. 1976. *Cognitive development: its cultural and social foundations*. Cambridge, Mass.: Harvard University Press.

Osgood, C. E., May, W. H. and Miron, M. S. 1975. *Cross-cultural universals of affective meaning*. Urbana, III.: University of Illinois Press.

Segall, M. H., Campbell, D. T. and Herskovits, M. J. 1966. *The influence of culture on visual perception*. Indianapolis: Bobbs-Merrill.

Triandis, H. C. 1972. *The analysis of subjective culture*. New York: Wiley.

Whiting, B. B. and Whiting, W. M. 1975. *Children of six cultures*. Cambridge, Mass.: Harvard University Press.

Chapter 12

The Bases of Fluent Reading

J. E. MERRITT

INTRODUCTION

The term 'reading' will be used here to refer to all of those responses that an individual makes to a text, whether consciously or unconsciously, in seeking to extract any meanings that interest him. In order to extract meaning a reader must process the text at a number of different levels, e.g. at the level of individual letters, spellings, syntax, etc. The information obtained at each level is normally combined in such a way that the fluent reader is much more aware of the meaning he extracts than of the processes involved in arriving at these meanings. In fact, most aspects of the reading processes are quite automatic. This article will present illustrative material which is designed to provide subjective insights into the different aspects of the reading process together with examples of current research in each area. When the focus switches from the underlying processes to observable behaviour we shall refer to reading 'skills' rather than reading processes.

It is convenient to make a distinction between three major categories of skill and these can be defined as follows:

Primary Skills: the ability to recognize letters and common letter groups at a glance, i.e. in a single fixation, and to associate these with any sounds, words, or meanings that they may represent in different contexts.

Intermediate Skills: the ability to anticipate linguistic sequences and structures in fluent reading so that words and phrases and their specific contextual meanings are rapidly identified.

Higher Order Comprehension Skills: the ability to extract larger units of meanings from texts by noting the various possible relationships between any smaller units of meaning, such as words and phrases, that are significant in relation to the reader's interests or purposes. Higher order comprehension skills are not always included in definitions of reading on the grounds that they are general cognitive skills and not therefore specific to reading. They do, however, depend upon the examination and re-examination of sections of text. This calls for a highly selective use of skimming, scanning and intensive reading strategies and readers of comparable intelligence are not equally adaptive in making these responses. There is an important text-specific element in this behaviour and it seems sensible, therefore, to regard the processes involved as aspects of reading.

Reading may also be defined within a broader context of purposeful behaviour. This would include the definition of specific reading goals, the planning of reading activities, the scrutiny of one or more texts, and the evaluation, integration, and appropriate application of meanings in relation to purpose. Whether or not these are classed as 'reading' there is little value in reading research that fails to take them into account.

An even broader view of reading would locate this kind of behaviour cycle within a broader cycle of information seeking behaviour. This would include the definition of information needs, the location and selection of relevant sources, the effective use of these sources and development of personal storage systems to facilitate later retrieval. This review will limit attention to primary and intermediate skills as these are the most important components in fluent reading. It is important to remember, however, that fluent reading is affected by all other aspects of the reading process in everyday reading, and this much more complex pattern of behaviour is the ultimate focus in all reading research.

PRIMARY SKILLS

Letters

Javal (1878) demonstrated that words in which only the upper part is visible are easier to read than words in which the lower part is visible.

(i.e. 'as in this example', and 'and this example').

Spencer (1969), reproduces an alphabet designed by Brian Coe which demonstrates that quite large sections of letters can be deleted without seriously affecting legibility. Evidence of this kind suggests that the fluent reader does not scrutinize every single detail of a letter but merely notes the distinctive features, i.e. only those features which need to be observed in distinguishing between one letter and another. These features vary according to the particular comparison to be made, for example, in comparing *hat* and *mat*, the ascender of the *h* is obviously a critical feature. In comparing *hat* and *bat*, however, the reader must note the completion of the curve in the 'b'. Massaro and Schmuller (1975) provide a detailed analysis of experiments and theories concerning more detailed investigations of the nature of distinctive features and how they are processed by the fluent reader.

There is still a great deal of controversy as to whether or not readers scan words on a letter-by-letter basis (Gough 1972). The evidence against this however is fairly strong. Kolers and Katzman (1966) presented one letter at a time to subjects at varying rates and found that letters must appear for about one quarter of a second for correct identification to occur. They argue, therefore, that fluent readers cannot scan on a letter by letter basis, as this would limit reading speed between thirty and forty-two words per minute, whereas college students read at about 300 words per minute.

Evidence of this kind emphasises the importance of some kind of grouping principle in the perception of words in fluent reading. At the same time, the fluent reader must be capable of making fairly fine discriminations, e.g. in distinguishing between words like 'better' and 'bitter'. The problem in the early stages of learning to read, therefore, is how to develop accurate letter perception without building in habits that interfere with the perception of letters as parts of larger groupings.

Phonemes

Our present alphabet derives from the Greek alphabet in which each vowel and each consonant were represented by a separate letter. However, the relationship between letters and speech sounds, or phonemes, is not quite as simple as it may seem. In addition, the representation of speech sounds has become much more complex over the centuries. This is partly due to the use of a restricted alphabet to represent the wider range of speech sounds of English, continuous changes in pronunciation over the centuries, and the continuous enrichment of our language by the introduction of foreign words and neologisms. First, then, let us consider the extent to which a letter could be said to represent a particular sound.

The acoustic properties of consonants vary in different contexts. For example, if the words 'dim' and 'doom' are recorded it is possible to cut the tape to separate the /im/ or /oom/ from the /d/, and when this is done, all that is left is 'two different kinds of whistles' (Smith 1971). Smith goes on to say that 'if the first part of the tape-recorded word "pit" is cut and spliced at the front of the final /at/ of a word such as "sat" or "fat", the word that is heard is not "pat", as we might expect, but "cat" '. Liberman (1970) points out that phonemes are not, in any case, separate segments strung together in a simple sequence but overlapping elements.

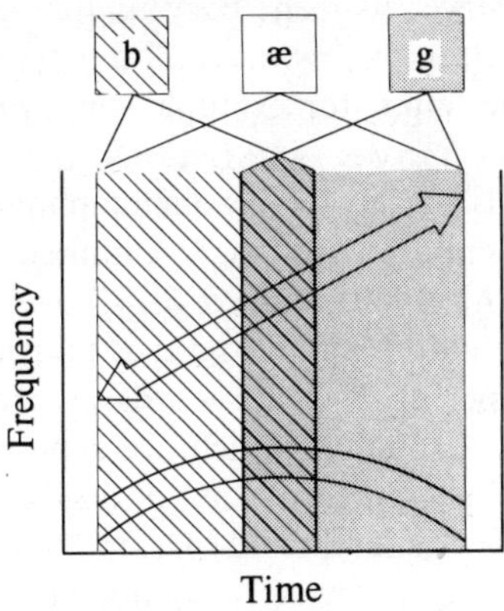

Figure 12.1

In this example, the influence of the /æ/ sound extends the whole length of the acoustic signal, thus affecting the quality of the consonant /b/ at the start and /g/ at the end. The /b/ and /g/ overlap in the middle so elements of all three segments are then being transmitted simultaneously.

In view of this it is rather misleading when a teacher tells a child that /k/ – /æ/ – /t/ 'says' /kæt/ for it clearly does not. To teach by this so-called 'synthetic' method may not be wholly misguided, for the mediated learning that takes place may arguably be of some help in the early stages. A potential disadvantage, however, is that the mediating elements may be built in to such an extent that they interfere with the fluent reading requirements of perceiving groups of letters, rather than individual elements. In other words, a limited sight vocabulary might be acquired at the expense of fluency.

A further disadvantage of the synthetic method is that it represents a limited view of the nature of the English spelling system.

One problem with our spelling system is that there are more phonemes than there are letters. There are twenty-six letters in the alphabet but about forty-three or four phonemes. We have to compensate for this deficiency by using combinations of letters to represent the extra phonemes, e. g. ch, aw, oo, etc. If a child learns to read by attempting to synthesize words from the sounds of individual letters, this strategy soon leads to difficulties, for /t/ – /h/ – /e/ – /n/ does not say 'then'.

This problem need not be too serious for it would be a simple matter to teach the small number of extra combinations. A major problem, however, is the variety of possible spellings for a given phoneme. Note, for example, these different spellings for the phoneme /ɪ/; vill*a*ge; pr*e*tty; br*ee*ches; p*i*t; s*ie*ve; w*o*men; b*u*sy; g*ui*lt; n*y*mph: i.e. a-e; e; ee; i; ie-e; o; u; ui; y. Alternatively, note all the phonemes that can be represented by a single letter, for example; *o*ne; *o*nly; t*o*n; t*o*p; t*o*; d*o*; w*o*men; *o*r: i.e. /wʌ/; /əv/; /ʌ/; /ɒ/; /ə/; /u/; /ɪ/; /ɔ/.

It is argued that this variety of grapheme-phoneme relationships becomes less chaotic if children are taught a limited number of phonic rules. Berdiansky *et al.*, (1969) studied 6,092 one- and two-syllable words used by young children and found that they needed 166 rules – and this still left ten per cent of the words as exceptions. Sixty of these rules related to consonants, which are generally thought to be reasonably regular in their representation of phonemes.

This is rather a lot of rules for a child to learn, but it is the exceptions that complicate the issue, for words do not come 'tagged' with a reference as to which phonic rule they follow, or ignore. Now, it is obvious that the young reader must draw on a considerable understanding of the phoneme-grapheme relationships, utharwize ue, aw a yung reedar, cud nat reede this fraze, but to concentrate on phonics as the royal road to effective reading is to ignore other factors that are no less critical.

Morphemes

If a fluent reader is asked to read aloud his pronunciation will often be determined by the morphemic structure, rather than phoneme-grapheme correspondences. He will have no difficulty, for example, with *'reach'* and *'react'*, because he can see that the 're' and 'act' are two separate morphemes, and he knows their separate pronunciations. Similarly, in the case of 'heard', he recognizes 'hear–' and '–––––––d' as two morphemes, the latter signalling the past tense, and he already knows from his spoken language that the past tense of 'hear' is pronounced /h3d/. By responding to morphemic spellings, therefore, rather than attending solely to phoneme-grapheme correspondences, the reader can pronounce words correctly by drawing on his existing knowledge of language instead of trying to construct words from ill-fitting segments of sound. A systematic consideration of these problems is provided by Venezky (1967), Chomsky, N. (1970), and Chomsky, C. (1970).

These writers point out that our writing system is very much more systematic than it appears – provided that the analysis is not restricted to grapheme-phoneme correspondences. Nevertheless, this still leaves many problems for the young learner, who is not, of course, a highly qualified linguist. His knowledge of language would have to be very considerable before he could respond to the morphemic cues in words such as 'creator' and 'creature,' and if he generalizes from 'hear' and 'heard', what will he make of 'bear' and 'beard'? The substitution of 'morphemics' for 'phonics' as the major element in teaching reading is obviously not very promising – yet morphemic insights, like phonic insights, are clearly of vital importance. Their role becomes more apparent when context cues are taken into account, and these will be considered in the latter part of the next section.

INTERMEDIATE SKILLS

It is difficult to establish the relative importance of the different cues which a person may respond to in normal fluent reading. The best that can be done at the present time is to identify the cues that are available and demonstrate that they can affect the reader to a greater or lesser extent. Certainly, the cues examined so far do not of themselves seem to be sufficient to account for reading behaviour, important though they undoubtedly are. Rather, they seem to depend on the effective operation of other processes which will now be examined.

Anticipation of Letter Sequences

Anyone who knows the alphabet could easily complete the following sequence: A:C:E:G: – : – : etc. Similarly, a fluent reader would have little difficulty in identifying the missing letter in the following sequence: r:i:g: – :t. In the latter case, however, there is a degree of uncertainty as the letters could represent a word that is not in the reader's vocabulary. If this were a serious possibility then the reader might possibly anticipate that the missing letter was perhaps *a, e, i, o, u,* or even *s.* Instead of the absolute certainty of the alphabetic sequence the reader falls back on the probability that certain letter sequences are more or less likely to occur in written English.

The importance of anticipation was demonstrated by LaBerge (1973) who found that latency times for matching unfamiliar letter-like shapes were no different from the latency times for matching familiar letters when the subjects were expecting the particular letters which were presented. A difference between latency times for shapes and real letters only occurred when subjects were not expecting the particular letters or shapes.

It is by no means certain, however, that letter anticipation is based solely on the frequency with which certain letters follow other letters. An examination of figures for digram and trigram frequencies produced by Mayzner and Tresselt (1965) shows that most of the high frequency letter sequences occur in a small number of short high frequency words. When these are excluded, most of the remaining high frequency digrams and trigrams occur little more than 2-300 times in the 20,000 word corpus. This is hardly enough to affect anticipation to any significant extent if we restrict our attention solely to letter sequences, and ignore other organizing principles which might be operating when we scan letters, e.g. associated phoneme-grapheme sequences and morphemic spellings.

Anticipation of Phoneme-grapheme Sequences

In the experiment reported by Kolers and Katzman (1966) it was found that when the presentation time for each letter of the six-letter words was very short (125 msec) the subjects did better naming words than letters. When the presentation time was longer (250 msec) the reverse was true. In the letter naming task, Kolers and Katzman also found that at shorter presentation times, subjects would often report all the letters correctly but in the wrong order. Sequencing errors, however, never occurred when the presentation times were longer, even though subjects still made errors in identifying some of the letters, so sequencing is evidently a separate kind of process.

Kolers (1970) suggests that there are three stages involved in the perception of letters which are presented successively: *scanning*, to form a schema; *ordering* of the elements; and *impleting*, or filling in of the elements within the structure. If we could assume that the processes involved in scanning words in fluent reading resembled those in identifying successive letters, we might suppose that the reader would normally scan to form a schema and pass straight on to the next word if this schema were acceptable. If not one might suppose that a secondary process would take place in which the order of the elements is identified, and if this is unsatisfactory, the reader would not necessarily re-examine the word but fill in the missing letters on the basis of some kind of probabilistic estimate. This line of reasoning takes us well beyond the evidence. It is the kind of conjecture that is worth taking into account, however, in considering the possible implication of this type of research.

It is almost a century now since Cattell (1885) found that words could be identified as speedily as single letters and suggested that 'general word shape' served as the cue for the recognition of a word. The evidence cited above shows that this valuable contribution of Cattell's must now give way to a more detailed analysis of the basis for 'whole-word' recognition. In fact, each of the three stages presented by Kolers now poses as many interesting problems as those presented by Cattell's original research. How, for example, does the reader produce a 'schema'? If letters are presented in succession we may rely on one process (Kolers ibid), if we see a nonsense word which is pronounceable as exemplified in the next section, we may use another (cf. Gibson, Shurcliff and Yonas 1970), and if we see a real word in a particular context, we may use another (Goodman 1969).

One contributing factor in producing a schema might be the relative probability of different sounds occurring in different positions in a word. Only five different sounds, for example, make up more than fifty per cent of words that end in consonants and eight sounds comprise fifty per cent of our initial consonants (Miller 1951). There is also evidence that the initial letters provide a stronger cue than letters in subsequent positions (Marchbanks and Levin 1965), at least with young children. If these two factors are combined then the number of possibilities is considerably reduced. If word length is also known, as in the Kolers experiment, and in normal reading, then the reduction in the number of possibilities is dramatic:

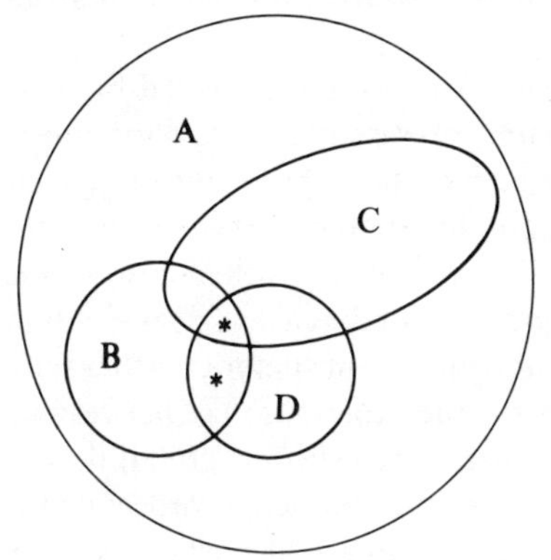

A = Words in the reader's vocabulary

B = Words beginning with a given letter

C = High frequency initial sounds

D = Six-letter words

* = Possible words

Figure 12.2

If we now add a final letter, and perhaps a medial letter we can see that the mathematics of cue combination make access to a large number of possible schema not too difficult to handle. (See Merritt 1970). So much attention has necessarily been devoted to the question of which cues a fluent reader may respond to that this powerful effect of combining cues has been seriously neglected.

Once the schema has been selected the matching of the letters must fit into an acceptable grapho-phonemic pattern. The reader is not at this stage concerned with how letters may be pronounced. He is concerned with whether or not the letters he has seen are among the acceptable spellings for the word he has selected. Then at Kolers's third stage, letters can be 'impleted' according to the speaker's internalized spelling system, and this may well take precedence when letters were not clearly identified.

Support for the idea that the perception of phoneme-grapheme correspondences plays an important part in word recognition was provided by Gibson *et al.* (1962). They carried out an experiment in which lists of pseudowords (letter strings that are not real words) were presented tachistoscopically to skilled readers. In one set, the letters were organized so that they could be pronounced fairly easily. In another set, the letters of each pseudoword were re-arranged so that they were not so readily pronounceable. The pronounceable pseudowords were found to be more readily perceived than the unpronounceable pseudowords. Gibson (1964) checked her results taking into account the possible effects of digram or trigram frequencies. She found that they did not predict success in reading the pseudowords when pronounceability was partialled out and length held constant. Alternatively, however, one might partial out the pronounceability contribution.

At that time, Gibson argued that words were recognized because the subjects responded to the phonemes represented. In a subsequent experiment, Gibson *et al.* (1970) repeated the experiment with deaf subjects and found that they too responded better to the 'pronounceable' pseudowords. As there is no way in which grapheme-phoneme correspondence could facilitate performance in the case of deaf children Gibson proposed that certain kinds of regularity in spelling, rather than pronounceability, provided a more plausible explanation of her results. The fact that we can pronounce nonsense words such as grebdink, veb or fropint does suggest, however, that grapho-phonemic processing is a continuing feature in the case of readers who are of normal hearing, otherwise it seems highly unlikely that we should retain such a high level of skill.

Anticipation of Morphemic Sequences

It was pointed out earlier that the pronunciation of a word may be determined by its morphemic structure, rather than by a direct correspondence between graphemes and phonemes, e.g. reach – react. The process by which this is achieved, however, is another matter. If the fluent reader encounters an unfamiliar word in isolation he will not know whether to respond at the morphemic level or at the phonemic level. For example, should 'pretent' be pronounced by analogy with 'prevent' – or 'present.'?

Although ambiguity of this kind cannot be resolved in the case of unfamiliar words there is some evidence to suggest that morphemic elements do provide a basis for word recognition in the case of familiar words. Pearson and Kamil (1974) investigated the effects of form class (nouns and verbs) stem length (3-10 letters per word) and affix length of inflected words ('ø', '–s', '–ed', or '–ing') on recognition latency. Their data supported a letter-by-letter interpretation of the recognition process, modified by a possible morphemic strategy for affixes. They suggest that subjects may scan the word for length first, then segment the word morphologically, although another possible explanation they considered is that a letter-by-letter analysis is used for the stem, then the first letters of the inflected ending are used to identify the whole ending.

All of these observations are of importance in that they throw light on mechanisms which may be available to the fluent reader in word recognition. (See Morton 1964.) In order to decide which cues are actually used we must consider additional information based on studies of word recognition when the words are in running texts.

Anticipation of Word Class

If one reads a phrase such as 'The big––––' one may have a fairly strong tendency to anticipate that a noun will follow. There is a high probability that a noun will follow an adjective, that an article will be followed by a noun, and so on (Open University 1977). In the case of young readers, Weber (1970) showed that ninety per cent of errors made by first-graders were grammatically acceptable substitutions. Kolers (ibid) reports a similar finding with adults in an experiment in which subjects were asked to read texts which had been transformed in various ways in order to see what kinds of errors resulted. These transformations included the rotation, reflection or inversion of individual letters, words, or whole lines of print. This is a fairly severe test as fluency is greatly impaired in these conditions. Even so, the proportion of grammatically acceptable substitutions was high and completely unacceptable substitutions were rare, e.g. a verb was rarely offered in place of an article, or a noun in place of a conjunction.

As Kolers pointed out, the classification of parts of speech into the traditional categories is a rather unsatisfactory procedure, although useful information was obtained in spite of the occasional ambiguities. A further check was therefore carried out in which words were checked for acceptability against the antecedent word and also against the whole clause. For example, the word 'the' cannot be substituted for 'them' in the way that a pronoun, say, might substitute for a noun; but given the antecedent word 'gave', both words are equally acceptable: yet in a clause such as '---who gave them some tea', the substitution of 'the' for 'them' would be unacceptable. Substitutions were assessed for acceptability in terms of class, form and meaning. Kolers reports that in the case of errors that were visually similar, e.g. 'paid', substituted for 'said', eighty-eight per cent of substitutions were syntactically and semantically acceptable. In the case of errors that were visually dissimilar, the figure was ninety-eight per cent. Nine per cent were syntactically acceptable but distorted the meaning of the passage ('Emerson once *paid* that' instead of '. . . *said*') and only one per cent preserved meaning at the expense of syntax ('Emerson once *say* that'). Thus, anticipation of grammatical relations evidently plays a dominant part in fluent reading, to the extent, even, of causing the reader to ignore the physical characteristics of words.

The figures are rather different when the whole clause is taken into account. Against this larger context sixty per cent of substitutions violated both meaning and syntax. Although Kolers does not make an issue of this, it would appear that in tackling a very demanding text, the reader makes use of less information than is available. It is arguable, perhaps, that an undue stress on within-word cues, or even the immediate antecedent, is not the best strategy in teaching reading. The most powerful cue is provided by the meaning of the whole sentence, and failure to emphasize this may simply lay the foundations for a maladaptive regression to earlier habits when reading under stress conditions, e.g. in reading a contract, or an income tax form.

CONCLUSION

It is a chastening experience to look back at some of the research carried out eighty years ago, and to read the ideas expressed by Huey (ibid) at the beginning of this century. Only in the last fifteen years has research in psycholinguistics begun to make real advances in reading theory, and in the practical field, many of Huey's ideas would sound remarkably like contemporary viewpoints, so limited is our ability to provide adequate courses on reading in the initial training of teachers.

Fortunately, the student of reading can now turn to some excellent collections of research papers and seminal articles, the most notable, perhaps, being those of Kavanagh and Mattingley (1972), Levin and Williams (1970), Massaro (1975), and Singer and Ruddell (1976). For the teacher, the current expansion of in-service education may, in time, provide the kind of link between theory and practice which is vital if standards of reading are to be improved.

Finally, it must be remembered that this review of current thinking has covered only a small segment of the reading field (see HMSO 1975), and even in this small segment the selection of research and its interpretation could have been very different in the hands of another writer. It is to be hoped that it will at least provide a reasonable starting point for a more systematic study for those interested in this area.

REFERENCES

Berdiansky, B., Gunwell, B. and Koehler, J. 1969. 'Spelling – sound relationships and primary form-class descriptions of speech comprehension vocabularies of six to nine year olds.' *Southwest Regional Laboratory for Educational Research and Development Technical Report 15*. Cited in Smith, F. 1971 *Understanding reading*. New York: Holt, Rhinehart and Winston

Cattell, J. M. 1885. 'Über die Zeit der Erkennung und Bennenung von Schriftzeichen, Bildern und Farbern.' *Philosophische Studien 2,* 635-650, cited in Huey, E. B. 1968. *The psychology and pedagogy of reading,* Cambridge, Mass: M.I.T. Press.

Chomsky, N. 1970. 'Phonology and reading.' In Levin, H. and Williams, J. P. 1970. *Basic studies in reading*. New York: Basic Books, 3-18.

Gibson, E. J., Pick, H. D. and Osser, H. 1962. 'A developmental study of the discrimination of letter-like forms.' *J. comp. physiol. Psychol. 55,* 897-906.

Gibson, E. J., Shurcliff, A. and Yonas, A. 'Utilization of spelling patterns by deaf and hearing subjects.' In Levin, H. and Williams, J. P. (eds), *Basic studies in reading*. New York: Basic Books.

Gibson, E. J. 1964. 'On the perception of words.' *Amer. J. Psychol. 77,* 668-9.

Goodman, K. S. 1969. 'Analysis of oral reading miscues: applied linguistics.' *Reading Research Quarterly 5, 9-30.*

Gough, P. B. 1972. 'One second of reading.' In Kavanagh, J. F. and Mattingley, I. G. (eds). *Language by eye and by ear: the relationships between speech and reading*. 331-58. Cambridge, Massachusetts: M.I.T. Press.

HMSO. 1975. 'A language for life'. Committee of Inquiry appointed by the Secretary of State for Education, under the Chairmanship of Sir Alan Bullock. London: HMSO.

Javal, E. 1878. 'Hygiène de la lecture.' *Bulletin de la Société de la Médecine Publique* cited in Open University 1977 *Developing fluent reading*. Post-experience Course PE231 Reading Development.

Kavanagh, J. F. and Mattingley, I. G. (eds) 1972. *Language by ear and by eye: the relationship between speech and reading*. Cambridge, Massachusetts: M.I.T. Press.

Kolers, P. A. and Katzman, M. T. 1966. 'Naming sequentially presented letters and words.' *Language and Speech 9,* 84-95.

Kolers, P. A. 1970. 'Three stages in reading.' In Levin, H. and Williams, J. P. 1970, *Basic studies in reading* 90-118. New York: Basic Books.

LaBerge, D. 1973. 'Attention and the measurement of perceptual learning.' *Memory and Cognition 1,* 3, 268-76.

Levin, H. and Williams, J. P. 1970. *Basic studies in reading*. New York: Basic Books.

Liberman, A. M. 1970. 'The grammars of speech and language.' *Cogn. Psychol. 1,* 301-23.

Marchbanks, G. and Levin, H. 1965. 'Cues by which children recognize words.' *J. educ. Psychol. 56,* 57-61.

Massaro, D. W. and Schmuller, J. 1975. 'Visual features, preperceptual storage and processing time in reading.' In Massaro, D. W. (ed.) *Understanding Language* 207-237. London: Academic Press.

Massaro, D. W. 1975. *Understanding language*. London: Academic Press.

Mayzner, M. S. and Tresselt, M. E. 1965. 'Tables of single and diagrams frequency counts for various word lengths and letter position combinations.' *Psychonomic Monograph Supplements 1,* No. 2, 13-22.

Merritt, J. E. 1970. 'The intermediate skills.' In Gardner, K. (ed.) *Reading skills – theory and practice*. London: Ward Lock Educational.

Miller, H. A. 1951. *Languages and communication.* New York: McGraw Hill.

Morton, J. A. 1964. 'A model for continuous language behaviour.' In *Language and Speech 7,* 40-70.

Open University 1977. 'Developing Fluent Reading.' *PE231 Reading Development,* Block 1, Units, 1, 2, 3 and 4. Open University Press.

Pearson, P. D. and Kamil, M. L. 1974. 'Word recognition latencies as a function of form class, stem length, and attix length.' *Visible Language VIII, 3,* 241-6.

Singer, H. and Ruddell, R. (eds) 1976. *Theoretical models and processes of reading,* 2nd edition. Newark, Delaware: International Reading Association.

Smith, F. 1971. *Understanding reading*. New York: Holt, Rhinehart and Winston.

Spencer, H. 1969. *The visible word.* London: Lund Humphries.

Venezky, R. L. 1967. 'English orthography: its graphical structure and its relation to sound.' *Reading Research Quarterly 2,* 75-106.

Weber, R. M. 1970. 'First graders' use of grammatical contexts in reading.' In Levin, H. and Williams, J. P. (eds) 1970. *Basic studies on reading*. New York: Basic Books.

Chapter 13

Occupational Psychology

PETER WARR

Occupational psychology has developed rapidly in recent years and shows every sign of continuing to do so. Work is one of the central means through which any society functions, and it plays a major part in most people's lives. This does not mean that they always enjoy it, but it does make occupational questions of clear importance to the psychologist.

A growing recognition of this fact within the psychological profession has been accompanied by an increasing awareness on the part of managers, administrators, trade unionists and work-people that psychology has something valuable to offer them. The problems facing people at work are of many kinds but psychological issues loom large in any organization, and the concepts, theories and procedures of occupational psychology are increasingly finding their way into industry, commerce and public authorities. This development is taking place against a background of growing attention by government and by scientists of all kinds to the encouragement of applied research in addition to the promotion of more basic investigations.

A second reason for the progress of occupational psychology arises from within the discipline itself. Psychology is gradually turning its research spotlight onto the activities and experiences of *people in their everyday lives,* and research of that kind needs both a setting and the interest of would-be participants. The central position of work in society and the growing public interest in occupational psychology mean that work environments may be particularly fruitful sources of knowledge and methods of study. Substantive and methodological developments here are likely to have a value which is transferable to other areas beyond occupational psychology itself.

The title of this chapter warrants an introductory comment: what should this field of psychology be called? The adjective 'industrial' is too limiting, in that we are also interested in what happens in hospitals, offices, shops and other work environments which are not appropriately described as 'industry'. Many North American psychologists have adopted 'industrial and organizational psychology' as a general title, but in Britain 'occupational psychology' has become the traditional label.

Definition of an area, especially one in growth and change, is difficult. Instead, I have attempted a broad classification of the components of occupational psychology, using five overlapping categories as follows:

Personnel psychology
Man-machine systems psychology
Industrial relations psychology
Occupational social psychology
Organizational psychology

A chapter of this brevity cannot give equal treatment to each component without becoming tediously abstract and general. Therefore I have rather arbitrarily decided to devote a larger amount of space to the fourth component than to the others.

PERSONNEL PSYCHOLOGY

The sub-area of personnel psychology was the first to become established, covering selection, training and vocational guidance.

Many large organizations use some form of psychological test as part of their selection process. It is obvious that tests cannot provide all the information needed for decision-making, but their value is nevertheless established. Like most decisions, a selection decision rests upon the integration of a wide variety of small pieces of evidence, and the person making a decision has to build situations where these small items of information can be generated.

A psychological test creates just such a setting, where people can behave in ways which might be relevant to their behaviour elsewhere. There is ample evidence that many tests have moderate predictive power of this kind (Ghiselli 1966; Guion 1965; Schneider 1976), yet numerous challenging problems, both conceptual and practical, face the psychologist in this area. Some of these are psychometric issues to do with the measurement of ability, aptitude, achievement or personality (Anastasi 1976), and the psychologist's skills and techniques here will be similar to those of social, statistical or educational psychologists. We also sometimes face difficult 'criterion problems': against what criteria should tests be validated? Consider the selection of new graduates by a large company: should the company be trying to predict performance in a graduate's first job or later? What measures of performance are available at each stage? Are they statistically acceptable? Do the criteria intercorrelate at different points in a career? Are some criteria more important than others?

But the selection process involves much more than psychological tests. Some form of interview is almost always used, both for the potential employer to gather additional information and for the candidate to learn something about the company. Early research on interviewing concentrated on the reliability and validity of interviewers' decisions (Ulrich and Trumbo 1965), but many studies were methodologically weak. For instance, some investigations employed experimental interviews lasting less than three minutes and others used a pen-portrait instead of a real candidate. The most appropriate overall conclusion is the same as that applicable to psychological testing: moderate validity is attainable by systematic, trained and cautious users.

Other research into interviewing has examined the process of information exchange itself and the factors influencing decision-making. For example, there is evidence that an interviewer's early implicit decision to reject a candidate is more resistant to subsequent change than is an early implicit decision to accept (Bolster and Springbett 1961).

A second element of personnel psychology deals with training, and the acquisition of knowledge, skills, values and interests. This area derives in part from psychologists' longstanding interest in learning and adaptability, and many traditional concepts and issues have been taken up by occupational psychologists. Research into training covers a wide range of topics: manual skill acquisition, apprenticeships, task analysis, age effects, computer-assisted instruction, knowledge of results, simulators, social skills training, foremen training, to name but a few. One or more of these aspects are dealt with by Bilodeau and Bilodeau (1969), Davies (1971), Deese and Hulse (1967) and Rackham and Morgan (1977).

A similarly brief mention is all that is possible for the third element of personnel psychology. This has long been known as 'vocational guidance', where the psychologist and the client work together to choose types of work for which the latter might be particularly suitable

(Crites 1969). Such guidance may be especially important at clear transition points, for example on finishing full-time education, after being seriously injured, or on being made redundant. In recent years this area has broadened into occupational counselling more generally, covering many aspects of career development and the continuing relationships between a person and his or her employment (Watts 1977).

MAN-MACHINE SYSTEMS PSYCHOLOGY

The second main component of occupational psychology, 'man-machine systems psychology', is sometimes known as 'human factors psychology', and in North America there is use of the term 'human engineering'. A related discipline in Europe is 'ergonomics', made up of psychological, physiological and anthropometric approaches to work and environments.

Anthropometry deals with the measurement of physical characteristics of the body: dimensions, weight, volume, range of movements and so on. A great deal of material has been gathered about the population distributions of relevant bodily features, and this is extensively used by ergonomists in designing motor vehicles and other environments where comfort and efficient performance are required.

Psychophysiological studies have been concerned with the effects of different working environments and work loads upon performance. For example, level and quality of illumination have been much studied, as have noise, heat, humidity, dust and combinations of these. Related research has covered different forms of movement, acceleration, vibration and speed; and other programmes have analyzed bodily reactions to varying hours of shift-work or to time-zone transitions.

Parallel developments have been in terms of the interaction between an operator and the machine he has to control. It is here that man-machine systems psychology comes closest to applied experimental and cognitive psychology, since research questions are often framed in terms of information reception, storage and processing and they may deal with issues of motor co-ordination and response feedback. Studies have been made of varied types of information presentation and the effects of these upon response efficiency under different types of work pressure. Other investigations have determined optimal response requirements, in terms of levers, foot-pedals and so on.

More recently the emphasis has moved from studies of a single man-machine interface to studies of man-machine systems as a whole.

The change is only one of degree but it is nevertheless important, since a more complete understanding now becomes possible. For example, studies may examine the job of a steelworks crane driver or furnace operator, not only in terms of his interaction with his own machine but also in terms of his place in the broader steel-making system both technological and social.

Man-machine systems psychology is well served by standard text-books, among which are DeGreene (1972), Howell and Goldstein (1971), McCormick (1976), Meister (1971) and Poulton (1970). One development is in terms of 'cognitive ergonomics', where the system control requirements are more in terms of information than physical energy. This is notably the case with computers, especially those operated in an interactive mode, for example in production scheduling, airline seat reservation, medical diagnosis and similar processes. Some research issues in this area are reviewed by Rose and Mitchell (1975), Shackel (1978) and Sime, Arblaster and Green (1977).

INDUSTRIAL RELATIONS PSYCHOLOGY

Practical problems and research issues in everyday life do not present themselves in tidy professional packages, this one for the psychologist, that one for the economist, the third for the sociologist. An investigator will usually have his preferred approach and his principal skills and knowledge within one discipline, but he will need to be alert to questions and ideas from outside that discipline. This is clearly true for industrial relations psychology, where the psychologist's skills need to be augmented by an understanding of sociological, economic and legal matters.

'Industrial relations' itself is a multidisciplinary academic area which has been strongly influenced by economic historians, lawyers and sociologists. Psychology has recently joined this group, and the last two decades have seen a growing number of psychological studies. Many of these have focussed upon the role of the shop steward, the part-time trade union official elected from among his or her colleagues to represent them at factory level (Nicholson 1976; Pedler 1974). Shop stewards have a difficult task, sometimes made harder by a lack of experience and training since there is often a rapid turnover in the position.

Another strand of research has examined the interpersonal and inter-group processes in bargaining between unions and management. There are obviously practical problems of gaining research access and maintaining confidence in this area, but a number of issues have been explored. One of these is the mechanism whereby experienced individual negotiators exchange concessions as they move towards agreement. Some shifting of positions by both parties is usually necessary if agreement is to be reached, yet to make a concession is often a risky step involving both position and image loss. Negotiators adopt several procedures to tackle this dilemma, one of which is a coordinated pattern of concession-exchange. They gradually move their demands through the consecutive mutual exchange of limited concessions, whilst holding firm to issues which are central to their position and image (Pruitt 1971).

Other studies have looked at *groups* of shop stewards and managers in negotiations. Early application of social psychologists' category systems for recording behaviour in groups turned out to be less than satisfactory, and behaviour analysis techniques have been designed especially for negotiating groups (Morley and Stephenson 1977). Less formal recording procedures have been applied in observational studies, for example leading to a model of group development similar to that appropriate for T-group training and other group activities (Warr 1973).

Other investigations have examined the way in which people assess the adequacy and fairness of their pay. This process of judgement has many features in common with other important social judgements, and knowledge is gradually being accumulated about the influence of social comparisons, changes in aspiration levels, social influences and several forms of expectancy and reward associated with goal attainment (Lawler 1971).

OCCUPATIONAL SOCIAL PSYCHOLOGY

These issues bring us to the fourth component of occupational psychology. Social psychologists' concerns for interpersonal influence, group membership, leadership and social attitudes of all kinds are mirrored in the occupational field by a large and growing number of research developments.

Early studies examined cohesiveness and norm-formation. It is now established that cohesive groups are more likely to initiate and sustain norms of behaviour and opinion than are less cohesive groups. All work groups have norms of several kinds, some of which concern the quantity and/or quality of work which is deemed appropriate. Whether or not employees are paid by results (so that more output yields more pay), there is often a norm or quota beyond which further work is discouraged. This is especially likely for cohesive groups.

More recent studies have examined groups or committees of managers and administrators. It may be suggested that effective groups need to undertake an identifiable range of tasks, in terms of generating ideas, testing suggestions, summarizing options, maintaining momentum, detailing plans and so on. Ongoing groups can be studied to see how the several tasks are successfully undertaken by individual members and to improve effectiveness through training or the reconstitution of groups to meet the full range of requirements.

Other types of social influence come about through formal or informal leadership activities. A manager or foreman is explicitly identified as a leader, but many work groups have their own network of leadership and informal status patterns. It is not surprising to find that people prefer their leaders to be considerate to them, showing an interest in and understanding of personal aspirations and abilities, but research has also pointed to the fact that subordinates recognise a need for decision-making and structuring on the part of their managers. To some extent this is a function of the leadership role itself, implying co-ordination and encouragement of group member activities, but it may also be viewed in terms of a 'path-goal theory' of leadership (Hammer and Dachler 1975). This suggests that the successful leader is someone who identifies major goals of his subordinates individually and collectively and who creates situations which open up paths to these goals. The goals may be in terms of higher productivity or pay but also be less overt in terms of personal and group satisfactions.

Occupational social psychologists have also devoted much attention to the study of work attitudes, their determinants and outcomes. Research in this area has traditionally been described in terms of 'job satisfaction', and it is usual to identify six main components. These are:

satisfaction with the work itself, what you actually do in your job (make motorcars, program computers, study psychology, etc.)
satisfaction with your boss
satisfaction with your pay
satisfaction with your working conditions
satisfaction with your colleagues (and with your subordinates, if you are a manager)
satisfaction with your employing organization as a whole.

Other attitude components can of course be of interest in some studies, for example attitudes about promotion prospects or about your trade union.

More recent research has been directed towards making work more interesting and satisfying. Many employees are required to undertake repetitive, limited, simple tasks. Is it possible to establish work settings and demands so that the needs of an organization and its employees can be more closely matched?

This question has been tackled in many ways under several banners. 'Job enrichment', 'job design' and 'work structuring' are common terms, and more general approaches have been viewed in terms of improving 'the quality of working life' or enhancing 'psychological well-being at work' (Davis and Cherns 1975; Warr 1976; Warr and Wall 1975). Related research has examined aspects of occupational stress (Cooper and Marshall 1976; Cooper and Payne 1978).

A central requirement is an understanding of the principal dimensions of difference along which jobs might vary: in what psychologically-important respects is one job different from another? One research programme (Hackman and Lawler 1971; Lawler, Hackman and Kaufman 1973; Oldham, Hackman and Pearce 1976) has drawn attention to five major dimensions of difference:

Skill variety: the degree to which a job requires a variety of different activities and skills.

Task identity: the degree to which a job requires completion of an identifiable unit of work.

Task significance: the degree to which a job has a substantial impact on the lives or work of other people.

Autonomy: the degree to which a job provides freedom, independence and discretion.

Feedback: the degree to which a job provides clear information about personal effectiveness.

There is substantial research evidence that these job dimensions are in general significantly associated with people's feelings about their work. This means that psychologically undesirable jobs can be identified and attempts at improvement can be considered. The general pattern of findings also opens up a question of major importance: what personal and situational factors influence the degree of association between, say, skill variety and psychological well-being at work?

One group of studies has focussed upon personality differences, for example on what Hackman and Lawler (1971) describe as 'growth need strength'. This is the degree to which a person has a strong need for personal growth and development at work. Within the overall positive relationship between the above-mentioned job characteristics and psychological well-being, there appear to be closer associations for those people who are high on measures of 'growth need strength'. However, this question is not entirely settled, and several methodological and practical questions require further attention (Stone 1976).

One possibility is that additional moderating variables might be more influential. For example, Sims and Szilagyi (1976) reported that the attitudes of higher occupational groups (administrators) were more influenced by amount of skill variety than were those of service, clerical and technical staff. A particularly interesting illustration is the study by Oldham, Hackman and Pearce (1976). Their basic research design was one which examined the relationships between psychologically-important job characteristics and several outcome measures (found to be generally positive, as summarized above) as well as the moderating influence of 'growth need strength' (also described above). But they went beyond this design to look at an additional variable, the extent to which employees were satisfied or dissatisfied with factors *extrinsic* to the job itself such as pay, security and colleagues.

The assumption was that people who were dissatisfied with these extrinsic factors might treat this dissatisfaction as more salient than any concern for intrinsic factors like variety, identity and significance. As a result it was expected that satisfaction with extrinsic factors would moderate the overall relationship between intrinsic job characteristics and job reactions, and this expectation was found to be supported to some degree. The final analysis brought together all the variables, looking particularly at whether 'growth need strength' and extrinsic satisfaction had a combined influence on the primary findings. The results were (not surprisingly) complicated, but in general gave support to the hypothesis of a combined influence. For example, the correlations between a measure of job characteristics and a measure of motivation were as follows. 'GNS' refers to the index of 'growth need strength' and 'PS' to an index of pay satisfaction, one of the extrinsic factors which was examined.

Employees with low GNS and low PS	Employees with low GNS and high PS	Employees with high GNS and low PS	Employees with high GNS and high PS
·08	·32	·30	·52

Research has thus reached an interesting and sophisticated stage. More investigations with alternative measures are urgently needed, and a broader range of samples must be studied. Most research is of North American origin, and white-collar employees are studied with disproportionate frequency. Particularly important is the need to complement cross-sectional, correlational designs with more experimental research.

A similar set of issues confronts the investigator in the related area of employee participation. This is of great topical concern, and much weight has been placed upon correlational evidence that subordinate employees who can exert influence on the decisions taken in their organization have more positive feelings than others about their work. Experimental studies which actually increase the level of subordinate participation indicate that the personal, social and institutional factors affecting well-being at work are more complex than the bivariate correlational data would suggest (Lawler, Hackman and Kaufman 1973; Wall and Lischeron 1977).

ORGANIZATIONAL PSYCHOLOGY

The final component in the classification suggested earlier is one where interest is directed to the broader context of individual behaviour at work. How might organizations (a university, a factory, a local government department) be characterized, and how might they be designed and changed?

One element of organizational psychology has been concerned with the definition and measurement of organizational structure and climate. For example, research has investigated the features and consequences of operational specialization and formalization and the beneficial and troublesome aspects of bureaucracy. Other studies have looked at people's perceptions of the 'climate' in which they work, its supportiveness, conventionality, risktaking propensity and so on. Reviews of this area have recently been provided by Payne and Pugh (1976), Payne, Fineman and Wall (1976) and Schneider and Snyder (1975).

The second element of organizational psychology is concerned with the ways in which organizations might be changed for the better. The emphasis is upon personal and interpersonal effectiveness, and the wide range of issues to be studied requires a broad perspective extending into other areas of psychology and other disciplines. This field is sometimes known as 'organization development'.

The style of investigation is often that of 'action research', where the investigator gains his data and introduces experimental changes through a closer involvement with study participants than is sometimes the case. Such a style of 'aided experimentation' is often necessary if scientific progress is to be made in complex social situations (Warr 1977). The organization development psychologist employs a number of procedures with a basis in social psychology; two illustrations will be noted.

One of these is 'survey feedback'. The goal here is to obtain data about the views which members have of their organization's effectiveness and climate. These views may be gathered by questionnaire or interview and will then be 'fed back' in terms of group averages in a way which opens up discussion about possible improvements.

A second psychologist's role is as a 'process consultant', where he attends meetings and discussions both to observe and record and also to promote examination of the processes of interaction during the meeting. He may thus comment on the group leader's behaviour, upon the group's approach to reaching agreement, or on procedures to ensure that decisions are followed up. Such a role is of course potentially stressful, since the psychologist is regularly involved in situations of conflict and disagreement.

Limitations on space prevent further examination of this challenging area. More comprehensive discussions are provided by French and Bell (1973), Friedlander (1976), Margulies and Wallace (1973), Warr, Fineman, Nicholson and Payne (1978) and others.

FURTHER READING

I am conscious that this brief chapter has merely scratched the surface of occupational psychology. In addition to references in the text, you may wish to consult the more general presentations in Dunnette (1976), Fleishman and Bass 1974, Korman 1977, Landy and Trumbo 1976, Porter, Lawler and Hackman 1974, Warr 1971, 1978, and elsewhere.

REFERENCES

Anastasi, A. 1976. *Psychological testing*. New York: Macmillan.

Bilodeau, E. A. and Bilodeau, I. M. 1969. *Principles of skill acquisition*. New York: Academic Press.

Bolster, B. I. and Springbett, B. M. 1961. 'The reaction of interviewers to favorable and unfavorable information.' *J. appl. Psychol. 45,* 97-103.

Cooper, C. L. and Marshall, J. 1976. 'Occupational sources of stress: a review of the literature relating to coronary heart disease and mental ill health.' *J. Occup. J. Psychol. 49,* 11-28.

Cooper, C. L. and Payne, R. (eds) 1978. *Stress at Work*. London: Wiley.

Crites, J. O. 1969. *Vocational psychology*. New York: McGraw-Hill.

Davies, I. K. 1971. *The management of learning*. New York: McGraw-Hill.

Davis, L. and Cherns, A. B. 1975. *The quality of working life*. New York: The Free Press.

Deese, J. and Hulse, S. H. 1967. *The psychology of learning*. New York: McGraw-Hill.

DeGreene, K. B. 1972. *Systems psychology*. New York: McGraw-Hill.

Fleishmann, E. A. and Bass, A. R. (eds). *Studies in personnel and industrial psychology* (3rd edition). Homewood, Illinois: Dorsey Press.

French, W. L. and Bell, C. H. 1973. *Organization development*. Englewood Cliffs, N. J.: Prentice-Hall.

Dunnette, M. D. (ed.) 1976. *Handbook of industrial and organizational psychology*. Chicago: Rand McNally.

Friedlander, F. 1976. 'OD reaches adolescence.' *J. appl. behav. Sci. 12,* 7-21.

Ghiselli, E. E. 1966. *The validity of occupational aptitude tests*. New York: Wiley.

Guion, R. M. 1965. *Personnel testing*. New York: McGraw-Hill.

Hackman, J. R. and Lawler, E. E. 1971. 'Employee reactions to job characteristics.' *J. appl. Psychol. Monogr. 55,* 259-86.

Hammer, T. H. and Dachler, H. P. 1975. 'A test of some assumptions underlying the path-goal model of supervision.' *Organizational behavior and human performance 14,* 60-75.

Howell, W. C. and Goldstein, I. L. 1971. *Engineering psychology*. New York: Meredith.

Korman, A. K. 1977. *Organizational behavior*. Englewood Cliffs, N.J.: Prentice-Hall.

Landy, F. J. and Trumbo, D. A. 1976. *Psychology of work behavior*. Homewood, Illinois: Dorsey Press.

Lawler, E. E. 1971. *Pay and organizational effectiveness*. New York: McGraw-Hill.

Lawler, E. E., Hackman, J. R. and Kaufman, S. 1973. 'Effects of job redesign: a field experiment.' *J. appl. soc. Psychol. 3,* 49-62.

Margulies, N. and Wallace, J. 1973. *Organizational change; techniques and applications*. Glenview, Illinois: Scott Foresman.

McCormick, E. J. 1976. *Human factors in engineering and design* (4th edition). New York: McGraw-Hill.

Meister, D. 1971. *Human factors: theory and practice*. New York: Wiley.

Morley, I. E. and Stephenson, G. M. 1977. *The social psychology of bargaining*. London: Allen and Unwin.

Nicholson, N. 1976. 'The role of the shop steward: an empirical case study.' *Industrial Relations Journal 7,* 15-26.

Oldham, G. R., Hackman, J. R. and Pearce, J. L. 1976. 'Conditions under which employees respond positively to enriched work.' *J. appl. Psychol. 61,* 395-405.

Payne, R. L. and Pugh, D. S. 1976. 'Organizational structure and climate.' In M. D. Dunnette (ed.) *Handbook of industrial and organizational psychology*. Chicago: Rand McNally.

Payne, R. L., Fineman, S. and Wall, T. D. 1976. 'Organizational climate and job satisfaction: a conceptual synthesis.' *Organizational behavior and human performance 16,* 45-62.

Pedler, M. 1974. 'The training implications of the shop steward's leadership role.' *Industrial Relations Journal 5,* 57-69.

Porter, L. W., Lawler, E. E. and Hackman, J. R. 1974. *Behavior in organizations*. New York: McGraw-Hill.

Poulton, E. C. 1970. *Environment and human efficiency*. Springfield: Thomas.

Pruitt, D. G. 1971. 'Indirect communication and the search for agreement in negotiation.' *J. appl. soc. Psychol. 1,* 205-39.

Rackham, N. and Morgan, T. 1977. *Behaviour analysis in training*. London: McGraw-Hill.

Rose, J. and Mitchell, J. H. (eds) 1975. *Advances in medical computing*. Edinburgh: Churchill Livingstone.

Schneider, B. 1976. *Staffing organizations*. Pacific Palisades: Goodyear.

Schneider, B. and Snyder, R. A. 1975. 'Some relationships between job satisfaction and organizational climate.' *J. appl. Psychol. 60,* 318-28.

Shackel, B. (ed.) 1978. *Man-computer interaction*. Amsterdam: Sijthoff.

Sime, M. E., Arblaster, A. T. and Green, T. R. G. 1977. 'Structuring the programmer's task.' *J. occup. Psychol. 50,* 205-16.

Sims, H. P. and Szilagyi, A. D. (1976). 'Job characteristic relationships: individual and situational moderators.' *Organizational behavior and human performance 17,* 211-30.

Stone, E. F. 1976. 'The moderating effect of work-related values on the job scope – job satisfaction relationship.' *Organizational behavior and human Performance 15,* 147-67.

Ulrich, L. and Trumbo, D. 1965. 'The selection interview since 1949.' *Psychol. Bull. 63,* 100-16.

Wall, T. D. and Lischeron, J. A. 1977. *Worker participation*. London: McGraw-Hill.

Warr, P. B. (ed.) 1971. *Psychology at work*. Harmondsworth: Penguin (2nd edition, 1978).

Warr, P. B. 1973. *Psychology and collective bargaining*. London: Hutchinson.

Warr, P. B. (ed.) 1976. *Personal goals and work design*. London: Wiley.

Warr, P. B. (1977). 'Aided experiments in social psychology.' *Bulletin of the British Psychological Society 30,* 2-8.

Warr, P. B. and Wall, T. D. 1975. *Work and well-being*. Harmondsworth: Penguin.

Warr, P. B., Fineman, S., Nicholson, N. and Payne, R. L. 1978. *Developing employee relations*. Farnborough: Saxon House.

Watts, A. G. 1977. *Counselling at work*. London: Bedford Square Press.

Chapter 14

Environmental Psychology

CHARLES MERCER

Psychologists have been very slow to realize – and many are still not convinced – that the physical environment and the behaviour which occurs in that physical environment, form part of a system. During the first part of this century, following the Zeitgeist, psychologists wanted to convince everyone, themselves included, that 'psychology-is-a-science'. Behaviour of people could somehow be extracted from the physical environmental context in which it occurred, be transmuted to the laboratory, and studied using artificially-created stimuli presented under rigorously controlled conditions. Thus it would be possible to uncover quite general laws of perceiving, thinking, learning, remembering and the like – general laws, devoid of a context. Even the doyen of what could be considered as an 'environmentalist' psychology – B. F. Skinner – has used the word environment to denote reinforcement contingencies rather than a physical environment as such. His fictional excursion (Skinner 1948) into the creation of an experimental society – Walden Two – placed far more emphasis on the institutionalized reinforcement schedules in the encouragement and development of 'correct' and 'appropriate' behaviour of the settlers, than the physical environment in which such behavioural engineering was made possible even, though, quite clearly, such a set up could NOT exist without the specific physical structure he envisaged.

Herein lies the first difficulty – the definition of the environment. The traditional psychologist often uses 'environment' to refer to the people, events, etc. which affect the individual. Thus the boy who has been subjected to a certain kind of environment – say large doses of physical abuse – will be more likely to develop into a physically aggressive adult due to his early *environment*. Apart from the early industrial psychologists, and later the ergonomists, there was little attention given to the other meaning of the environment – the physical environment – before the 1960s.

Many other disciplines are, of course, concerned with this other meaning of environment. Geographers, planners, architects, urban designers have the physical environment as a central focus. In such disciplines it is the covert assumption that climate and topography are an influential determinant of life style, that the built environment can facilitate or prohibit certain kinds of behaviour, or that the physical ambience of a New Town can contribute to its community viability and indeed whether migrants will be attracted in the first place. It is somewhat paradoxical that a specialty called environmental psychology – where the focus is on the physical connotation of environment rather than the reinforcement contingency connotation – has now become so firmly established. Psychologists have taken to the environment only recently and the bulk of the work that constitutes environmental psychology is not (although this is becoming less true) to be found in the prestigious psychology journals, but in journals specially created for the purpose or in the journals of the other contributing disciplines. It would of course be better to adopt a disciplinary neutral term like man-environment studies so that members of any discipline could make forays into the area, without the feeling that they were trespassing on someone else's territory or indeed losing their disciplinary affiliation. The built environment, does after all serve as a central issue, a focus of concern, about which all disciplines *should,* at this stage in the history of man, be making a contribution. The development of both practical solutions to environmental problems and theoretical models which can aid in the provision of more adequate man created physical environments in the future, represents one of the most worthwhile of contemporaneous challenges.

Before environmental psychology emerged, psychologists were to be found working in Ergonomics. The founding of the Ergonomics Research Association in Britain during the last war was an explicit recognition of the importance of the physical environment, particularly the working environment. Working environments could be improved to the benefit of both the 'worker' and production. If the heating, lighting and acoustics were right, the machine designed to fit the man, or the sink to fit the housewife and if there was quite a lot of rest pauses, all would be well.

A specific beginning to environmental psychology in the U.K., however, was probably the setting up in 1966 of the Building Performance Research Unit at the University of Strathclyde. It was multidisciplinary in orientation, and, because sponsored by 'doing' bodies, was committed to turning out information and tools that designers could use in their attempts to make buildings more appropriate and successful for the people who would eventually use them (Weaver, undated). In the United States, environmental psychology grew because psychologists who had high standing in traditional psychological fields began to realize that the physical environment is a rich source of behaviour variability and that psychology as such, ought to extend its boundaries to include the environment (Higginbottom 1974). There was also a notable upsurge of questions about behaviour being asked by the design professions.

Any innovation can only get properly started when the establishment criteria of respectability are fulfilled. International conferences, journals, newsletters and comprehensive textbooks make up such criteria. The EDRA conferences (the eighth in 1977) in the United States now provide a major forum, the Environmental Psychology conferences in the U.K. and the Architectural Psychology conferences in Sweden allow a similar purpose. (Details of these, together with evaluation, can be found in the *Architectural Psychology Newsletter,* see refs). Environmental psychology was first reviewed comprehensively by Berkeley psychologist Ken Craik in 1970 (Craik 1970). In 1973, it had gained enough weight to be included in the *Annual review of psychology* (Craik 1973) and is to appear again in 1978 (Stokols 1978). David Canter, a leading British environmental psychologist, reviewed the empirical research in 1974, produced the first comprehensive U.K. text in 1975 and directs the first post graduate environmental psychology degree course at the University of Surrey. Professor Terence Lee, also of the University of Surrey gave us the mini-text *Psychology and the environment* in 1976. The first comprehensive American text – *An introduction to environmental psychology* – was published in 1974 by members of the Environmental Psychology doctoral program at City University of New York (Ittelson *et al.* 1974) who have also produced two editions of collections of important source papers in the area (Proshansky *et al.* 1970, 1976). Downs and Stea edited a major collection of papers drawn from geography and psychology – *Image and environment* in 1973. The American Psychological Association now have a separate division (division 34) devoted to Environmental Psychology and Population, which produces its own newsletter. Thus environmental psychology symposia are now a regular feature of the annual APA conventions, as indeed they are becoming at the annual BPS conferences.

METHODS IN ENVIRONMENTAL PSYCHOLOGY

The methods used in environmental psychology are exactly the same as the methods of mainstream psychology but with extensions, elaborations and shifts of emphasis due to the nature of the phenomena under study. [See Lee (1976) for a listing, and Ittelson *et al.* (1974) for a broad coverage]. For example the 'traditional' area of personality, where both idiographic and nomothetic methods of assessment are available, has been extended so that it is now possible to talk about 'environmental personality' (Sonnenfeld 1969) – 'the predisposition to behaviour within the context of the non-interacting environment – the geographic environment of space, resources and landscape'. Sensitivity to, mobility in, control over, and risk taking in, are four factors that have so far emerged from the analysis of environmental personality. Such endeavours (see also McKechnie 1970) will allow understanding and more importantly forecasting, of people's behaviour with respect to leisure and recreational resources and natural hazards, and could be of enormous use in aiding resource management and policies of relocation, in situations of environmental threat.

By substituting the building for the person, a *building's* personality can be appraised. The problems are essentially the same – that is, making sure that what you measure has both validity and reliability. Canter *et al.* (1975) gives an excellent overview of the theoretical and methodological underpinnings of such 'building appraisals' and of their use in diagnosing the strengths and weaknesses of buildings currently in use, thereby providing information, which not only could feed forward into future buildings, but suggest modifications – either in administrative policy or physical modification – to current buildings.

A shift in emphasis, as opposed to an extension of a method, was given by Barker (1965, 1968) in his formulation of ecological psychology. Barker's approach does at least two things – it orientates psychologists towards using T- methods (psychologist as transducer) which leave the behaviour under scrutiny undisturbed, rather than O-methods (psychologist as operator) which systematically alter (e.g. by controlled laboratory experimentation) the phenomena that the psychologist as transducer leaves intact. Secondly the approach provides a theoretical cornerstone in the theory of 'behaviour-settings'. Although couched in unnecessarily complex language, it asserts that the behaviour and the setting in which the behaviour occurs, are interacting parts of a total system which has its own programme. The parts cannot be understood in isolation from the system. The approach has so far been used in a variety of settings – schools, churches, housing projects and small towns. Its application is almost unlimited, and as Craik (1973) says, Barker's influence on environmental psychology would be difficult to overestimate.

If environmental psychologists are going to have an impact on the physical environments of the future, they must at some point provide workable solutions to actual problems. Altman (1973) in an excellent paper summarizes the difficulties that behavioural scientists have in functioning in this mode, and ways of overcoming the difficulties, while Jameson (1974) suggests that a useful role of the environmental psychologist is not to find out what people want, but to find out what people *might* want or be *persuaded* to want. In other words begin to utilize the methods of the market researcher.

CONTENT OF ENVIRONMENTAL PSYCHOLOGY

When we move to the content of environmental psychology, we find that the area is now too large for any one person to cover, and that any attempt to do so in brief would result merely in sentences composed of people's names and dates with a few key words interposed between them. Rather than do this, I will try to give the flavour of the field by picking out a limited number of behaviour settings and leave the reader to pursue the further readings.

Hospitals

There has been much concern recently about the hospital environments. The furore that surrounded the exposure of conditions at Ely Hospital, Cardiff in 1968 and Pauline Morris' book *Put away* (Morris 1969) focussed attention on the hospital provisions for the mentally handicapped. Le Boyer (1975) in his advocation of birth without violence, directs attention to the physical milieu surrounding birth and the high technology versus home delivery debate, while Canadian psychiatrist H. Osmond (1966) has for many years maintained and campaigned for the view that the psychiatric outcome and the physical setting are intimately related. The research program at City University, New York (Ittelson *et al.* 1976) attacked this relationship specifically and in so doing generated a new method – that of behavioural mapping – in which patient behaviour is time sampled and grouped into six categories, e.g. 'isolated passive' behaviour which includes sitting alone, sleeping; 'mixed active' behaviour like making the bed, watching the television with others, etc. The kind of people on a ward, the administrative policy and the physical structure of the setting were seen to be the major determinants of patient behaviour and findings like patients displaying more behaviour variability in small rather than large rooms was provocative. A similar kind of paradigm was adopted by Aumack (1969, 1967) in the development of the Patient Activity Checklist which was used to record the changes in patient behaviour following ward upgrading schemes. One clear implication of this work was that ward management has to be trained in the use of new environments if upgrading schemes are to be successful. The necessity for management training of staff is also a message embedded in the approach of Gunzberg and Gunzberg (1970) to the physical milieu provided for the mentally handicapped. Upgrading of wards – normalization – is futile unless both client and staff are trained to use it maximally. Such schemes bring out very clearly the dynamic interaction that takes place between people and space, and force an explication of the goals of such therapeutic environments. In studying a children's ward Canter (1975) reinforces this assertion in the finding that a ward described by the designer as 'open plan' has a very definite pattern placed upon it by its users, which if understood, would enable the designer to 'anticipate usage and plan more effectively for it'.

Schools

Before the second world war, school design was based largely on medical requirements of heating, lighting and ventilation. After the war, according to Medd (1972), architects under the influence of Piagetian orientated educationalists, attempted to design schools to facilitate 'discovery learning'. According to the Plowden Report (1967) on primary education, discovery learning is the best method of attaining three main objectives of primary education a) transfer of learning b) positive attitudes towards learning c) sociable and autonomous human beings. In order to make such discovery learning possible, it was thought to be necessary to open up space, and over the last decade hundreds of schools have been built using open plan designs. This is all very well until discovery learning is specifically defined because of course definitions are legion. The problem is enhanced when we ask the embarrassing question of whether such learning *logically* requires an 'open plan' – and anyway what is meant by open plan? Medd (1973) suggests (without apparently much evidence) that such plans should incorporate five ingredients – a) a home base b) an enclosed room c) general work area d) particular bays e) veranda and covered bay. From research that is going on in the Welsh School of Architecture (e.g. Mason 1977) it appears that when you ask teachers to say what they understand by discovery learning there is either ignorance or a tremendous divergence of views, and ask them how such a concept relates to physical design and there is a fairly general incomprehension. Both 'traditional' and 'progressive' teaching – depending on the particular teacher and the ethos of the school – can take place in a cellular plan school or any variety of open plan school. This kind of environmental research (and see also Durlak and Lehman 1974) again points up the vital point that the relationship between space and people is interactive. Even if discovery learning as a method, is taken seriously, the people who use environments specifically designed to facilitate such learning must be trained how to do so most effectively.

Residential Environments

Much attention in the past has focussed on relatively straightforward variables such as site layout (Festinger *et al.* 1950, Kuper 1953) density (see Fischer 1975 for a review) and the like, but in 1972 Newman came on the scene promising to reduce crimes of opportunity in residential areas (particularly in the public housing sector) dramatically, through design. Both in the U.K. and the U.S.A. there have been large increases in the amount of such crime taking place in residential urban environments, vandalism, muggings and burglary, particularly in low income housing sectors. Many people argue that whilst there is an inequality of opportunity and rewards in society, crime rates will always be high. Such a view implies the only solution is a socio-political restructuring of society to iron out disadvantages. Other people (Newman is an example) argue there is nothing so wrong that tinkering about with the system will not put right. Tinkering about with the system in this case refers to more appropriate design of residential environments. Newman's thesis is basically that Man is a territorial animal who has a need for territorial ownership in the same way he has a need for food and water. Ownership means that a person – resident – is able to delineate, survey and use 'his' area. On many high rise developments, or open plan housing projects these conditions are not fulfilled. Who 'owns' the territory surrounding the super block, whose responsibility is it, and how is it to be used? Newman argues that where such questions cannot be answered unambiguously the areas are 'indefensible' and serve as an incentive for criminal activity. Make them defensible (delineate areas, fix function, provide visual surveillance, etc.) and crime is automatically reduced. Newman's work has raised a lot of controversy. His critics maintain that he is, in his recommendations (Newman 1976), simply supporting the status quo, and thereby making it more difficult to bring about structural social change. He maintains he is designing better accommodation and at the same time reducing 'crimes of opportunity' substantially. Newman's work nicely illustrates that when someone makes a practical, easy to grasp, recommendation, which involves money, they quickly get swept into the political arena.

Neighbourhood

Overcrowding in Britain was appalling by the end of the last century; it was inevitable that radical solutions to the problem were necessary. Ebenezer Howard, 'a humble London shorthand writer', proposed his radical solution in 1898 in his book *A peaceful path to real reform.* This provided the theoretical basis for the *Garden city* and later the *New town.* When Howard died, after thirty years of propagandizing the idea, there were only two such developments – Welwyn and Letchworth. The New Towns idea only really caught on after World War Two when new housing, redevelopment, and relocation became a paramount government objective. The solution in the United States came from Clarence Perry in his proposal of a Neighbourhood Unit Formula (Perry 1939). Perry laid down very specific parameters for a neighbourhood unit, that if followed would promote desirable social objectives. The parameters included population size, distinct boundaries, recreation facilities, siting of shops and schools, and traffic loads. Many of Perry's injunctions were incorporated in post war British New Town policy. Even so, as late as 1961, Goss was able to write that although New Towns did provide people with a successful physical environment, the assessment of their social success was problematic because of the 'general lack of information about how communities work' (see Mercer 1975). This provides a wonderful challenge to the environmental psychologist. Does 'neighbourhood' have salience for people, is it a valid planning concept for promoting social objectives or, as at the new town of Milton Keynes, should it be done away with? A first requirement here of course is the measurement of neighbourhood. Lee (1954, 1968) provided one of the first inroads and generated, using a cartographical technique, a measure which he called a Neighbourhood Quotient (NhQ). With this measure he was able to say whether planning doctrines would be likely to lead to greater or less community involvement and viability. Later work (e.g. Spencer 1973) has shown up some rather big methodological problems in the elicitation of neighbourhood maps, not of sufficient weight to abandon the quest, but instead, to increase the sophistication of method and theory. Looking at people's cognitive maps (socio-spatial schemata as Lee calls them) can of course be done on any level. Kevin Lynch, (1960) though not the first person, attempted to do so at the level of the city, and in some exceedingly imaginative work, Gould and White (1974) have developed methods for doing so, at the level of region or country. The development of cognitive maps of children is also an area in which much work has been done. The work of Blaut and Stea (1970) who have shown that cartographic understanding in young children is quite advanced, could have important educative implications. Key sources in the environmental perception area are Goodey (1971), Hart and Moore (1973) and Downs and Stea (1973).

I have limited myself mainly to behaviour settings of man-made environments, and to only four of these. That of course is the tip of the iceberg. What could be described as environmental issues are just as much good fodder as behaviour settings – pollution, population, energy and so on. Population psychology is already launched (Fawcett 1970, 1973) and logically belongs in environmental psychology. If so included it would prevent environmental psychology from developing parochialism towards buildings and nature reserves. By adopting a broad view of the environment, environmental psychologists are in a key position to generate new enthusiasms in mainstream psychology, cutting across nationalist boundaries.

Johnson (1973) claimed that it was in 1963 that 'environment' became more than just a trendy topic. It became a matter of public concern and an issue to be taken seriously in the political arena. It was finally institutionalized in 1972 with the UN conference on the 'Human Environment' in Stockholm. Population was given the UN treatment (for the third time) in Bucharest in 1974, Human Settlements in 1976, Dessertification in 1977. Clearly there is an international consensus that there will be catastrophic consequences if our tampering with the environment continues to be done unthinkingly and without international cooperation and understanding. It could well be that Mankind in this decade is at a turning point (Mesarovic and Pestel 1975) where decisions taken now, and decisions not taken now, will effect the viability of our children's future. Just as clearly it is necessary for all educational institutions to respond in radical ways to the culturation of the next generation in ecosanity – of seeing environment in its broadest meaning and nurturing self constructive behaviour rather than the reverse. Environmental education (see Swan and Stapp 1974) will, it is hoped, be one of the biggest growth points of what is already proving to be an exciting, challenging and progressively useful field of inquiry.

REFERENCES

Altman, I. 1973. 'Some perspectives on the study of man-environment phenomena.' *Representative Research in Social Psychology 4,* No. 1 109-26.

Aumack, L. 1967. 'Social psychological research in mental hospital settings.' *Technical Report 67-2,* Veterans Administration Hospital, Danville, Illinois.

Aumack, L. 1969. 'The patient activity checklist: an instrument and an approach for measuring behaviour.' *J. Clin. Psychol. 25,* No. 2 134-7.

Barker, R. G. 1965. 'Explorations in ecological psychology.' *Amer. Psychologist 20,* No. 1 1-14.

Barker, R. G. 1968. *Ecological psychology.* Stanford University Press.

Blaut, J. B. and Stea, D. 1970. 'Studies of geographic learning.' Paper for the annual meeting of the Association of American Geographers.

Canter, D. 1974. 'Empirical research in environmental psychology: a brief review.' *Bulletin of the British Psychological Society 27,* 31-7.

Canter, D. 1975. 'Behavioural maps or cognitive maps?' Paper to ISSBD, University of Surrey.

Canter, D. *et al.* 1975. *Environmental interaction* Surrey University Press in association with International Textbook Company.

Craik, K. H. 1970. 'Environmental psychology.' *New directions in psychology 4,* 1-121. New York: Holt, Rhinehart and Winston.

Craik, K. H. 1973. 'Environmental psychology.' *Annual review of psychology 24,* 403-22.

Downs, R. M. and Stea, D. 1973. *Image and environment.* London: Edward Arnold.

Durlak, J. T. and Lehman, J. 1974. 'User awareness and sensitivity to open space: a study of traditional and open plan schools.' In D. V. Canter and T. R. Lee (eds), *Psychology and the built environment* 164-9. London: Architectural Press.

Fawcett, J. T. 1970. *Psychology and population.* New York: The Population Council.

Fawcett, J. T. (ed.) 1973. *Psychological perspectives on population.* New York: Basic Books.

Festinger, L. *et al.* 1950. *Social pressures in informal groups.* New York: Harper and Brothers.

Fischer, C. S. *et al.* 1975. 'Crowding studies and urban life: a critical review.' *J. American Institute of Planners 41,* No. 6, 406-18.

Goodey, B. 1971. 'Perception of the environment.' *Occasional paper no. 17.* University of Birmingham Centre for Urban and Regional Studies.

Gould, P. and White, R. 1974. *Mental maps.* Harmondsworth: Penguin.

Gunzberg, A. L. and Gunzberg, H. C. 1970. 'Practice in Living.' *British Hospital J. and Social Service Review,* November 14th, 2274-6.

Hart, R. A. and Moore, G. T. 1973. 'The development of spatial cognition. A review.' In *Image and environment,* R. M. Downs and D. Stea (eds), 246-88. Chicago: Aldine.

Higginbottom, N. 1974. 'David Canter's research in architectural Psychology: an overview and bibliography.' M.Sc. in Environmental Psychology mimeo.

Howard, E. 1898. *Tomorrow: a peaceful path to real reform.* This was reissued in 1902 as *Garden cities of tomorrow.* Since published by Faber and Faber in 1965.

Ittelson, W. H. *et al.* 1974. *An introduction to environmental psychology.* New York: Holt, Rhinehart and Winston.

Ittelson, W. H. *et al.* 1976. 'The use of behavioural maps in environmental psychology.' In H. M. Proshansky *et al.* (eds), *Environmental psychology 2nd Edition.* New York: Holt, Rhinehart and Winston.

Jameson, C. 1974. 'The impact of social research on planning procedures.' In *Man environment: a better fit?* Dennis Donnelly (ed.) Research memorandum No. 26, Centre for Urban and Regional Studies, University of Birmingham.

Johnson, S. P. 1973. *The politics of environment: the British experience.* London: Tom Stacey.

Kuper, L. (ed.) 1953. *Living in towns.* London: The Cresset Press.

Le Boyer, F. 1975. *Birth without violence.* New York: Alfred Knopf.

Lee, T. R. 1954. 'A study of urban neighbourhood.' Unpublished Ph.D. dissertation, University of Cambridge.

Lee, T. R. 1968. 'Urban neighbourhood as a socio-spatial schema.' *Human Relations 21,* No. 3, 241-67.

Lee, T. R. 1976. *Psychology and the environment.* London: Methuen.

Lynch, K. 1960. *The image of the city.* Massachusetts: MIT Press.

Mason, B. 1977. 'Discovery learning and design.' Mimeo, Welsh School of Architecture, Cardiff.

McKechnie, G. E. 1970. 'Measuring environmental dispositions with the Environmental Response Inventory.' In *EDRA Two: proceedings of the 2nd environmental design research association conference.* J. Archea, J. and Eastman, C. (eds), Pittsburgh.

Medd, D. 1972. 'The design of primary schools.' *Built Environment, May,* 104-10.

Medd, D. 1973. 'School Design.' *Trends in Education 31,* 26-34.

Mercer, C. 1975. *Living in cities.* Harmondsworth: Penguin.

Mesarovic, M. and Pestel, E. 1975. *Mankind at the turning point.* London: Hutchinson.

Morris, P. 1969. *Put away: a sociological study of institutions for the mentally handicapped.* London: Routledge and Kegan Paul.

Newman, O. 1976. *Design Guidelines for Creating Defensible Space.* National Institute of Law Enforcement and Criminal Justice, United States Dept. of Justice, Washington.

Osmond, H. 1966. 'Design must meet patients human needs.' *The Modern Hospital, March.*

Perry, C. 1939. 'The Neighbourhood Unit Formula.' In *Urban housing.* W. L. C. Wheaton *et al.* (eds). New York: The Free Press, 1966.

Proshansky, H. M. *et al.* (eds) 1970. *'Environmental psychology – man and his physical setting*. New York: Holt, Rhinehart and Winston.
Proshansky, H. M. *et al.* (eds) 1976. *Environmental psychology, 2nd edition*. New York: Holt, Rhinehart and Winston.
Report of the committee of inquiry into allegations of ill-treatment of patients and other irregularities at Ely Hospital, Cardiff, Cmnd 3975, HMSO, March 1969.
Report of the central advisory council for education (England). Vol. 1 Children and their Primary Schools, HMSO, 1967. (The 'Plowden Report'.)
Skinner, B. F. 1948. *Walden Two*. New York: Macmillan.
Sonnenfeld, J. 1969. 'Personality and behavior in environment.' *Proceedings of the Association of American Geographers 1*.
Spencer, D. 1973. 'An evaluation of three techniques of image representation; a study of neighbourhood perception in Selly Oak, Birmingham.' Unpublished thesis, Centre for Urban and Regional Studies, Birmingham.
Stokols, D. 1978. 'Environmental Psychology.' *Annual review of psychology 29*.
Swan, J. A. and Stapp, W. (eds) 1974. *Environmental education. Strategies toward a more liveable future*. New York: Wiley.
Weaver, M. undated. 'The Environmental Psychology of David Canter and the Building Performance Research Unit.' Unpublished paper, M.Sc. in Environmental Psychology, University of Surrey.

FURTHER READING

Canter, D. *et al.* 1975. *Environmental interaction*. Guildford: Surrey University Press.
Canter, D. 1976. *The psychology of place*. London: Architectural Press.
Fischer, C. S. 1976. *The urban experience*. New York: Harcourt Brace Jovanovich.
O'Riordan, T. 1976. *Environmentalism*. London: Pion.
Ittelson, W. H. *et al.* 1974. *An introduction to environmental psychology*. New York: Holt, Rhinehart and Winston.
Mercer, C. 1975. *Living in cities*. Harmondsworth: Penguin.

Author Index
(italicised numbers are references)

Subject Index

Table of Contents of Psychology Survey, No. 2